CHURCH
AND
STATE

CHURCH
AND
STATE
UNEASY ALLIANCES

STEWART LAMONT

THE BODLEY HEAD
LONDON

For my mother, Morag

A CIP catalogue for this book
is available from the British Library

ISBN 0 370 31341 0

Copyright © Stewart Lamont 1989

Printed and bound in Great Britain for
The Bodley Head
31 Bedford Square
London WC1B 3SG
by Mackays of Chatham PLC

First published in Great Britain in 1989

Contents

Acknowledgements

Foreword

1 Caesar and the Ungodly Commonwealth   5

2 Reinventing the Church: Brazil   26

3 The Jefferson Wall: The United States of America   55

4 Hot Wax and Melted Ice: Russia   86

5 Black, White and Shades of Grey: South Africa   106

6 Capitalism, Communism and Christendom: Europe   139

7 The Naked Empress: England   173

8 Conclusion: The High Road and The Low Road   197

Index   208

Acknowledgements

In preparing this book I relied on a number of journals and books, but perhaps the most worthwhile parts of it are those which depend on first-hand experience from a round-the-world trip I undertook in the winter of 1987–8. In addition, I would like to offer thanks and acknowledgement for help and/or hospitality to the following people: in Brazil, Fr John McGuire and parishioners, Rev Dr Jaime Wright, Cardinal Arns of Sao Paulo, Robin Dilkes and Jan Rochas of the BBC, and Mr Dougie Woods. In the United States, Dr Jerry Nims in Atlanta; Rev Mary Gene Boteler, Dr Rick Nutt, Dr Bill & Carole Pugh in Alabama; the American Family Foundation. Bishop Krister Stendahl of Stockholm; Rev Dr Villy Molngaard, Knud and Dodi Masden in Denmark; Rev Prof Lukas Vischer in Geneva; Very Rev John Fitzsimmons in Rome; Very Rev Dr Duncan Shaw, Metropolitan Alexei of Leningard, Prof Zabotlotsky; Keston College; Michael Fry. Rev Douglas Aitken; the Ambrose Reeves Trust; South African Consuls General, Sandy Shaw and Annette Joubert; Tony Benn MP and Norman Hogg MP. My agent Andrew Hewson, and at the Bodley Head Corinne Hall, and especially Derek Johns for taking the book there with him.

S.J.L., Glasgow, the Ides of March, 1989

Foreword

Everyone must obey the state authorities because no authority exists without God's permission and the existing authorities have been put there by God. Whoever opposes the existing authority opposes what God has ordered and anyone who does so will bring judgment upon himself. For rulers are not to be feared by those who do good, but by those who do evil ... for this reason you must obey the authorities – not just because of God's punishment, but also as a matter of conscience. That is also why you pay taxes because the authorities are working for God when they fulfil their duties.

Epistle to the Romans, Chapter 13, v. 1–3, 5–6

These extraordinary verses have been used as justification for all kinds of tyranny over the 1,940 years since they were written. Emperors, kings, princes and prelates have all used them to subdue dissent and justify compliance with the established authority no matter how tyrannous that was at times. The instruction is even more extraordinary if we consider the circumstances in which the verses were written. Paul had yet to experience the conditions of the Roman Christians who, within a few years of his writing this letter, were to undergo persecution by Nero. No matter how much we may excuse Paul in retrospect because his thoughts were dominated by the idea that the world was about to end and that Christians should not waste their energies in earthly pursuits, we cannot absolve those who were later to use these words to quash prophetic protest. They are in marked contrast to the attitude to the state shown by Jesus in the gospels. He would neither be tempted into the ranks of the 'freedom fighters' opposed to Roman rule, nor would he give the

Emperor his unqualified allegiance. 'Render unto Caesar the things that are Caesar's,' he quipped when asked if he believed in paying his taxes. In Matthew Chapter 17 v. 26 he gives an even more ambiguous response when he seems to advocate paying taxes so as not to offend the Roman authority. The nub is that there is no sanction given by Jesus to any specific form of relationship between his followers and the state. In practice, it was the thinking of the paranoid Paul in Romans Chapter 13 which was to determine the form of church/state relations in the period after the persecutions. Ideally suited to provide a basis of justification for emperors to claim the loyalty and obedience of Christians, it was seized upon by popes who saw the need to modify it in order to protect their power base. In AD 494 Pope Gelasius I contended in a letter to the Byzantine emperor that his interference in church affairs was illegal. He put forward the theory of the 'two powers', a separation of the power of church and state, which was then taken to ludicrous lengths in the clericalism of the Middle Ages and led to claims of papal supremacy. Pope Innocent III saw the state deriving power from the church in the same way as the moon reflects the light of the sun. These pretensions reached their zenith in the bull *unam sanctam* of Boniface VIII in 1302 which claimed the superiority of the spiritual sword over the secular in all matters.

The balance has also see-sawed to the supremacy of the state over the church. Charlemagne argued that the state's duty was not only to support the church but also 'to strengthen within it the knowledge of the Christian faith'. Today that solution is known as Erastianism after Erastus, the doctor of medicine, who was Calvin's biographer and successor at Geneva. He developed the theory that excommunication was the preserve of the state since it was not sanctioned by the Bible and because punishment was the role of the magistrate. His theory assumed the magistrate acted in a Christian state in which all believed the same 'right doctrine' and that therefore the magistrate did not have to set himself as the arbiter of doctrine. Such theories have long since been washed aside by the tide of secularisation which has swept over Europe in the last century, but they have left islands of Erastianism which preserve a church/state model close to Romans Chapter 13. State taxes which finance churches are still in force in many countries and in England parliament is still constitutionally the arbiter of the Prayer Book.

Papal supremacy has not fared much better in the face of secularism but there are still countries where Roman Catholic teaching on contraception and abortion is strictly enforced by law. The present pope has shown by his policy of appointing bishops who will toe his conservative line, that he shares the mindset of some of his powerful predecessors if not their power. Yet in Europe the nations whose church/state relationship was determined by historical factors no longer in play often cling to these models as if this were the only possible mode in which they could co-exist. Yet as this book illustrates, different continents have developed other systems which are valid and relevant for our own age and which make the European models seem anachronistic. The growth of transnational power blocs, such as the EEC or NATO and the division of the world into the communist bloc and the Third World have both eroded the sovereignty of the nation states upon which the church/state concordats were built. The 'global village' which the mass media have created has given people a chance to experience forms of religious belief other than the monopoly culture of centuries ago. Then there was no such thing as toleration of alternative belief systems, never mind an ecumenical movement. Population migrations, freedom of travel and inter-faith marriages have all contributed to a changed religious climate. These changes and the stress on human rights, including the right to believe and practise the religion of one's choice, have changed the context in which church/state systems operate. Special arrangements for one religion or church over another can no longer be held up as normative and final, but this is not a call for nations to abrogate their Christian heritage and regard church/state pacts as a thing of the past. On the contrary, the interaction between religion and politics and the necessity for a spiritual dimension in the life of any nation, make it essential to have a framework in which religious bodies relate to their state authorities. The absence of such a framework can result in the abuse of human rights and drive the churches into a dissident role. However, in order to preserve the independence of the spiritual realm, any such arrangement is better at one remove from the political process.

An illustration of these changing factors occurred early in 1989 when a parliamentary committee considered a Church of England proposal to allow divorcees to become vicars. At first the committee blocked it, then allowed it through by one vote. It signalled yet another round in the escalating battle between the church and the Conservative government in Britain, a battle which may yet end in disestablishment. In the same week the multifaith nature of modern Britain was brought home by the footage of the novel *The Satanic Verses* being burned not in Bagdad, but in Bradford. That too was possibly an early indication of a future clash of cultures which may well put a strain on Britain's understanding of itself as a Christian country. One way to avoid sterile confrontations between the Christian Church and the state and give acknowledgement to a substantial presence of other faiths in Britain would be to set up a National Religious Council which would act as broker and reconciler between the state and religious bodies. Failure to renegotiate these arrangements on an equitable basis now will, in my opinion, lead to a messy divorce detrimental both to the churches and the British nation.

1 Caesar and the Ungodly Commonwealth

The autumn sun was breaking intermittently through the sky, its yellow light edging the rainclouds that were massing to the north of Rome. Five miles from the city on the Via Flaminia, the leader of a group of men looked up anxiously. The churning in the pit of his stomach eased as he looked towards the clouds. There, unfolding before him, was the symbol of victory. He felt a surge of confidence. Within hours his adversary had foolishly compromised his superior forces outside the safety of the Aurelian walls and was in retreat. Fleeing with a mob of fugitives, he met his death in the Tiber as the victorious army marched across the Milvian Bridge.

The conqueror was hailed as emperor and the chi-rho symbol he had seen in the sky was held high on the shields of the victorious army as they entered the imperial city. From now on, the persecuted Jewish sect would enjoy the status of being the official religion of the Roman Empire.

That is how many histories portray the dramatic turnabout that occurred on 26 October AD 312. Just as Constantine the conqueror saw divine favour in his vision of the chi-rho symbol and the inner voice which told him that through it victory was his, so also many Christians have seen the events of AD 312 as part of the divine plan for their faith. But for others, what Constantine established was not Christianity but Churchianity, a sham version of the gospel which enslaved the church to the state and endowed it with the powers to perpetrate atrocities such as the Inquisition or to decide that it could adjudicate on astronomy *without* the aid of a telescope better than Galileo could *with* one. Whichever view you take, AD 312 was a fulcrum point when the balance tilted and Christianity assumed a predominant place in world history.

It does not matter that the chi-rho symbol was not yet in use by Christians in 312. Whatever legends were added retrospectively to accounts of the battle of Milvian Bridge, and no matter how much Constantine's conversion may be derided as superstitious or calculating, the fact remains that Constantine acted afterwards in a manner that gave consistent support to Christianity. The Bride of Christ, the Christian Church, has had many relationships with many Caesars and suitors since Constantine. She has played the part of widow in atheistic states where Christ officially is dead or does not exist, and has enjoyed friendships, partnerships and ménages, ranging from sister-confessor to adultress and prostitute. Occasionally the church has seen the state as anti-Christ and there are still parts of the Christian Church today which regard a state church or established religion as rendering to Caesar the things that belong to God.

This book will look at a number of different forms of contemporary church/state relationships in countries in which Christianity is the major religion (some of them in which it acts as an adversary of the state). When the Pharisees first asked Jesus (Matthew 22:17) whether it was 'lawful' to pay taxes to Caesar, they did so as Jews within the Roman Empire for whom the Torah (Holy Law) was the prime rule of faith and life. Jesus' reply ('Render unto Caesar . . .') was an apt one for the situation. It is still often quoted as the ideal formula for separating the proper spheres of influence of church and state. But, alas, it does not provide a guide for deciding when the limits of these respective areas of influence have been reached.

The other tablet on which church/state dealings are based is 1 Peter 2:13–17 which was used by the Protestant Reformers as justification for the church/state system that they evolved. It exhorts Christians to be subject to human institutions whether it be the emperor or those imposing punishment in his name and is summed up in verse seventeen: 'Honour all men. Love the brotherhood. Fear God. Honour the emperor.' This goes further than the gospels and appears to imply that obedience to the state is the duty of Christians. However, the first letter of Peter is not exactly the most popular document of our age, with verses such as 'wives be submissive to your husbands'. The most serious objection to it as a theological justification of state authority is that it was clearly written with the expectation that the world was about to end. (Ch. 4:7. 'The end of all things is at hand.') It must therefore be placed in the context of a speech by the ship's chaplain to passengers on the *Titanic after* it had hit the iceberg, rather than as a draft maritime regulation to govern crew and passengers for all time. To use it as the basis of church/state constitutions in subsequent ages is like putting faith in the unsinkability of the *Titanic* even after we know her fate.

If we know anything from subsequent centuries, it is that *no* form of church/state relationship is without its dangers. That is not to say that such concordats ought not to be entered into. After all, 'Caesar' is in most cases no longer a single person or monarch who claims a divine right to rule, but a democratic state composed of citizens. If you define the church as the body of believers (the body of Christ), then in a very real sense the church/state dichotomy comes down to resolving the ethical issues not as a power struggle between two institutions or between prime minister and primate, but as a function of two different aspects of the individual – one as citizen and voter, the other as church member and believer. The positive way of viewing this is to regard it as a parable of the incarnation, i.e. just as Jesus was both human and divine (the 'two natures' doctrine), so we are mini-churches and mini-states without ourselves, corpuscles of the Body of Christ and little Caesars. It is often difficult to tell which role we are being called upon to play and there is much overlap in the area we call 'human rights'. Ghandhi put it thus: 'I claim that the human mind or human society is not divided into watertight compartments called social, political, religious. All act and react upon one another. I do not believe the spiritual law works on a field of its own. On the contrary, it expresses itself only through the ordinary activities of life. It thus affects the economic, the social and political fields.'

In agreeing with that, I side with those who maintain that it is impossible to avoid interaction between religion and politics. But that need not mean that religion has to have expression in a state-sanctioned institution. As we shall see, it is possible for fruitful partnerships between state and church to exist where the link is not constitutional. It is also all too clear from the lessons of history that when the king's head was on one side of the coin and Christ's on the other, state religion often became the Church of Janus Christ – facing two ways and serving two masters, the house divided against itself. There are other situations when the church will stand out against the state as a prophetic or critical voice and the state will be forced to listen – not because a church/state bond exists, but because of the moral force or majority mandate behind the church.

Is there an ideal form of church/state relationship? Or is the ideal to ensure that there is none? Both ideas have had currency from the time of Constantine onwards and in the final chapter I will draw on arguments in favour of both, based on the examples throughout the book. But the arguments are many and varied. One is tempted to sympathize with Kipling's world-weary observation: 'There are nine and sixty ways of constructing tribal lays – and every single one of them is right.'[1] But no one can pretend that any of the forms of church/state relationship in today's world are 'right': the good, the bad and the ugly would be a better way of describing the models that are available for study.

To begin with, the notion of 'state' differs greatly from continent to continent. The concordats which were built on medieval ideas of sovereignty are hardly appropriate when applied to a Latin American generalissimo. The nation state has given way in Eastern bloc countries to a kind of dependence on Russian communism. And where does one put the USA, the nation 'under God' which forbids any form of state co-operation with churches but so many of whose citizens are zealous church-goers?

Clearly there can be no one definition of 'state' which would apply throughout this book. That might at first sight seem equally true for the notion of 'church'. Can there be any similarity between bodies as diverse as the Dutch Reformed Church in South Africa and the Roman Catholic Church in Holland? Or between the wild worship of black Pentecostals in the Deep South of the USA and the cold Calvinism of a Swiss canton? There is no common bond if we concentrate on style and system. But all of these bodies share belief in the supremacy of Jesus of Nazareth as the Son of God, in the Bible composed of the Jewish scriptures and in the collection of writings known as the New Testament which were adopted around AD 200. They owe common heritage to the church of Constantine's era and most of them would recognize one another as part of 'the Holy Catholic and Universal Church'. Rome has in practice (and also in theory if you read between the lines of the encyclicals) given up claims to be the sole custodian of the keys to the kingdom of heaven. And, despite the odd backwoodsman who insists on separating the wood from the trees, Protestant denominations and sects no longer identify Rome with anti-Christ and themselves as the elect. In other words, the Christian Church, fragmented as it is into communions and by national partitions, can be regarded as a distinct entity.

Those who have no belief in or admiration for the 'kingdom which is not of this world' to which the churches owe ultimate allegiance, will want to regard the churches as a diverse group of quasi-political

1. From Kipling's *In the Neolithic Age*.

organizations. At this point I must declare my interest and say that I take the view that there is such a thing as the universal church, even if it has no expression in institutional form. I am lukewarm about conglomerate bodies like the World Council of Churches which to my mind encourage people to think in organizational terms about their Christian faith, but I accept that without an earthen vessel to contain it, the essence of what the church stands for would lack a means through which to express itself. Thus I would make a distinction between the church as denomination or institution/organization and the church as the Body of Christ, a metaphysical notion which binds together people from widely different religious traditions and styles of worship.

Recognition of the latter is now more or less universal and given expression in ecumenical councils. These should be seen as expressing unity through diversity, not as a spurious search for a standardized church, achieved by a crude process of ecclesiastical joinery. Such a church would be a kind of Frankenstein monster, hardly likely to be capable of life and growth. It is tempting to look for reunification of the churches, but not only is it an energy-wasting process, and destructive of the diversity which has developed in Christian churches, but it is manifestly unnecessary since the unity is already there if we are prepared to make use of the mutual recognition which the concept of a universal church affords us. It enables many styles of worship and systems of authority to flourish without the takeovers and mergers which would make the church into a kind of religious multinational.

Sometimes the Vatican seems to treat parts of the Roman Catholic church in ways which make it look just like a multinational. However, the less central control or authority is maintained, the more able the churches are to develop in ways appropriate to the circumstances of different parts of the world. Balancing that devolution process is the notion of the universal church which prevents it becoming schismatic or sectarian. Indeed circumstances of the modern world, where the global village is the parish, reinforce this *oikoumene* or World Community. Those who adhere to the idea that there is a True Church which can be identified with a particular denomination will, of course, be appalled at such latitudinarianism and universalism, but this book is not intended for them. The assumption of the book is that we live in a post-ecumenical age. However, it is necessary to labour the point about the universal church because the policing of the semantic side of ecumenism is not as rigorous as it is for those other humanitarian *causes célèbres* of the late twentieth century, racism and feminism. Loose language is severely dealt with in these areas but no such strictures appear to be applied to denominations which use the word 'church' in a universal sense but are implicitly referring to their own denomination. For example, a recent book *The Trial of Faith: Theology and the Church Today* turns out, on closer inspection, to be a collection of essays by Anglicans who appear to be deaf and blind when it comes to recognition of other religious traditions within the UK. The Anglo-Catholic wing of the Church of England behave as if there were no other traditions but the Roman. Roman Catholics are guilty of semantic sins also when they refer to 'non-Catholics' (a rather imprecise term which seems to make no distinction between practising Christians of other denominations, atheists and Rastafarians) as if all who are not 'Roman' Catholic can be subsumed in one word. (A stalwart Protestant at the newspaper for which I write a weekly column is so incensed by this that he refers to the pope as a 'non-Protestant'!)

The absurdity of seeing one's own tradition as orthodox and normative, and all the others as heterodox, is demonstrated by the diversity of Roman Catholicism itself. A church which counts Archbishop Milingo, Cardinal Arns, Archbishop Lefevre and Cardinal Ratzinger among its hierarchy is hardly monolithic. Sadly there are sometimes attempts by the present pope, John Paul II, to act as if the old authoritarian structure were still in place. This has led to tensions between the Vatican and the Roman Catholic Church in certain countries, notably the Netherlands, the United States and Brazil in recent years. All three of these have developed very different ways of relating to the society in which they operate. My prediction is that these situations are straws in the wind, initial signs of a process which will bring about the loosening of bonds between Rome and her daughter churches in other continents.

However, it will not follow the pattern of the schisms of earlier eras when the separated brethern were consigned to isolation. The interdependence of the modern world through communications, the external pressure of secularization, and ecumenical movements will mean that Christianity will begin to develop different emphases in different continents across denominational lines. Inter-continental lines of authority will be weakened and conciliar centres will arise in Africa, South America, North America and Eastern Europe, each different in its culture and concerns. This too will have its effect on church/state relationships, some of which will be redrawn on the lines of the church playing an adversarial role towards the state.

I am not suggesting wholesale amalgamations to produce some

monster church of the future. Rather the demolition of partition walls in order to survey the world as it has evolved after 2,000 years of Christianity. The pantheon of Christianity has many different icons of Christ – Jesus the guru, Jesus the guerrilla, Jesus the prophet, priest and king. All different emphases according to different cultures or different needs of the people. All valid expressions and manifestations of God. No one need exclude another, any more than when Christ said he would appear in the guise of the outcast or the starving, He intended to confine revelation within human suffering simply to starvation.

I believe we are on the threshold of an evolutionary leap in religious history. Just as the Reformation broke the mould of monolithic Christendom, the church/state continuum which constituted the world and outside of which there was no salvation, and established choice and variation in church/state co-existence, so I believe we have arrived at another such threshold. Christendom's modern equivalent is unlikely to get much larger. In the main, churches have given up prayers for the 'heathen' and even the most active evangelical fundamentalist denominations are dealing in individual souls, not the conversion of whole nations. Short of a religious war and compulsory conversion, Christianity has reached the limit of its expansion in Europe. It is still growing fast in Africa and Latin America and it will not be long before the vibrant churches in these continents start asking why they are dominated by European thinking in their Christianity.

The early Christians inherited the Jewish respect for law, or codified religion. Allied to the Greek appetite for philosophy and the Roman talent for order, it meant Christianity was destined to be a rational religion. The Western philosophical tradition furnished the idea of propositional truth which came to its zenith in the scholastic theologians of the Middle Ages. Such thinkers were naturally disposed to believe that theology, 'the queen of the sciences', was able to pronounce about physics, which was then called 'natural philosophy'. The disastrous consequences of that were reaped in the nineteenth century when religion took on science on the rationalist battlefield and limped into the twentieth century badly wounded. Meanwhile science and philosophy developed in ways that were antagonistic to religion. Science took the reductionist path, splitting its subject areas into ever smaller specialisms understandable only in terms of themselves and without need for concepts such as God. Philosophy went into the cul-de-sac of linguistic analysis, abandoning concepts such as a loving God as meaningless. Christianity never quite recovered from those defeats in the Western world. Despite the fact that physicists began to talk in terms of matter and energy as interchangeable, of truth being stated as paradox, and of there being a ghost in the machine which, although they took it apart, they could not define, it was too late for Europe. The process of secularization had gone too far for Christianity to retain the unquestioned status it had enjoyed for 1,500 years. The Hungarian physicist and philosopher Michael Polanyi expresses this in a vivid metaphor. The last 250 years of European culture, he says, have been the most brilliant in human history, but their brilliance was created by the combustion of the heritage of a thousand years of Christian civilization in the oxygen of Green rationalism; the fuel is now exhausted, and pumping in more oxygen cannot produce more light.[2] Gone too are the notions of sovereignty which popes, kings and emperors had invoked as the means to retain power. The establishment of Christian religion which began as a divine right underwritten by theological rationale, ended up as an inheritance from the past, a convenient arrangement which it has not been necessary to disturb.

But increased secularization in Europe means that the century will end with only nominal numbers of practising Christians in countries which are officially 'Christian'. There is hardly likely to be fighting in the streets over this. State religion in Europe is liable to go out with a whimper rather than a bang. It has served its role well as a preserver and promoter of the faith during the years when Western philosophy ruled and Europe colonized and converted large sections of the world. But that is not the end of the story. The flame of faith is kept alive not only by the fuel of reason. In other parts of the globe forms of Christianity are flourishing which do not depend on propositional logic for their dynamic.

In Africa Christianity is growing faster than in any other part of the world. The most successful denomination is Pentecostalism, a spiritist and emotional form of worship which appears to be well suited to African souls. But now that the missionaries have taken a back seat, African influence seems to be growing within the Anglican and Roman Catholic communions in that continent. If proof were needed of the prophetic leadership coming from African Christians, then martyrs like Janani Luwum in Uganda or the Nobel Peace Prize winner, Archbishop Desmond Tutu, are prime examples of spiritual leadership being given worldwide recognition. From a European

2. Taken from *Mission and the Crisis of Western Cultures* by Lesslie Newbigin. Handsel Press 1989.

rationalist standpoint, African Christianity is intellectually unso-
phisticated and simplistic in its approach to the Bible, which might
seem to make it inferior to European versions. This view assumes that
more education will 'bring them up to our level' and ignores entirely
the spiritual strength of the African churches which provides them
with a perfectly valid foundation. We would not improve African
Christianity by taking away its bricks and leaving it to clutch at
the straws of our burnt-out rationalism.

In a similar way, Latin America 'liberation theology' is deemed
to be an aberrant form of the Christian faith. Some accuse it of
being Marxism hiding beneath a cassock or, more mildly, of being
a 'social gospel'. As we shall see, it is neither of these things but
springs naturally out of the way the Christian Church has developed
in Latin America. It gets its agenda from the concerns of people –
which in many ways makes it the antithesis of Vatican centralism.
It is no coincidence that Pope John Paul II does not like the smell
of it. Whether he likes it or not, during the past quarter century
many heroic deeds have been accomplished by Latin American
Christians at a time when atrocities were being perpetrated by
the military regimes in their countries. Martyrdom, poverty and
a sense of community – the churches of South America did not
learn about them from textbooks of the early church, they learned
them the hard way. They have their prophets of the poor like Dom
Helder Câmara and Dom Paulo Evaristo Arns in Brazil and their
martyrs like Archbishop Romero in San Salvador. They have their
revolutionary priests who have pioneered an extraordinary form of
church/state bond by participating in the governments of Marxist
states like Nicaragua. They have their theology of liberation of which
the best known proponent was Leonardo Boff, suspended by Rome
who considered him to be teaching heresy. He wasn't, but it was
not orthodoxy either, it was just different. Boff's brother, Clodovis,
is also a theologian and wrote one of his books on theology in the
form of a diary of a safari to the interior of Brazil with the title
Feet-on-the-Ground Theology. He sums up the clarity and the relevance of liberation theology, '. . . Don't be surprised if my attitude
is one of basic sympathy with the common people. Unless there is
an act of faith in the people, a people that is both oppressed and
religious, you cannot understand anything about that people. Only
love can see well.'

If Latin America has suffered, it has also emerged, like Africa,
with a stronger faith than other parts of the Christian communion.
In both continents the Christian Churches have acted as advocate for

the poor and the oppressed and have not been compromised by their
dealings with the state. That is not so for the Orthodox Churches. In
1988 the millennium of Christianity in Russia was celebrated, but the
distinctive Orthodox faith has been around since earliest times. Since
AD 330, when Constantine designated Constantinople as the capital
of the empire, the ecumenical patriarch has been based there. Today
Turkey is a secular state and the patriarch is still in Istanbul but he
does not have authority to interfere in the affairs of other Orthodox
Churches.

To the west, the Orthodox Church of Greece has been involved
in wrangles with the state in recent years. Long eclipsed by the
Ottoman Empire, church/state issues are now to the fore in Greece
with quarrels over the disposal of church land by the Greek state.
In Russia, the relationship was a stormy one particularly during the
time of Peter the Great, but today an uneasy truce exists between the
Russian Orthodox Church and the atheist Soviet state. The Russian
Orthodox Church is not so much established as licensed to operate
through a state official. Here, more than anywhere, the ornament is
made of delicate porcelain and is closely monitored from outside the
Soviet Union by those determined to see the freedom granted to the
church as a barometer of Gorbachev's policy of *glasnost*. As well as
reflecting the different character of the Russian people, Orthodoxy
has its own distinctive polity and theology. The term 'byzantine
complexity' aptly derives from this part of the Christian tradition. It
is difficult to decide whether Orthodoxy is a dinosaur of the faith or
a chameleon which can adapt to any form of church/state bond and
survive and it remains to be seen whether it will take an evolutionary
leap forward.

Of the countries which have had strong church/state bonds from
the Renaissance onwards, Italy, Spain and Eire all guarantee the
Roman Catholic Church a special role in the affairs of the nation.
They have a predominantly Catholic culture and have played an
influential role in RC history. All have had to contend with bitter
civil conflicts in the twentieth century. Their Christian leaders have
been and are on the side of reactionary thinking in theology and
recent Vatican appointments to bishoprics have set out to confirm the
hold of the traditionalists who would uphold the church's position in
the state. By keeping a stale crust on the pie, the Vatican and pope
may think they have sealed in the flavour but underneath the meat
is rotting away. These churches are stalwart in keeping faith with
'traditional' teaching on birth control, divorce, married priests, and
women priests.

While all churches are equal in the sight of God, as far as Caesar is concerned some are more equal than others. The march of history has left some churches in anomalous positions with regard to their arrangements with various states. It is anomalous because although the constitutional position has not changed and the nation state retains the same boundaries as when the deal was struck, external circumstances have changed considerably. This raises the question of whether the constitutional position is any longer appropriate. For example, part of the arrangement in England prohibits a Roman Catholic ascending the throne and is quite out of keeping with the changed situation in Roman Catholicism or the tolerance of the population at large.

The fact that there is little or no desire within the Church of England (despite its involvement in various ecumenical organizations) to do anything about this is a reflection of its moribund state. Much as I admire some aspects of it and its clergy, past and present, there is a curious amalgam of complacency and pride which seems to prevent it taking any step that might move it forward (e.g. unity with other churches or acceptance of women priests). It has grown so accustomed to having a foot in both camps that it has ended up doing the splits, and become an ecclesiastical eunuch.

Elsewhere in the British Isles, things are not much better. In Scotland the national church has the emblem of a burning bush. The Church of Scotland is semi-established, having fought its battles over patronage and property last century and hammered out a deal which is an equitable model of church/state partnership. Alas, the Church of Scotland seems to be a burnt-out bush when it comes to utilizing the resources of people and territorial bases at its disposal. With the Church of England and the Roman Catholic Church it has found an increasingly high profile role in cautioning against the effects of policies by the Thatcher government. Apposite as many of its criticisms are, like those of the Church of England, its mandate is waning as people in the pews vote with their feet, while the Tory government was returned with a substantial majority in 1987. The Kirk is unlikely ever to enter a union with the other sizeable church north of the border, the Roman Catholic Church, so it is content to keep its position as a 'national' church.

I argue in Chapter 8 that the way forward for Britain as a whole might be to adopt some form of constitution which allows a National Conference of Churches to have a special relationship with the state. However, I don't delude myself that there is an appetite for change. Ostriches don't pull their heads up out of the sand unless there is a threat of slaughter or it is feeding time at the zoo. As to the threat of slaughter, it is unlikely that any latter day Caesar would want to persecute the state churches of Britain – and it is tempting to agree with the churchman who said this was what was wrong with them.

As we shall see, there are a number of incentives for the churches to remain with the status quo. Neither of the British state churches is dependent on taxes delivered via the state to survive financially, and could possibly survive more effectively if disestablished. But the church/state relationship has been compared to a delicate ornament which is liable to slip through the hands of those who try to clean it too vigorously and smash into little pieces. Many within the churches fear that if the whole issue were up for grabs, then the ornament might get some rough handling indeed or even be stolen by the secular lobby and Britain would find itself no longer a 'Christian country'. That is a pragmatic argument but it is surely also a negative and defensive one. Any church which kept its privilege as a minority to promote mission from the safe niche of establishment would have ceased to be a church of living faith and have turned into an icon of the past.

Another consequence of disestablishment in Britain would be that in both Scotland and England the present national churches would be forced to take account of a sizeable Roman Catholic presence (as different in style from one another north and south of the border as the C of E and C of S are from one another). No doubt a lot of the old prejudices would surface if Roman Catholics were to be brought into any future National Conference of Churches which was recognized by the state. One has only to look across the Irish Sea to see how unwilling some parts of the Roman Catholic or Presbyterian communions are to change or compromise with other Christians. Until recent years it was unlikely that steps would be taken to update the British Constitution unless a crisis forced it upon us. (For instance, if Prince Charles became divorced or the Church of Scotland sponsored some form of civil disobedience against Mrs Thatcher's government to assert independence.) Recent events may indicate that the climate is ripe for disestablishment (see p182).

In the ABC of church/state relationships, the African and Brazilian pattern is basically anti-establishment, whereas the relationship in those European countries whose origins go back into the heyday of papal power is one of connivance with the state. It is usually based on a concordat between church and state and truly deserves the letter C in the alphabet – it is Catholic, conservative, cultural. Because of these attributes it is not easily swept aside. But a new middle 'C' has become the dominant tone in these concordat countries – complacency. There is unlikely to be a violent overthrow of the concordat but gradually it will become less relevant as secularization advances. (For example divorce was eventually permitted in Italy despite the concordat.)

The church/state relationship in North America is completely different from the European pattern. Although the New World has embraced technology, mobility and pluralism, there a different kind of secularization is at work. The American Catholic is much more liberal about sexual theology. There is no state church. Indeed, as we shall see, the United States maintains separation between church and state in its Constitution. This has allowed it to tolerate diverse religious groups including some bizarre cults, all of which enjoy freedom under the law and tax exemption. But this toleration has been bought at a price – the substitution of the symbols of the state as sacral elements and the surrender of the vacuum between church and state to the Electronic Church. If not repelled by its Cadillac gospel, we have at least been given cause in recent years to question its morals.

At the other end of the spectrum from the United States of America is the Lutheran model in Scandinavia. In Denmark, Norway, Sweden and Finland the Lutheran Church is the state church. It is run like a civil service and paid for by taxation. This results in ludicrous anomalies. Technically 95 per cent of Swedes are members of the Church of Sweden but only a tiny minority of them ever attend it. There is no severe discontent about this situation, no foment to cut off the church's money. But it is difficult not to conclude that despite a rich and omnipresent church, the widespread secularism which pervades Nordic life is in direct relation to the quiescent role of the churches. Further south in Europe, the Calvinist Reformation produced a church/state bond which has been described as theocracy. The power to punish moral offences no longer belongs to the Reformed churches in Switzerland but its ministers are paid through state taxes. The country is divided into Protestant and Catholic cantons, the church tax going to the officially recognized denomination in that area. It would be open to a Swiss citizen to opt out of this system and elect for his church tax to be paid to a charity fund, but few do so. The 'penalty' for this might be the withdrawal of the right to the services of a minister for funeral rites. Excommunication is seldom an issue since most adolescent Swiss take advantage of the communicant classes which permit them to take time off school, and after confirmation they retire to a limbo of non-involvement.

A similar situation pertains in West Germany, except that the tax-payer lists his or her denomination and the taxes are allocated to that or to a charity register. It means that the Swiss and West German churches are rich and do not need to worry about attendances (which are better than in Scandinavia) but one cannot avoid the impression that their material prosperity has been bought at the price of relegating their position in society to a peripheral one. It is a far cry from the days when Boniface VIII could write in his bull *unam sanctam* of 1302: 'He who denies that the secular sword is in the power of Peter does not understand the words of the Lord . . .' That kind of papal monarchism, or its vain equivalent after the French Revolution, ultramontanism, is now thankfully a historical curiosity. Modern church/state relations in central Europe are a far cry from Caesaro-papism. But although the modern system may keep the churches solvent, it is not combating indifference towards religion. To paraphrase a well known text: 'What does it profit a church to gain the whole establishment and lose the souls for which it exists?'

That point is highlighted if we look from central Europe to the north and east. In Poland the Roman Catholic Church is not established but is all-pervasive in what is officially a Marxist state. It has played no small role in achieving some of the social and humanitarian reforms which have been wrung out of the state. The Polish people won these reforms not simply because the Polish pope had put his divisions on their side; the strength of witness of the Church was the determining factor, and it raises again the question of whether the Christian Church is truest to itself when it is under attack rather than allied to power structures.

East Germany, or the DDR, does not receive attention later in this book, so it is worthwhile here to contrast the church/state situation in the two Germanys. In the DDR, there is no state support for the clergy but state grants are made available to religious charities. Freedom of religion is guaranteed under the 1974 Constitution and of 17 million people in the DDR 11 million are Christian, the overwhelming bulk of these being Protestants following Luther's heritage. Indeed in 1983 the 500th anniversary of Luther's birth provided an opportunity for the DDR to show that, with the exception of Poland, it was leading the way in religious *glasnost* in the Eastern bloc. This openness has rebounded upon the state, for the growth in East Germany of peace movements has propelled the church into the role of critic. The East German church has been reluctant to accept the role and the peace campaign is much more low-key than the rallies and fence-cutting activities in the West, but as one Lutheran pastor puts it, 'It is a challenge and a sign or symbol of another mentality without anger or tension and that is why it is seen as being so dangerous to the state.'

Numerically, the 58 million of West Germany's 62 million population who are 'Christian' are more significant, but in terms of the effect they have within the country as a whole, it is the weaker church which wields the greater influence on the way people are thinking about the future. If we look at examples of countries in which the church has a prophetic role – sometimes in open defiance of the state, as in Poland, South Africa and parts of Latin America – we see that as well as their becoming a focus of dissent within those countries, they tend to win the admiration and support of international opinion. The church assumes a role of moral leadership because it leads by assent internally and externally. This could, of course, be by default. If there is no political opposition (if dissidents are in gaol or banned or in exile) and the church has occupied the vacuum, it has done so perhaps out of necessity or by invitation or because it cannot resist getting involved in politics. The last motive is one that is often ascribed to the church when the 'social gospel' becomes almost indistinguishable from a socialist manifesto. But the same trap can befall those on the political right who reinterpret the gospel as patriotism or 'decency' or bourgeois standards of behaviour.

Religion as a force for change is difficult to assess, particularly in a society in which there is widespread agnosticism about the existence of a Supreme Being. Some will see the church as a leftover from history, a club which has at various times appeared in the guise of the Ku-Klux-Klan and the Pilgrim Fathers, the penniless monk and the proud prelate. Or as a multinational business which claims allegiance from millions of customers. Or again as an institution like the police or the banks which exists to promote orderly dealings between members of society. They will not judge it on a metaphysical basis but on its history. If that was all there was to assess, then it is probable that most people would regard the church as at best neutral and at worst an evil influence.

Ecclesiology is the word used to describe what we believe the church to be. In the first few centuries the church was the community of believers who were called together for worship and fellowship. As the notion of monarchial bishops developed, the concept of church became more identified with a hierarchical organization with doctrines and regulations governing faith and practice. Such an infrastructure existed by the time of Constantine and the organization was well suited to becoming the state church of the Roman empire.

Before beginning a survey of several current models of church/state relationship, we should review briefly the major landmarks in the evolution of the Christian state after AD 312. Early in 313, Constantine and his co-emperor Licinius issued the Edict of Toleration at Milan which made religion a matter for individual conscience to decide. It went further and restored property not only to Christians but to the church, the first evidence of the church being treated as a corporation although the tone suggests it had this status already. Following hard on this came measures to pay Christian clergy out of state funds and exempt them from public office, a further privilege. All these applied only to Catholic clergy, and when the Donatists in North Africa lost their case to excommunicate any who had renounced Christianity under the persecutions, they seethed against the Constantine deal as an ungodly compromise and as a result were marginalized with no privileges.

Constantine convoked the Council of Nicea in 325 because of the crisis in the church over the views of the theologian Arius (who taught that Jesus was not fully God because of his essential humanity). There is no suggestion that the emperor directed the Council which was run by the theologians. The Nicean Creed united the church but already the disputes with those who would not admit any division between spirit and matter were casting their shadows. Eusebius of Caesarea, a gifted bishop/historian, proclaimed Constantine as 'vice-regent of God' whose duty it was to develop his high calling and incidentally to coerce heretics into submission. However, Constantine in 328 was warning the high-handed Athanasius on his appointment to the important see of Alexandria that he should not exclude heretics from his services, an interesting example of an early tug-of-war between the church, which wanted purity of faith, and the emperor who wanted to keep his empire together. It was a tension that was to persist for centuries.

It should not be thought that everything changed overnight. Constantine retained his pagan title of Pontifex Maximus (ironically now borne by the pope) and many major festivals remained pagan. However, in 330 he designated Constantinople the Christian capital of the empire. The difficulty with Christianity was that it did not allow its followers to be relaxed about pagan customs. It refused to tolerate Roman paganism or bless a state apparatus which endorsed pagan cults. A Christian emperor could not continue to claim divine status, but if he did not do so, the pagan gods would not exercise protection over the state. It placed the emperor in a no-win situation. Counsellors like Eusebius did much to encourage Constantine until his death in 337, but by then it was becoming clear to the Christians that in order to consolidate their privileged position they would need to take over the Constitution and restructure it, so that they called the shots. How successful they were in doing this is demonstrated by the complete failure of Julian the Apostate to turn the clock back. Christianity was too strong to be tampered with. In 360 its property became exempt from taxation. In 378 the Bishop of Rome received legal immunity. In 373 Ambrose forsook a top civil post to become Bishop of Milan, a sign that high-fliers were attracted to a church career and of how power was shifting from the state to the church.

A century after Milvian Bridge, the wheel had come full circle. Pagans were now barred from civil posts and mobs acting in the name of the church were plundering and even murdering pagans. The persecuted had become the persecutors. It was at this time that Augustine wrote *The City of God*, a key work on the role of the church in history which was realistic about the human imperfections which went with establishment and less idealistic than Eusebius and his followers about Rome as God's instrument for Christianising the world. However, Augustine was not averse to using the state's power to compel obedience to Rome. His see was in North Africa and the precariousness of empire was brought home to him by the sack of Rome by the tribes from the north in 410. The Western church was, however, strengthened by these successive incursions. It became the legitimizing agent of Constantinople for the barbarian kings who ruled in the western half of a now broken empire. This led to an attempt by Constantinople to assert itself, but Pope Leo I saw his chance to establish supremacy for the see of Peter and his Tome (AD 449) formed the basis of the Council of Chalcedon in 451, which marks the high point of Roman influence in the east – but the cost was schism between Constantinople and Alexandria. (The issue was the old Christ:God/man dichotomy; the protagonists Cyril and Nestorius. The latter was partly vindicated, but Rome was the real winner.) The next years were spent battling over whether or not Chalcedon should be upheld, with a continuous see-sawing of power plays between Rome and Constantinople. The seventh century brought the incursion of Islam and only the pro-Chalcedon parts of the empire remained.

In the West the empire finally lost out when the Franks took Italy in 751 and gave the former Byzantine territories to the pope who became their temporal sovereign. From that time on, the Christian state in the West would appear as a papal creation and a new historical era had begun. In one sense it made the papacy a subservient power, but in another it freed the papacy to stake legal claims to supremacy as it paraded the forged Donation of Constantine, a document in which a grateful emperor grants the western half of his empire to the pope who had allegedly cured him of leprosy. It was exposed by Renaissance scholars because of its use of anachronisms such as a papal crown which did not exist in the fourth century.

It matters little that the claim of Rome to be top dog in the Christian world rested on a fraud since there was no one to dispute it for the next three hundred years. Islam might have overrun the Holy Roman Empire (and ended the partnership between Charlemagne and the pope) but it had reached the end of its lines of supply. As it was, from Bede to Luther, from the Dark Ages to the Renaissance, the papacy became the dominant institution in Western Europe. In the form of the papacy, the ghost of the Roman Empire was sitting crowned upon the grave.

The two main characteristics of medieval government, whether secular or ecclesiastical, were to dispense benefits and justice. The papacy was uniquely placed to arbitrate in disputes, deal with both sides and profit from the transaction. To us it may sound like extortion, but benefits and justice went hand in hand and the papacy could often deliver. R W Southern cites the case of a dispute about a parish church in Lingfield in 1144, during a period of acute civil war in England when relations with Normandy were severed. The case went from England through Normandy to Rome and back, and the pope had his judgement implemented two thousand miles away while wars raged in between. Little wonder that the papal courts became favourite venues for the medieval obsession with litigation. A result of the pay-off system was the growing wealth of the monasteries which were exempt from taxes.

In the era of the crusades there were attempts to re-unite Christendom. This would have brought the emperors based in Constantinople back into partnership with the papacy. Between 1054 and 1274 the popes pursued a policy[3] of keeping channels open to the emperor and grinding down the Patriarch of Constantinople. These attempts failed, and it is intriguing to speculate on what might have happened if they had succeeded and the partnership had turned its joint might upon a Holy Land crusade and established Christendom around the Mediterranean. As it was, nothing came of these moves despite the busy traffic in legates and ships and crusaders. 'In a sense 1274 was the last hopeful year in the Middle Ages. Henceforth the Greek church/state was engaged in a losing struggle for survival against external attack, and the Latins were beset with the rising difficulties of internal disintegration.'[4]
The Greek church/state disappeared when it was engulfed by the conquerors of Islam and the Western papacy developed the infamous tool of the Inquisition to deal with the enemy within. From 1274 on, the popes were in a seemingly powerful position. They controlled the disposal of benefices and thus vast wealth, and had developed the system of indulgences. But other factors acted against them. The growth of monasteries had got out of hand and a ban on new religious orders resulted in unofficial 'hippy' cults like the beghards and flagellants. The pope had also lost his touchstone of church/state power, the emperor. The pope claimed the right to crown the emperor and in many ways derived his command of the secular arm from his ability to manipulate the emperor's authority as guardian of the church. Indirect power meant nothing unless it could be backed by secular action and it was increasingly apparent that kings were determined to run things their way without interference from the pope.

The English Reformation is an example of this trend. Henry VIII set up his own church. The Lutheran Reformation was driven by theological fuel but it was effected by the desire of the German princes to assert control over the rich lands and benefices of the papacy. They were only too ready to do business with Luther, as were the Swiss to adopt the Calvinist theocracy which left religion with income but no control, except over morals and doctrine. In retrospect, therefore, Boniface's vain boast in 1302 ('He who denies that the secular sword is in the power of Peter does not understand

3.   1054. Great Schism between Rome and Constantinople. Pope excommunicates patriarch. Then in 1274, Council of Lyons attempts to re-unite Rome and Constantinople. Mendicant orders discouraged.
4   R W Southern *Western Society and the Church in the Middle Ages*, Pelican 1970.

the words of the Lord'), represents the zenith of papal pretensions.[5]

The doctrine of the two swords survived in some ways through the centuries of the divine right of kings, a clear case of the emperor stealing the pope's clothes. But after the gunpowder smoke of the seventeenth century had cleared, ideas which depended on allying secular power to divine sanction seemed to have lost their credibility. A new rationalism which saw 'rights' in humanistic terms rather than in *ex officio* powers was growing. The French Revolution and the American Revolution put further nails in the coffin of papal monarchy. The former made the Roman Church pay for its sins of complicity and the latter made sure that no religion could get its hands on secular power in the new America. However, there is an important factor underlying the church/state relationships which have developed in this period of modern history. In sweeping away the old theocracies and papal monarchies, the constitutional arrangements which were made to accommodate various state churches relied on inherited assumptions about the right of the church to operate as the arbiter of correct religion. It was natural that they did not take account of pluralism or individual conscience. These were not ideas that had much currency when the constitutional arrangements were being made in Britain.

In other words, concepts such as human rights and freedom of religious belief, which are part of international law and United Nations charters in today's world, played little part in the church/state concordats of many of today's nations. Little wonder that when constitutional reform is on the agenda, religious establishment is seen as an anachronism. In 1900 there were 145 countries in the world which regarded themselves as officially religious, but this had declined to 101 by 1980. In the same year 1,307 million people lived under these religious states; 1,579 millions under secular regimes; 1,488 millions under atheist regimes. The numbers of Christians in these three categories were 662, 513 and 524 millions respectively. It is estimated that half the people of the world live in conditions in which religious freedoms are curtailed; and 60 per cent of all Christians are in this situation.[6] But after we have digested all these statistics, what is to be said? Persecution does not make for a greater number of saints (martyrs, perhaps), but it does appear to result in an energizing of the church towards a more dynamic expression of faith. The 'Gideon syndrome' comes into operation and the core of

5   In the bull *unam sanctam*.
6   Figures from *World Christian Encyclopaedia*, OUP 1980.

believers appears to be more highly motivated than its counterparts in states in which the church is in a majority position. Standard of living is no guide. Who is to judge but God between the witness of churchgoers in an African village, in a Brazilian barrio or a South Carolina suburb? All have active religious practice and all have vastly different forms of church/state systems.

Contemporary church/state relationships seem to fall into the following categories:

1. Inherited from a 'Revolution' settlement or constitutional arrangement based on the medieval state.
2. An accommodation between church and state giving special privileges to one church.
3. Secular state which recognizes church interests.
4. Secular state which does not recognize any official religion.
5. Secular state which licenses religion and may grant status to a particular church.

There is only one nation in which the state officially promotes atheism (Albania). Although the situation in many Marxist states falls into category 5 which may be seen as state control of religion, it is arguable that this is no different from how things were in many periods in history up to and including the rule of Constantine. No state can afford to ignore a church which commands the allegiance of substantial numbers of its citizens. The question is whether it is right to enshrine this relationship in the constitution and whether the church is compromised by accepting privileges from the state. Although much has changed since the time of Constantine, that question is still very relevant today.

2 Reinventing the Church: Brazil

It has been called 'upside-down theology'. It is reviled, revered and misunderstood around the world. In liberal circles it is a buzz-word to affirm solidarity with the oppressed. In the Vatican it is a by-word for communism. Liberation theology is nothing if not talked about. What it stands for, is another matter.

To listen to many of the groups in Britain who fight racism or campaign for the Third World or for disadvantaged groups, liberation theology is the religion of the downtrodden who will obtain justice when power is transferred to them. That makes liberation theology sound like a power play and a cloak for political action, which is precisely the accusation that its opponents level against it. Yet despite the appearance of being all things to all people, liberation theology has a very definite context. That context is Latin America, a vast continent which was trodden beneath the imperial feet of Spain and Portugal and converted to Catholicism. As might be expected, the rulers exported an authoritarian brand of religion which was granted state privileges in a concordat with the state. The twentieth century saw the rise of military dictatorships which took over the reins of power and continued the arrangement. Coca-Cola imperialism from North America brought evangelical Protestantism into some states in Latin America, but in general the continent was thoroughly Roman Catholic and that church was thoroughly pledged to uphold the state. In the 1960s something happened which resulted in a profound change in church/state relationships.

The military juntas had become too oppressive. The use of torture and murder by police in certain states had become epidemic. It came at a time when there was renewed emphasis on human rights issues. The Second Vatican Council (Vatican II) had made a fundamental shift in the self-definition of the Roman Catholic Church. Its priests and nuns in Latin America made use of that to develop a response to the oppression which gave some hope to the people. Some became identified with human rights movements. Within a decade, more and more Roman Catholic priests came to see themselves as servants among the estate workers rather than chaplains to the lord in the manor. The emphasis was on practical charity and political solidarity. When the Mass was translated into Spanish and Portugese, for the first time, literally and metaphorically, the priests spoke a language that their people could understand.

The profound implications of this were the subject of reflection by priest theologians who had received their training in the scholastic tradition of European Catholicism. It led them to abandon the traditional 'top-down' hierarchy of authority. Since the concerns and the needs of the people were foremost in their minds, these concerns became the agenda. Action was followed by reflection – an inversion of the traditional theological process. It was truly theology turned on its head. *Praxis* – or action – was the measure of orthodoxy, not the dogmas of the church. Not only was this attitude novel, but it turned the authority of the church upside down.

In this brief phase in the history of Latin America the church/state relationship had radically altered. Church was now aligned with people against junta and generalissimo. The small minority who controlled the wealth and the land in South American dictatorships felt betrayed. They were shocked when the local priest came as spokesman for peasant farmers who wanted permission to buy land for a school. They refused and were appalled that the priest did not take no for an answer. He rolled up his sleeves and started to lay the foundations himself. Occasionally, a landowner would take the law into his own hands and shoot someone on his land. Still that did not deter the meddling priest. But he stopped coming with requests. Instead he aligned himself more completely with the peasants. Incidents like that were all too common during the birth of liberation theology and nowhere more common than in the country that dominates South America geographically and demographically, and lays greatest claim to the creation of liberation theology – Brazil.

Brazil is synonymous with Samba and sunshine – and soaring inflation. No amount of the first two can seem to counteract the inexorable rise of the third. Like a huge dammed lake, the national debt lurks in the dark mountains behind the sunny beaches, threatening one day to burst and flood the land. The metaphor is illustrated every time the rains come. Red rivers, coloured by the soil of the coastal cities, sweep away roads and houses. The first victims are inevitably the *favela* dwellers, the flotsam and jetsam of Brazilian society whose homes are made literally from cardboard scavenged from the local rubbish tip. A *favela* is not merely inadequate housing. It is not just a slum or a shanty town. It is worse than these. It is one step up from the rubbish heap, a crack in the industrial landscape into which people have crawled for shelter and fallen through to hit rock bottom on the standard of living scale. From a total population of 120 million in Brazil, it was estimated that in 1982 four million lives in *favelas*, begging or stealing food and breathing air that grew more fetid each day. Approximately 10 per cent of Brazilians live in one city, the industrial capital of São Paulo. The archdiocese of São Paulo undertook a survey in 1975 which revealed 26,000 unregistered dwellings, 5,000 secret subdivisions, one million homes without sanitation and 2 million with inadequate facilities. Of these, 95 per cent had television. That is just one of the paradoxes of Brazil, a glorious country of hot sun and rainforests, of beaches and mountain plateaux, of shrinking currency and burgeoning population. A Third World country with modern industry, Brazil has been called 'Belindia' because a quarter of the population enjoy the standard of living of Belgians, a quarter just get by; and half live in abject poverty such as is widespread in India.

The church is trusted in Brazil in a way that the state is not. My first experience of this was on arrival when I was given a quick lesson on the vagaries of the Brazilian currency. Brazil used to have the *cruzeiro* as its currency, a word which spoke of the close connection to the cross of Christianity in the past. The military regime had further driven home the parallel by their vicious torture campaigns against dissidents in the early 1970s. Then came elections and hope surged of a renaissance in Brazilian life. But the new president, Tancredi, died before assuming office. President Sarney took his place and promised to stabilize prices which had soared when the effect of the regime's debts filtered through to the economy. He announced overnight a gigantic devaluation – and a new currency, the *crusado*, which was to be worth 1,000 *cruzeiros*, while the old notes were overstamped and kept in circulation. For a while Sarney's 'crusade' worked – that is what the word *crusado* means – but soon its alternative meaning came to the fore – 'uppercut'. Brazil is still reeling from that blow but is not yet counted out.

Brazil has all the vices and virtues of the Latin American continent – and it has them in greater abundance. But it also has a unique phenomenon which has had a revolutionary impact on its religious life – the *communidades ecclesiales de base* (CEBs). Commune, congregation, parish – none of these words quite describes the role of the base communities which now number over 120,000 in Brazil (they are common in Nicaragua also). Their flexibility makes them difficult to define, but their importance goes further than role or number. They represent a profound revolution in thinking about the church. In many ways they are a return to patterns of church which were evident in the early Christian communities. Theologians, in trying to explain them, often use terms like *koinonia* or *communio*, but more important than titles or theories is their function, which is *praxis*, the acting out of faith.

In an interview in *Latinamerica Press* in January 1983, an Irish-born nun, Sister Gabriela O'Connor, described how she had worked for twelve years in Brazil doing the conventional work of the 'top-down' church. Then, at Villa Monte Santo one day in the late 1960s, a parishioner came to her lamenting that the garbage truck had not come for weeks and that the village was drowning in rubbish. From the self-help group that grew out of that need came a regular litter patrol, a campaign for a road so that the truck would not baulk at the journey, and eventually requests from the people to have Bible study relevant to their needs. Seven years later Sister Gabriela reflected: 'It was just something that happened naturally. People are very religious here. I've seen the community's faith deepen over the years. They used to be horrified when they were called "communists". They'd say, but we don't even know what communism is, other than living communistically together. But we do know that the Lord said . . . and then they'd quote scripture at you. We no longer feel that we have to defend ourselves when we are branded revolutionaries. On the contrary, in such an oppressive situation we *must* be revolutionaries – we wouldn't be Christians if we weren't. A miracle is taking place here and all over Brazil.'

Is that hype? Over-zealous pietism? Gilding the lily on the garbage patch? I knew that I could not understand the books on liberation theology or the claims like those of Sister Gabriela unless I saw something of what was going on for myself. My destination was Carapicuiba, a dense suburb of Sâo Paulo where 400,000 people are concentrated into 35,000 square metres. It has all the deprivation of the worst parts of Brazil and yet is only a short distance from the big industrial plants at Sâo Bernardo. Just beyond is a ghetto of new housing built behind a security fence with armed guards at the entrance, where the more prosperous citizens huddle in order to minimize their chances of being robbed. My host was a down-to-earth Scots priest, John McGuire, whose garb never varied from jeans and a T-shirt (except for slacks and a summer shirt on the day we went to see the cardinal). But he was recognized everywhere he went in his white VW van by the 'fans' as he affectionately called the people – not a reference to their being *his* fans but drawn from his own intense love of football. He eschewed a starring role for himself. He was more like a football manager but thought of himself as a 'punter' on the terraces. His current project while I was with him was the building of a crèche whose foundations would support the sanctuary for a new church. Currently he was using a kind of double garage beneath his flat for one of his four sanctuaries. A warm and witty man in his early forties, he had been nearly thirteen years in Brazil and has not lost his sense of humour or his sense of perspective about the frustrating side of Brazilian life which he usually met with the expostulation, 'Mickey mousery!'. Such an earthy Scot was the essential witness I needed to convince me that liberation theology was not a con. I found, by listening and living inside his parish, that it is not.

At night from the balcony of the priest's flat in Carapicuiba you can see the lights of downtown Sâo Paulo twinkling on a lake. At least it looks like a lake at night, but when the hot sun beats down, it is revealed for what it is – a sandpit which has flooded. Around the edges, between the railway and the water, are heaps of rubbish which create their own miasma of rot and stench. Yet as each load arrives, figures emerge from the camouflage of the heap to rake over the contents. They retire with the pickings – often decaying food which they devour desperately before anyone else can get at it – back to the camouflage dwelling, the *favela* that is indistinguishable from the cardboard of the rubbish.

Further up the hill, in the high *favela* (plywood and breeze-block dwellings with water and electricity), Fr McGuire is paying a call. He has as his parish half the 'village' of Carapicuiba. Today, two of his parishioners are in a bad way. The woman who greets us outside her *favela* is coughing in an ugly way. Her skin is wizened, her eyes dull. A badly rolled cigarette burns in her fingers. She looks seventy and is fifty.

Inside, her husband lies on the bed he has occupied since a bullet shattered his spine seven years earlier. He greets us cheerfully with a handshake in the normal Brazilian manner. The other hand nurses the plastic bladder barely concealed by the dirty bedclothes. There is no welfare, but he is entitled to a small allowance of rice and beans – survival diet. But it has not been delivered this week.

Padre John promises to investigate or to give the woman some food from the cache he keeps for the purpose at the back of his flat. We climb into the van and swing downhill past the children of the family we have just left. Pretty young girls, whose soft skin will soon be affected by vitamin deficiency and who will be under pressure to sell their bodies when they have nothing left to sell in their home.

Our next call was to buy a huge order of beer. This was not for the padre but for one of his flock who runs an *adega*, a hole-in-the-wall shop, and who cannot get the discount that is available to the padre who knows that the saving will come back to the church. So I am enlisted to load the crates as a labourer in the beer-garden of the Lord. We do not have time to enjoy the fruits of our labour before we leave for the next visit, passing on the way the school which has just been built next to a *favela* so that some of the children can have a chance of education. Not all will take it. Their parents will demand that they go on the road to collect cardboard instead of going to school. The van gives a toot and we wave to a group of boys playing the Brazilian version of cricket with beer cans for wickets. Remembering our own load, we bump over the 'sleeping policemen' placed at regular intervals in the road to deter the young men from emulating Brazilian hero and world champion driver, Nelson Piquet. Not all the policemen are sleeping. Some are out stopping cars to inspect documents, hoping for a bribe from those whose papers are not in order. In the matrix of Brazilian society, police and politicians are enmeshed in a web of graft, bureaucracy and favouritism. Dollars double your chances of slipping through the net.

But it is not only the church that is trying to help those who have sunk to their knees. Part of the country's trouble is the difficulty of raising taxes for the immense public expenditure which is necessary to maintain the infrastructure of roads and bridges that an industrial economy needs as much as schools and health centres. Luiz Carlos Neves, the Prefect (Mayor) of Carapicuiba brought that home to me when I went to see him. His suburb contains 400,000 people, 126,000 of whom have the right to vote, and he administers a budget of 300 million *crusados*. But the neighbouring suburb of Barureiri, with roughly the same social profile and a third of the population, raises three times that amount in taxes. Another neighbour has double the population and ten times the revenue. He showed me photographs of the teeming streets. 'Forty per cent of the people who live here are from the rural north-east. They come here because they've been told the streets are paved with gold.

'The railway attracts them here like a magnet. Street hawkers are a problem. A lot of them come from the north. I tried once to make a hole in this problem by calling some of them together and asking what their trades had been. Then I gave them jobs doing the same thing in Carapicuiba and one I gave his fare back to the north. Within weeks they were all back where they started. Brazil is rich in land and in people. But it's not always a question of giving the people land. That has been tried and sometimes they sell the land and migrate back to the city. It's easier dealing with a community, so the government gives incentives to communities.'

Looking behind him in his office I caught sight of a large crucifix, the wounds painted in tiny rivulets on the body of the Christ. It stood between a photograph of the pope and the three large flags – state, nation and party. I asked him how church/state co-operation worked at the local level. 'If someone belongs to a religion, any religion, the administration is happy to help. Suppose a church starts a programme for children or a school, we will help with teachers, food for lunches, things like that.' I put it to him that those at the bottom of the pile needed positive initiative perhaps more than the kind of top-up help he had outlined. The prefect agreed. 'We have some projects for the poor. But some powerful minorities like the farmers and landowners are against them because it means they will lose profit. I can get a grant for 1,000 self-build houses but I need land and—' The prefect waved his hand towards the window, indicating the congested landscape packed with houses. He continued, 'I am trying to urbanize the *favelas* but it is not easy. My wife promised some of the people who live down by the rubbish dump a rice and beans allowance if they left there. But they won't budge. Greed and cunning have taken them over. We built a school between one *favela* and a council estate and hoped that the *favela* children would attend. But their parents send them out collecting cardboard because they lose usefulness if they are at school. And the other side of it is that the council-house people refuse to send their children to that school because they will be mixing with the *favela* children.' The prefect looks back resignedly and I begin to see what someone later described to me as the never-ending wheel of Brazil's problems.

We take our leave of the prefect and emerge into a mêlée of people streaming out of the bus and train stations which back on to the rather anonymous prefectura. It is a reminder that the ten-hour working day is coming to an end and we must be on our way to the local foundry before it closes at six o'clock.

Padre John can't afford to be late as we are going to order eight tons of iron from this foundry. Not any old iron, but rods of specific measurements which will be used for the reinforced concrete for the foundations of the crèche and new church he is building on the vacant site behind the flat. All the building will be done by workers from the parish. They have already built two halls for different parts of the parish and a health centre. They have enough cement, so our next call is to order more sand. On the way back we pay a pastoral call on an AIDS sufferer who contracted the disease from a blood transfusion and has been sent home to die in the 'village of the frog', part of the parish down by the 'lake' which invariably floods the village when the rains come.

Sunday service is packed in the village of the frog, mainly by young people. A violinist and guitarist accompany the lady who leads the singing. With the shortage of priests so acute in Brazil, the laity lead and organize almost everything but the Mass itself. In parts of the country they well nigh do that, too, but more of that later. Padre John goes down well. He is fond of football but today's sermon mentions Nelson Picquet. In front of me are two young newly-weds. The girl stands out, not just because of her bright yellow sleeveless dress but because her face could easily have been a cover for *Vogue*. John tells me she was brought up in the village and has opted to carry on living there. They are lucky, both she and her husband have jobs. The factory where we go for lunch no longer provides jobs. The machines have been taken away and it is deserted. The automotive parts industry is in decline. Upstairs in the management offices the four brothers who run the factory wait to learn if their schemes for diversifying their product will succeed. They are in cheery and optimistic mood. 'We have a saying – "God is Brazilian" – he'll sort it out.' 'Even the burglars here are religious,' claims another brother. 'They say, "If God wills it" before they steal anything.'

There is a great appetite for religion but, alas, also for burglary in Brazil. Beneath us on the factory floor is the spot where Padre John keeps his VW van safe inside the security gate to discourage the thieves who stole his last one. The inequalities in Brazilian society breed desperate men. One of the village policemen was shot outside the prefectura in the centre of Carapicuiba that very week. It was a revenge killing and the victim's relatives know who to look for. 'They'll catch him, shoot him and that will be the last of it. No investigation,' the padre predicted with a distinct lack of relish. For once he was wrong. They did catch him the next day, but they didn't shoot him. Instead they left him to die in the cells, his private parts having been amputated.

The next day there was a Mass for the dead policeman. 'I shall take the opportunity to talk about the need to forgo violence and revenge,' said Padre John, who has conducted last rites for many victims of murder. When the Mass is over, it is time to go off for the next of many meals I was to enjoy in the homes of a circle of key families of the parish. In the hectic life that Padre John leads, it is a chance for a breather, but there is always church business to be talked about and the opportunity to keep in touch. But there is even more to it than that, as I soon became aware.

Tonight we go off for a meal with a family from the congregation which resembles the Marx Brothers. Grandma has been at the sugar-cane brandy and a good time is being had by all. They are boisterous, generous with their hospitality – and very poor. Laughter and conversation (conducted at bellowing level) give way to cabaret. Guitars are produced and Grandpa Nilso and his son Jochin sing their own compositions – one in praise of St Joseph who was the channel of prayers for the curing of a past illness. This is not the only minor miracle. Nilso's brother sings a solo for the first time in twenty years. Our spirits are high as we head the van up the one in two incline of the muddy road for home. When we get there a few figures emerge from the dusk. The padre disappears into his store and emerges with several plastic bags filled with rice and beans which are grabbed by grateful hands and vanish into the night. Then it is time for the padre to turn in. The next day he has to do the round of three parishes for Mass.

You may be wondering what all this has to do with church and state, why the experience of one particular parish in Brazil deserves mention in these pages. Fr John McGuire would not claim that he or his parish is special. Indeed there are more spectacular examples of successful parishes in Latin America. But there several reasons for dwelling on it here, and it illustrates a number of things about liberation theology. First, it is not the 'unusual' parishes in which the effects of the 'liberation' experience are to be found, but in the ordinary ones. Although there are variations between church/state relationships throughout Latin America and between brands of liberation theology, one factor predominates above all others – experience precedes theory. Gustavo Gûtiérrez puts it thus: 'Practice leading to theory, leading to practice – that is the vehicle of truth.'

Much of what is written by the liberation theologians is abstract and might seem to contradict this. I must confess that when I first read their books, the abstractions about '*praxis*' and 'liberation' and 'community' were not easy to relate to. It was difficult to see what all the fuss was about. Were they codes for Marxist ideas? Or were the liberationists, like many theologians, keen to see reality in terms of ideology and validate their experience by that means. Nothing could be further from the truth. The ideas are not Marxist. Occasionally they touch on some of the same methods but they do not share the underlying presumptions.

Second, it is a facet of Latin American life that the social conditions about which they are writing are so common and so intrusive into ordinary experience that they are taken as read. If proof were needed that these are not ivory-tower theologians then one only has to look at the personal life of the leading exponents of the theology. As well as holding professorships they hold pastoral positions in places in which they can hardly avoid being aware of the nitty gritty of life. Nor is the reverse true. That they are 'pastoral priests' who have swallowed a theological lexicon and, like the sorcerer's apprentice, have let loose a demon they cannot control. The academic credentials of the theologians are impeccable. Most were *magna cum laude* at European institutions. But here is the nub. It is because they are not playing the European intellectual game that they are so reviled.

If they were simply sloganizers or closet Marxists these churchmen would have been exposed long ago. The controversial confrontation arises not because they are playing at semantics, nor as we shall see later because they are Marxist, but because they challenge the essence of the colonial Catholicism on which Latin American Christianity was built. As Alistair Kee writes in *Domination or Liberation: The Place of Religion in Social Conflict*:[1]

As a multinational monopoly, the hierarchy regulated supply from its head office in Rome by conditions of licence which were often stringent and in many respects arbitrary ... According to Boff, the Inquisition was little concerned with immorality but greatly concerned with heresy. The reason is quite clear. Immorality which leads to confession, penance, absolution and indulgences, actually stimulates the activity of religious monopoly capitalism. Sin is good for the religious business, but heresy

1. SCM 1986.

threatens the acceptance and credibility of the whole system. In
this approach we see the problem. The church is not guided by
theology or ideas or ideals. Its nature is determined by its mode
of religious production. It is therefore not possible to change the
nature of the church or relations within it at the level of ideas, for
example by exposing the condemning domination. The church and
relations within it can only be changed when the mode of religious
production is replaced.

This is what Boff and his followers have done. They have changed
the nature of 'production' by making the local community the centre
of initiative (and therefore authority). Kee's analysis points up nicely
the similarity with Marxist methods which has so aroused the fears
of the hierarchy. But what should be stressed is that Boff does not
replace the 'means of production' with a socialist political movement
but with a Bible-centred group. However, as we shall see when we
look closer at Boff's work, it would be naive to think that what has
been achieved in Latin America is superficial. It is as profound a
revolution in the concept of the church as occurred at the Protestant
Reformation, and to be fair to the pope and the Congregation for
the Doctrine of the Faith in Rome – they know it. It is simply that
they are trying to stick the wrong label on the reformers, which says
'Made in Eastern Europe' when the credit (or blame) belongs to Latin
America.
    How this peaceful revolution came about was explained to me
by a leading churchman and close friend of Cardinal Arns. He is
the Rev Dr Jaime Wright, general secretary of the United Presbyterian Church of Brazil. A tall man whose Yankee drawl betrays
his American parentage, Dr Wright has become an authority on the
'disappeared ones', those who vanished during the military regime in
the early 1970s. His interest is not academic as his own brother Paul
was one of those who vanished in 1973. The pain still shows in his
face when he speaks of how they used to meet in Republican Square
after exchanging a code over the telephone. Later he found out that
Paul (who was involved with the organization *Assent Populaire*)
was killed after forty-eight hours of torture. The human rights
campaigns of those days cemented Dr Wright's close relationship
with Arns. Both men are determined that Brazil's mini-holocaust
shall not be forgotten. Cardinal Arns has produced *Brazil – never
again!*, the most comprehensive study of the years of torture, which
summarizes a million pages of military court records over five years,
the first study since the Inquisition of oppression from the point of

view of the oppressor. Out of the evil of that half decade came the impetus to change the supportive role the church had played towards previous repressive regimes.

Brazil became a republic in 1891, Dr Wright explains, but there was separation of church and state, unlike in Paraguay and Argentina where Catholicism was the official religion (as was the case in Chile). There was another Brazilian constitution in 1964 but the military coup in that year produced a constitution (amended in 1967) in which Article 5 suspended all constitutional and civil rights and put everyone under the power of military courts. The regime wanted to hold the people down – but it didn't work because the state had no means of dealing with the Vatican - no concordat existed. So the Brazilian church was on its own and turned its back on the state for the first time since it became a colony in 1500. Since 1891 the church had blessed uncritically whoever was in power, but this was different. For the first time priests and nuns who supported the Vatican Council reforms were being attacked.

The secret is that the church is now putting the scriptures in the hands of the people. That is the main reason for the growth of the 'base communities'. It doesn't matter that it may also have been because of a shortage of priests, because when people study the word of God they no longer need an interpreter, because the Holy Spirit is their interpreter. They no longer need the bishop because they have a higher authority – and that undermines the Roman Catholic Church at a crucial point in its hierarchy. Boff doesn't see the bishop–priest–people trinity as a downward flow but a triangle in which the bishop/priest is not a *necessity* for revelation.

'Before Vatican II I don't remember Brazilian Catholics celebrating Easter. There was no joy for the Resurrection. It all ended in the gloom of Good Friday. They believed in a dead Christ and a baby Jesus, neither of whom had any power over death. I remember a crucial incident at the funeral of a student who had been tortured to death. People were warned not to attend by the military who surrounded the cathedral with cordons. Arns got up and spoke on the Resurrection and the importance of believing in a Christ who conquers death. The people were so moved that they exited the cathedral singing a contemporary hymn and spilled down the cathedral steps to face soldiers with sacks of tear-gas grenades. For the first time people had the guts to face the armed forces. It came from faith in a resurrected Lord. That moment was the beginning of the end of the dictatorship. Because dictatorship only ends when fear ends. And that day you could almost see the fear being transferred from the faces of the people surrounded on the cathedral steps to the faces of the soldiers.'[2] The deep voice paused for a time in his darkened lounge and it allowed me to savour that moment of only a decade ago. Jaime Wright then addressed the present situation.

'Today there are no political prisoners in Brazil. Working in the field of human rights is different now. Because it's the violation of the poor that you have to denounce. What happened during the dictatorship was that it was the sons and daughters of the middle class who were being tortured. They're off the hook now, and the church finds itself alone in defending the poor. In 1987 there was a massacre in a prison within sight of a television camera. Fourteen people were bludgeoned to death and the general assumption was that if they're in prison they're guilty, that you're guilty until proved innocent.

'The gap is widening daily in Brazil between the rich and the poor. Prices go up but the minimum wage is held down. What's that but a gross violation of human rights? People are aware of the national debt. But it's not their debt – it's the dictatorship's debt from buying arms and lining pockets. But even the present government can't produce an audit to say where the debt came from. The military won't allow it because it would embarrass them and their friends in North America and Europe who allowed the bill to mount.'

Jaime Wright is scornful of those who try to impose European thinking on Brazil's problems. Arns has already said that if the debt is to be paid, it should not be the people of Brazil who have to pay it. Could this be the seedbed of revolution? Wright thinks not. 'There's no way you can think this. Mobilizing would be difficult – worse than in the worst time of the dictatorship. Anyway, the peripheral poor do not want to overthrow capitalism. They want to be part of the consumer society. That's why, when some of them were given land, they sold it and migrated back to the cities. But until there is land reform that works, we won't move forward. The land can support the population of Brazil if we have reform. Population is not the problem. Nor is the political left which is so fragmented. We have a black joke here that there are forty-seven groups of the left – and they're all clandestine!'

Many people like Jaime Wright believe that the way forward for

2.   A similar confrontation occurred on May Day 1980 when soldiers surrounded on open-air Mass being held for striking car workers in Sâo Bernardo. Non-violence 'won' when the worshippers put flowers in the barrels of the soldiers' rifles.

Brazil lies in the use of the concept of citizenship. Two-thirds of the people pay indirect taxes but don't realize they have involvement and think themselves disenfranchised. It is the church with its stress on 'community' that has provided the dynamic for a change in this attitude, Wright argues.

'Brazil has the most progressive hierarchy in the world. Dom Paulo [Arns] is reluctant to be interventionist. His strategy is to get people involved. He has inverted the pyramid of canonical rights as a bishop. In Sâo Paulo, he held an assembly in 1987 to decide the goals for the next two years, because he believes that the church is the people and therefore he has confidence in the ability of people to determine their priorities. In the world's largest diocese, it must irritate the élite to have these sandalled, ragged people having an equal say with a university professor, but it works. If there is a two-thirds vote in favour of an option it becomes the priority for the whole diocese. Last year's one, not surprisingly, came out in favour of housing as the top priority.'

This process of consultation is practised by many of the pro-liberation Latin American bishops. Archbishop Romero of San Salvador consulted his priests about the sermon he preached in 1980 in the face of military oppression of church personnel which was to prove a fatal provocation to the murderous military.[3] Jaime Wright, despite his being a Presbyterian minister, has even been involved in Dom Paulo's democracy. When Pope John Paul II was paying his visit to Brazil in 1980 he followed his normal practice of inviting his host prelates to contribute notes for his sermon. Dom Paulo drafted Wright on to the committee of five who were writing the pope's sermon. Wright also recalls with affection the tour of the USA he undertook with Dom Helder Câmara in the late 1970s to alert people to the torture regime, when the saintly bishop used to introduce him in his unmistakable accent by saying, 'Thees man is not only a Protestant! More important – he ees the honorary auxiliary bishop of Sâo Paulo!'

Dom Helder is now living in semi-retirement in the north of Brazil and still holds a unique place in the affections of the nation. As the first man to document the torture, he was banned, denounced as a traitor, and his name forbidden to be mentioned in public. His mantle has fallen now on the equally charismatic Dom Paulo Evaristo Arns. Says Wright, 'I think these two men complemented each other. Dom Helder spoke out with great courage. Dom Paulo as a cardinal enjoys diplomatic immunity and is able to protect his back. I would hate to think of this period in Brazil's history without these men.' Not

3.   After the sermon posters appeared, saying 'Be patriotic – kill a priest'.

all Brazil's bishops displayed such leadership. Arns' predecessor in Sâo Paulo, Cardinal Rossi, at one point actually denied there was any torture taking place. He was kicked upstairs into the Vatican after Arns (then an auxiliary bishop en route for another episcopal appointment) was sent with a protest to Rome and was appointed by Pope Paul to fill the vacancy. Today the only staunch conservative in the Brazilian hierarchy is the Archbishop of Rio who did nothing to change his reputation as a reactionary by deleting the slogan issued for the Lent 1988 celebration of the centenary of the abolition of slavery in Brazil. 'I heard the cry of the people!'[4] fell on his deaf ears as he rewrote the liturgy to include patronizing prayers about 'black men being competent to achieve high positions' and entitled it: 'Many colours, one people'. Another stain on the church's record is the Mass said for the military junta in Argentina by the hierarchy there. However, these seem to be the exceptions that prove that liberation theology rules. But it took more than just the catalyst of the torture regime to bring about such a widespread reformation in the Brazilian church.

Born in the 1960s, matured in the 1970s, liberation theology faced its confrontation with its old-fashioned 'parent' in the eighties. But as occurs in so many clashes between offspring and their parents, the idealist youth was trying to follow to its logical consequences the high principles enunciated by the authority figure. In this case it was the Second Vatican Council and the encyclical 'Populorum progressio' written by Pope Paul VI in 1967. It was written in a period when the lid was beginning to rattle on all kinds of societies. 'Make love not war' was the chant as students and idealists protested against Vietnam and nuclear weapons, and 'dropped out' of a materialist society. The cool breeze of Paul's thinking was lost in the ferment of Europe and North America where it was described by the *Wall Street Journal* as 'warmed-over Marxism'. His credibility there suffered further over his 'Humanae Vitae' encyclical opposing artificial contraception, but in Latin America where there is not the same resentment over that issue, it was his statement dealing with the need for more time to be given to the agenda of human rights that claimed attention. It came just in time for a historic meeting of the Latin American bishops at Medellín, which many see in retrospect as the occasion of the birth of liberation theology.

4.   The title echoes that of a famous 1973 document produced by churchmen in the north-east to draw attention to human rights abuses. In 1988 it was applied to the racism issue.

As if to symbolize the change of emphasis, society was first on the agenda (a departure from previous practice), then the church, then theological matters. CEBs were mentioned, as was the phrase 'option for the poor', which was to become a rallying cry during the next decade of repression. Brazil 1964; Bolivia 1971; Uruguay 1973; Chile 1973; Argentina 1976; Peru 1975 and Ecuador 1976. These are the infamous milestones along the road of repression, marking the occasions when coups became a threat to human rights. When 9,000 were liquidated in Argentina in a dirty war, the silence of the church was a kind of complicity. Thus when the bishops met again in 1979 at Puebla, they had come a long and painful way since Medellin and were now speaking of 'a duty and right to be present in politics'. But they also had the presence of a new pope – Karol Wojtyla, John Paul II. The pope from Poland was well versed in oppression by the state but was less sympathetic to the way that many of the bishops talked about ideology. They found common ground in repudiating the 'false consciousness' of Marxist materialism which some states imposed on their citizens. They acknowledged that there were two kinds of political activity: the first concerned with the common good; the second with party affairs, which was properly the concern of lay people. In many ways Puebla was inconclusive in that neither the zealous supporters of CEBs nor the arch-conservatives triumphed, and the vast bulk of bishops unified around the middle. But the middle had shifted. In Brazil, Bishop Candido Padin had drawn attention to the classic 'national security ideology' which sees 'geopolitics' as central to the state's role. It views states as entering alliances with one another for convenience while constantly competing economically and culturally for supremacy. National security is the ultimate end; the method of achieving it through governance means that the individual must at all times be subordinate to the state. In such a society the agents of strategy are the élites of the military and the technocrats. Groups like workers and students are subjects. In defending against the 'enemy' from their superior position, such élites often expect the church to be an ally against Marxism and to lend moral force to the need to obey. When the Nazis of Europe raised such a national security ideology they did not receive church endorsement but neither did they get an orchestrated church campaign against their human rights abuses. Latin America has learned from that mistake. At Puebla, the bishops outlined 'national security doctrine' alongside 'capitalist liberalism' and 'Marxist collectivism' as ideologies which had been used to suppress human beings. 'States pass; the people remain,' they declared. 'We see the growing gap between rich and poor as a scandal and a contradiction to Christian existence. The luxury of a few becomes an insult to the wretched poverty of the masses.' Warning of the sinfulness of this and the prospects of structural conflict they went on to express, 'a preferential option for the poor', a slogan that has now found its way into the language. Puebla, the site of the CELAM (Latin American Bishops' Conference) meeting, was the birthplace aetiologically of '*El pueblo de los pobres*' (the people of the poor).

But the divergence between Rome's magisterium and the liberation theologians was fast widening. At Pueblo the pope had declared that the church did not have to resort to ideologies 'in order to love, defend and collaborate in the liberation of the human being', to which one bishop remarked: 'Let him who is without ideology cast the first stone.' For one does not have to be hostile to Roman Catholicism to be aware that much of its history and style has closely resembled that of a national security ideology in trying to defend Christendom. Phillip Berryman's excellent study *Liberation Theology*[5] draws attention to the work of two Latin American writers, Pablo Richard and Joseph Comblin, on the notion of Christendom. Comblin points out that the prophetic voice needs a structure like Christendom in which to express itself. Those who appear to call for the end of the game of pope versus emperor simply put another label on the box and start another game with new rules. Thus Luther, Calvin and the Puritans with their state churches. In his view the American church/state dichotomy simply led to 'civil religion', a kind of reverence for the state, whereas Richard sees Latin America in terms of Neo-Christendom, first colonialist then military—ecclesiastical. He predicts that something new will replace it (unless the military triumph), since the new popular religious movements reject any kind of Christendom as belonging to the old era of church/state relations.

Berryman sums up: 'Although he does not draw the conclusion, the upshot of Comblin's view is that it is not at all assured that what we are witnessing in Latin America is an end to Christendom. In Nicaragua it may be that the high level of conflict there and the fact that both supporters and opponents of the revolution use religious arguments and symbols, obscure a real move beyond Christendom, as Richards argues. I tend to think, however, that if the revolution is consolidated there and if revolutions occur elsewhere in Latin

5.   Pantheon, N.Y. 1987.

America, Christendom will not simply disappear but will assume another form.'[6]

One could argue that this has already happened. The continental consensus on liberation theology constitutes a kind of Christendom which counterbalances the national security states set up by the military regimes. To my mind, one of the most striking facets of liberation theology is that despite the diversity of countries and situations in which it has been an influence, it can be seen as a common system which has spread across the whole continent in less than two decades. Like Luther's ideas on justification by faith alone which sparked the Reformation, perhaps nothing travels as fast as an idea whose time has come. However, some of the credit should go to the World Council of Churches which did much to publicize the human rights abuses. The liberation theologians themselves emerged as heroes, but the role of the Vatican in helping them to achieve such fame by persecuting them should not be ignored!

I have now reached the difficult point of trying to distil the essence of what the liberation theologians developed in the last twenty years, for as I have already stated, much of their work is abstract and relies not so much on content as method, i.e. reflection on action, rather than *a priori* argument. This means no two CEBs are alike. It is sometimes thought that there is a broad spectrum of 'liberation theologies', some of which are acceptable to the Vatican and some of which are not. This is not so. Not only is there remarkable unanimity between the ideas of the various thinkers but it is not the fringe exponents who were carpeted by Rome but the central figures such as Leonardo Boff and Gustavo Gutierrez. Nor are we talking about hordes of theologians. There are maybe a dozen at most. Best known in the West are the Boffs (Leonardo and Clodovis); Gutierrez; Segundo; Sobrino, plus the two already mentioned, Comblin and Richard. Nearly all are Roman Catholic but Bonino, the Argentine Methodist, deserves mention. Nor need they all be theologians. The winner of the 1980 Nobel Peace Prize for his human rights work, Adolfo Perez Esquivel, is a sculptor. His book *Christ in a Poncho* describes how on a trip to Ecuador he had a dream of Christ on the cross wearing a poncho, and later saw it in reality at a community he was visiting. On emerging from prison he painted it as 'The Christ of the Poor'. Esquivel makes much of the fable of the ants and the elephant. 'There are so many more of us (than the elephant of the state). That's why the basic communities

6.   p 137 op cit.

are so important. They help each member to find himself as a person and it develops a sense of solidarity.'

This oblique approach, writing theology as a series of parables or incidents in life, is followed by Clodovis Boff in his journal *Feet-on-the-Ground Theology*, the product of a safari to the interior of Brazil in which he acquired an injured foot along with the following insight, 'In the heart of the cold and bare earth is hidden treasure – wheat and chaff. That's why it is important always to be alert to what's present and pulsating at the heart of life. The theologian is the diviner who examines the entrails of life in order to find there the signs of the divine. The theologian is the detective of mystery – the explorer of the kingdom in the midst of the world.'

My attempt to harvest the wheat from the chaff yields the following summary of liberation theology:

1.   Faith is interpreted from the point of view of the poor. This results in identifying with them in their struggles. But 'it is not a question of idealizing poverty but rather of taking it as it is: an evil. To protest against it and to struggle to abolish it' (Gutierrez).
2.   People are usually poor because of the way that society is organized, thus it implies a critique of society. It consists of 'unmasking' the anti-Christian elements which can be discovered in Christian society. For instance, it questions the morality of Sâo Paulo schoolkids from rich homes flying in a jet aircraft over *favelas* with no drinking water on their way to Disneyworld in Florida.
3.   This critique extends to the way that the church is organized (see below, p 46 on Boff's challenge to the church). Romero and Sobrino often used Iraneus' saying: 'God's glory is the living human being'. This primacy on the individual is quite distinct from Marxist collectivist authority or the church's hierarchical authority.
4.   Part of reflection is consciousness-raising, a weak English equivalent which does not do justice to the collective element in the term *conscientizacion*. This concept enables the leaders of the base communities (CEBs) to educate the peasants to be aware of the forces that are shaping them. Part of this is simple literacy training, but the intention is to relate this to the Bible and inoculate the peasants against 'popular religion' which tends to see sacraments like baptism as medicine.
5.   The Bible becomes a mirror of the people's reality: slavery in Egypt; exile in Babylon (the big city); Isaiah's prophecies

of liberation from oppression; the parables about the rich in the gospels; Christ's life of poverty among the poor. The list is endless, but the relevance is immediate and dynamic for a person who is taught to read and then given a Bible without prior cultural conditioning.

Whatever else it has been accused of, liberation theology has not been dubbed a failure. Indeed its very success across the continent has forced those who do not approve of it to explain their opposition. As could be expected, the opponents were some of the generals from the juntas who were arresting churchmen and women during the late sixties and seventies. They did not need to write a thesis to hit back when they had plenty of men with truncheons to hit people over the head instead. But the unkindest cut and potentially the most wounding came not from the juntas but from the Vatican. After a stormy visit to Nicaragua in 1983 in which he was caught in one photograph wagging his finger in rebuke at Father Ernesto Cardenal as he knelt to kiss his ring, the pope commissioned Cardinal Ratzinger, the doctrinal watchdog, to assess liberation theology. The result surfaced in a 1984 document 'Instruction on certain aspects of the "theology of Liberation" '. It was a stinging attack and to hammer it home, was issued on the eve of Leonardo Boff's being brought to Rome to be carpeted for his views as expressed in the book *Church, Charism and Power*[7]. Ratzinger's main objections to liberation theology were that (i) its diagnosis was faulty and Marxist, and it encouraged violent revolutionary elements; (ii) it took its agenda from an uneducated proletariat and reduced revelation to the lowest common denominator; (iii) it undermined the divinely ordained structure of the Roman Catholic Church.

The first reaction of many Latin American theologians to point (i) was to think that it could not refer to them, but when Boff was suspended they realized that this time the finger that was pointing belonged to Ratzinger, and it *was* pointing at them. The document reeks with contempt for the Latin American work. Two quotes will suffice: 'The "theologies of liberation" of which we are speaking, mean by *Church of the People* a church of the class, a church of the oppressed people whom it is necessary to "conscientize" in the light of the organized struggle for freedom. For some, the people, thus understood, even become the object of faith.' (IX.12)

'One needs to be on guard against the politicization of existence

7.   Orbis 1981

which, misunderstanding the entire meaning of the kingdom of God
and the transcendence of the person, begins to sacralize politics and
betray the religion of the people in favour of the projects of the
revolution.' (XI.17)

It must have left a very sour taste in the mouths of those who
had suffered a decade of murders of their priest colleagues to be
treated as traitors by their own church. A further nasty twist is that
when Boff had completed his doctoral thesis in Munich in 1970 it
was Ratzinger who had steered it to a publisher. Now the teacher
had turned against the pupil.

Many of the arguments against liberation theology turn on semantics and are in that sense misunderstandings. The charge of Marxism
is not fair when you consider the number of statements denouncing
the oppression of Marxist states in the liberationists' writings. As
for the violence, the theory and practice of the movement has been
non-violent. The argument that they take their agenda from ignorant
peasants does not hold, since the Bible study and *conscientizaćion* is
directed by those with years of theological education behind them.
When you read the story of Cardinal Arns mixing with the Xocos
Indians who had recaptured their statue of St Peter with slingshots,
and saying to them: 'The cardinal admires you and supports you
and seeks to learn from you', you realize that the pygmies of the
faith are not in the jungle, but in the Vatican.

If the first two objections are ill-founded in theory and fact it is
when we come to point (iii) that the trouble starts. Ratzinger: 'It has
to do with a challenge to the hierarchical and sacramental structure
of the church, which was willed by the Lord Himself . . . this position
means that ministers take their origin from the people . . .' (IX.13). If
you read *Church, Charism and Power* where Boff quotes a Brazilian
layman who draws the parallels between the Vatican and the Kremlin
you can begin to realize why it got up Ratzinger's nose so much. If
you then turn to Leonardo Boff's *Ecclesiogenesis: Base Communities
Re-invent the Church* (first published in 1977 in Portugese) and read
(p.7): 'The church sprung from the people is the same as the church
sprung from the apostles,' you begin to understand what Ratzinger
was getting at in IX.13. *Ecclesiogenesis* goes on to advocate circumstances for laity presiding at the Eucharist and a whole chapter on
the possibilities afforded by women priests!

In 1983 Boff gave an interview to *Istoe*, a leading Brazilian
news magazine in which he was asked if the world had become
as important for him as heaven and he replied, 'It's a question of
misplaced attention. One church thinks about God, prayer, Mass, the

sacraments. The other grounds itself more in love of one's neighbour and the practice of justice, more than talk about justice. One church does not exclude the other. Yet in the end we will be judged more for how we have loved than for the number of times we went to Mass or for our beliefs in such teachings as the Immaculate Conception and Papal Infallibility. All Christians would like an infallible pope – or even one who would declare, for example, that capitalism is an iniquitous system (as Paul VI defined it in 'Populorum progressio')! Our greatest challenge today is how to be Christian in a world of misery.'

As a Protestant I am excited by the ecumenical breakthrough that liberation theology brings with it, full of admiration of what has been achieved in Brazil and elsewhere and will happily shout amen as I thumb the pages, but I can quite understand why Cardinal Ratzinger doesn't see it that way. What the Latin Americans are bringing about is not a political revolution but a religious one comparable to the Reformation. There are a number of reasons why, after coming to public notice in 1984, this confrontation has not resulted in Boff and the others simply being fired. The first reason is that they are not marginal or unrepresentative, but central and popular. Declaring them heretics would probably start talk of a schism. No one likes to precipitate schism and it is a last option not a first one. The second reason is that the political situation has eased in South America (but not in Central America) and the church has had a chance to consolidate rather than fight for its life. The third and crucial factor is the person of Dom Paulo Evaristo Arns, Cardinal Archbishop of São Paulo, the uncrowned pope of Latin America. His office carpet was worn thin during the torture time with a procession of refugees from other countries whom he helped, and Boff is his protégé. It was Arns who insisted on going to Rome with Boff, accompanied by Cardinal Lorscheider, to help defend him in 1984.

His photographs show him as an unlikely looking rebel, small, dapper in his grey-sheen double-breasted suit. He greeted me warmly when I visited him, and immediately I became conscious of the charisma he exudes. He sat beside me on the settee and tapped my arm in a friendly manner as he emphasized points. 'Church and state,' he said in perfect English tinged with a French accent he picked up during his education in Paris, 'church and state were divided from the beginning of the Republic. We get no income from the government. But,' he added with a twinkle, 'we are free to protest!'

'Of course, it was very different in the time of censorship.

Some people didn't know about the torture because there was a total censorship. Now our task is to effect changes without being party-political. We are studying exactly this problem. We have produced books and audio-visual material on a whole range of issues. Laymen are in all the parties. Our Justice and Peace commission has five parties represented. That way it's impossible to have real influence without compromising the esse of the church. In the torture times we were the opposition fighting for human rights, dignity and the gospel. But they never knew my voting preference as a pastor. That is part of the positive way that the church can influence the state. Also, as a bishop I have had conversations with people who wanted advice on whether they should co-operate with the government. One was the secretary of health – and one of our best doctors. He came to discuss issues with me and whether he should continue to serve in the government. I said, "As a Christian you have to go and stay as long as you can." '

I ventured to suggest that the same advice could have been given in Nazi Germany. His reply was crisp. 'All these Christians left when they realized they were aiding torture.' We moved on to discuss the crucial issue of liberation theology which colours not only his life in Brazil but his relations with the Vatican. 'Base communities began a long time ago. Before liberation theology was ever known about. I was born in a base community. We did everything for ourselves – roads, schools, as they did in ancient Brazil. Our tiny village of forty families was so far from civilization, fifty miles from wild animals, but it had primary and secondary schools. Organized, people can do so much. Unorganized, they can do nothing. Liberation theology makes us conscious of the opportunities to do something through the gospel and complete the plan of God for the situation we are in. Our fathers opened that world to us. Liberation theology gave us the possibility of coming out of the colonial world of 1500 and making something of tomorrow. Until we do that, we are dependent, the way the black people, the Amazon people, were. When I came back from seminary in 1952 things were better in Brazil than in Europe but now 70 per cent of the population is living with $120 per month and it's impossible to live normally on that.' The twinkle came back into his eye. 'Those are government statistics, so they must be true!'

He went on to make a statement that could have been a cliché on the lips of someone else, but his life has lived the truth of it. 'I come from rich Sâo Paulo but I must fight for the poor in the north-east also. I can't just represent the bankers downtown.' His Eminence then demonstrated intimate acquaintance with the rates of pay for the car workers in Sâo Bernardo and in the multinationals. When we reached the subject of Boff and the Vatican, his memory was as clear but his words were more guarded. The experience has left its mark on him, but he put a cheery face on it. 'If you look at the sequence of the meetings you will see that we first went to Rome in September 1984. We had a further meeting in December when it was still a cool climate. We were determined to show that Rome was not right just because it was Rome. Then in March 1986 we had a meeting with the Holy Father and he gave us a homily at the table for thirty minutes. We discussed liberation as a biblical word, as a historical word and as it occurs in the patristic literature. Then in April 1986 he sent a letter describing "liberation" as useful, opportune and necessary.' Dom Paulo smiled as if it had all been a terrible misunderstanding. Reading between the lines and sensing behind the smile, there must have been a lot of subtle diplomacy and tough talking to get the pope and Ratzinger to back off. The truce resulted in the 1986 Ratzinger document 'Instruction on Christian Freedom and Liberation' which is much more conciliatory and stresses the acceptable uses of the word 'liberation'. Boff agreed to keep a low profile which seemed to suit him fine as he wanted to get on with *praxis*. Gutierrez called it at the time, 'a relaunching' of the movement, adding, 'It closes a chapter; a new, more positive period is beginning.' The impression was gained by many that the Latin Americans were taking the truce as victory. The cardinal would never be caught crowing over a victory, but there is no doubt he got the pope to call off the dogs. His strategy is to praise the pope for characteristics which are admired in Latin America. 'The Holy Father is an anthropologist. For him the human being is the centre and starting point to explain life and science. He approaches the Bible as an anthropologist. For example, he is conservative and dogmatic in theology but in 'Laborem et Exercens' he gives the worker a key role: he advocates participation at all levels in industry, and wants all to be owners. That anthropological approach to capitalism or socialism is very nice. I admire this Pole who is so strong and thinks about what is going to happen in 200 years.' You might almost think that the pope was an advocate of liberation theology as Dom Paulo expounded. Did I catch another twinkle in his eye as he added, 'Of course, it's not possible to have a full view from his background in Poland.'

The pope saw a little of the plight of Brazil when he visited the country in 1980. In a spontaneous gesture he entered a hut in the *favela* of Vidigal in Rio and embraced an old woman who was then overcome with emotion. The pope's heart was opened too, and he gave away the gold ring which Paul VI had given him on becoming a cardinal, to be used for the parish. In a sequel that my friend the padre would have described as 'mickey-mousery', the demon king and Cardinal of Rio, Archbishop Sales, took over the ring as the property of the archdiocese and it is now on exhibition rather than having been converted into liquid cash for the *favela*. However, the *favela* dwellers gained facilities in return.

Sales is not alone as an opponent of the reforms of the past twenty years. In November 1972 Bishop Lopez Trujillo used his position as general secretary of CELAM to attack liberation theology. Rumour has it that Dom Paulo dare not retire because he knows that the Vatican would replace him with an anti-liberation bishop. It is more than speculation, since the Vatican has in the past turned down several requests from Brazil for episcopal nominations and has implemented a policy of imposing arch-conservatives on hierarchies which it wants to bring into line, the most outstanding example being in the Netherlands. Dom Helder Camara's successor in Recife was a safe conservative. In another hammer blow to Arns' power base in 1989 the Vatican announced that the giant Sâo Paulo archdiocese would be split into several smaller units. All the bishops therefore will require to be reappointed by Rome.

In Brazil the Roman Catholic Church continues to carry the banner it took up twenty years ago and exercises a prophetic role towards the state. The pleas of 1967 and 1973 may have gone unheeded by the state, but the church has marched to the beat of a different drum. Despite its reputation for orgiastic excess at the samba season which ends as Lent begins, and the seductive emotionalism of the Spiritist churches whose tom-toms throb all year round for a significant slice of the population (up to five per cent), Brazil is a country hungry for religion as well as, in many cases, literally hungry. Statistically and spiritually Brazil's Roman Catholic Church is exerting leadership throughout the world. But it would be wrong to pretend that the story is guaranteed to be happy-ever-after. However, Brazil has made a successful transition from colonial Christendom to its new *modus vivendi* with Rome. It has moved from a turbulent relationship with the state to one of mutual tolerance if not liking. The Brazilian Bishops' Conference (CNBB) wrote to president Sarney in 1988 criticizing the level of corruption in government and the holding of state banquets when so many were starving. The President was stung. He had been hoping the church would back him in his attempt to extend his term from four years to five and he protested his own Christian belief and jibed that corruption crept in everywhere . . . even into the Vatican bank. Such exchanges are healthy in a democracy and demonstrate the strong position of respect that the church has achieved in Brazil despite all the troubles. What has been gained in the last twenty years will not be easily swept away.

The same cannot be said of all the countries with liberation theology movements. Some, like Argentina, have a divided hierarchy and are still emerging from their former passive role towards the state. Too much push from the reformers and a pull from Rome could split such churches asunder, which is another reason why neither side is being too forceful at present.

Nowhere is the situation more explosive than in the Central American state of Nicaragua. On the surface this is a model of liberation theology which has been as successful as that of Brazil. Not only are there CEBs in abundance, but there are priests participating in the Sandinista government which threw off the hated dictator Samoza whose family had crushed and squeezed the people and the economy for generations. These revolutionaries fought in the name of a romantic figure from the 1920s and 1930s, the charismatic Augusto Sandino, an amalgam of politician and prophet who was assassinated in 1934 by one of the Samoza clan who then ruled with American support until the revolution of 1979. But now Nicaragua, a small country the size of England and Wales, situated midway on the chord which joins the North and South American continents, has become the focus of several conflicting power plays, all of them with a distinctly different view of church/state relations. The outcome may well be critical for the way in which liberation theology is perceived in the future.

Although church and state were separated in Nicaragua at the end of the last century, the Roman Catholic Church has always been the predominant denomination. It adopted a cosy complicity with the various Samoza regimes until the 1970s, when the excesses became all too evident. Cardinal Bando Y Bravo initially welcomed the Sandinista revolution in 1979 but is now at odds with it. He denies that he has encouraged Americans to give money to the US-backed Contras (which consist of a large number of Samoza's former hated private guard) who are trying to overthrow the Sandinistas from bases in Honduras. It did not help when he held Mass in Miami at which Contra leaders were present. The Cardinal counterclaims that the Sandinistas have abused the Indians near the border by moving them away from their homes and have censored radio and television broadcasts. The feud reached farcical proportions in August 1982 when the cardinal's chief propagandist Mgr Bismark Carballo was photographed running naked down the street by a man who alleged that he had caught him in bed with his wife. (The monsignor claimed that he was the victim of a set-up and had been having lunch with the lady who was a parishioner when a gunman ordered him to strip and run outside, where by arrangement the media were waiting.) The next year the pope arrived. But an opportunity to mend fences was blown when he clashed with a crowd who had expected to hear him condemn a recent Contra terrorist bomb attack which had killed seventeen on the very spot from which he was speaking. When he said nothing, they began to heckle him. He also failed to say prayers for the leaders of the country who included four of his own priests. These are Miguel D'Escoto, who became foreign minister and minister of culture immediately after the revolution; Fernando Cardenal, minister of education; his brother Ernesto now minister of culture; and Edgar Parrales who ran social welfare until 1982 when he went as ambassador to the Organisation of American States. They had been suspended since 1981 and D'Escoto expelled from his order. Andrew Bradstock in his book *Saints and Sandinistas* sums it up by saying, 'Since the revolution, church and state have been caught in a perpetual spiral of suspicion.'

What makes this situation different, however, is that the 'church' is on both sides. On one side the bishops are emerging as the focus of political dissent against the government and on the other a substantial section of the Roman Catholic Church is pledged to the Sandinistas.

Indeed Fernando Cardenal has said that he regards his present job not only as an extension of his vocation but as more consistent with his calling than his previous job as a philosophy professor. His colleagues argue that their actions are an expression of solidarity with the poor. 'I don't think that the church needs to go looking for privileges and extraordinary rights in order to accomplish its mission,' writes D'Escoto.

Critics of the Nicaraguan government allege that it is Marxist and is simply stringing along the church in order to subvert it as a vehicle for communism. This appears to be the view in the Vatican. Humberto Belli, a Nicaraguan who was given a Vatican post in 1982, has written that his country faces the choice of being a Poland (where it is not afraid to confront the government) or a Czechoslovakia (where it has become subservient to the regime). It doesn't take much guesswork to conclude which model appealed to the Polish pope. But if John Paul II believed that he could regard Nicaragua as that model, he soon learned that there was a difference in popularity between the two governments among their people. One-third of priests attended a Mass which D'Escoto held at the end of a July 1985 fast to protest at US 'state terrorism' against his country. The following Lent he led a *via crucis* march across the countryside which attracted a vast following. It may not command the allegiance of everyone, but as long as D'Escato and his companions are there, the government cannot be said to be opposed to the popular church.

A more subtle criticism is the argument that by participating in the government these priests are causing a split in the church. Their reply would be that Christians must be present to preserve the Christian nature of the revolution. At first sight it would appear that it is unnecessary for this to be undertaken by ordained Christians and that the pope has a valid point in asking these men to step down. It appears to be the old medieval model rearing its head again. However, as we have seen from the views of Boff, the new notion of church does not see priesthood in the same way and their views are perfectly consistent with their thinking of the church as community not hierarchy. However, in terms of public relations, the Sandinista priests and their high profile could lead to many seeing liberation theology as yet another power play by the church.

The other charge is that they are Marxist. They do not conceal their sympathy for socialist methods or ideas. I have not been to Nicaragua, but I have met a number of Britons who have, and most were mystified by the bogeyman talk which the Reagan administration put out about Nicaragua. Some have said that you are far more likely to find a Bible in Nicaraguan homes than any socialist literature. The US attitude towards Nicaragua is seen as hypocritical when it is compared with their response to insurgency against Cory Aquino's government in the Philippines. It was regarded as right and proper of Cardinal Jaime Sin to have helped Mrs Aquino's efforts to gain power and perfectly proper for her to defend the sovereignty of the state with force when it was threatened. It would appear that a lie-down-and-die pacifism is required of the Sandinistas when their country is under military attack.

It is difficult for Europeans to appreciate the paranoia which seems to affect Americans about 'Soviets' and 'Marxists'. We can understand the Monroe doctrine of protecting American interests in Latin America, perhaps even understand the domino theory which sees any communist state close to the US border as a potential threat.

But the intense propaganda which promotes the activities of wild gung-ho heroes like Oliver North and scandals such as Irangate is difficult to understand unless we remember that McCarthysim is but a generation back. Anyone who has watched the Jimmy Swaggart telecast which is beamed by satellite to Latin America, with the obnoxious preacher's voice dubbed into Spanish, will know what I mean. Satan, Soviets and Sandinistas are used almost interchangeably in a hysterical display of hatred and paranoia which claims the authority of the Prince of Peace. Worst of all perhaps is the United States' support in Latin America for coups and regimes which have used torture, corruption and wholescale oppression of their people. These are justified by the protection of American economic interests or because the end (fending off communism) justifies the means. There are enough shameful examples which are a matter of record, but one word – Irangate – will suffice to sum up the hypocrisy and scoundrel mentality masquerading as patriotism which leads the USA to provide arms for terrorists and call them 'freedom fighters'.

In most of the conflicts around the globe the definition of guerrilla/freedom fighter/terrorist is a matter of which side you are on. But it would appear that the USA is alone in regarding the Contras as the 'goodies'. Such cowboy and indian diplomacy would be harmless if it did not affect the lives of nations – and of people. It is one other argument in favour of liberation theology that it has provided a net with which to exclude the predatory theology which many North Americans have tried to inflict on their South American neighbours. In his study of the Protestant Churches' response to the revolution in Nicaragua, *Faith in Struggle*,[8] David Haslam says that this fundamentalist faith which comes with the Coca-Cola imperialism is described by many Latin Americans as 'a theology of death'. 'It is biblicist, other-worldly, falsely pacifist and ideologically and economically captive to the USA. It ultimately involves external control, dependency, structural injustice and despair and leads to a state of mind which looks only outwards for salvation to an external god who is remarkably North American in character.'

Perhaps Nicaragua has become a victim of its success with liberation theology, but in a straight choice between it and the theology of death, I would choose life.

8.   Epworth Press 1987.

3 The Jefferson Wall: The United States of America

The border round the United States of America could be seen as a weird wall of two-way mirrors. Outsiders see inside the world's most powerful nation through television and movies which takes archetypes like JR from *Dallas* into homes around the world. The Philippines can enjoy New York Jewish sit-coms and Gaels in the chilly Isle of Lewis can repeat the latest surfboarder slang from California. But the image the American sees looking outward is a reflection of his or her own hopes and fears. Sustaining this amalgam of ethnic groups and states as 'one nation under God' is the Almighty who saw fit to give Moses the Law and, to his new Israel in the New World, the Constitution. This document has the effect of inspiring reverence from mid-west farmers and New York cabbies alike, and provides for a strict separation of church and state. Americans believe it is the best system yet devised for coping with the demands of God and Caesar. It has certainly been successful in preventing the persecution and bigotry which stained the record of the Christian Church in many other parts of the world but, as we shall see, it now poses dangers.

Nature, and politics, abhor a vacuum, and if there is no temple in the Forum, then Caesar himself becomes God. I will argue that the strict separation of church and state championed two centuries ago by the USA helped establish a just notion of religious liberty which acted as a chastening example to Europe. Alas, in this century it has led to an unofficial national religion being established by the tele-evangelists and their Electronic Church which has fomented much that is worst in the American character; and in other ways has led to the substitution of the American Flag for the Ark of the Covenant, and the Constitution for the Tablets of Stone.

The American news media (which are the main channels through which Americans see the world) are in the main isolationist. A traveller to the USA will look in vain through newspapers and television news programmes for news of his country. Foreign coverage tends to concentrate on Russia, the 'evil empire' as Reagan called it in the days before *glasnost*, and other enemies of democracy such as Iran and Libya. Israel is accorded a special place because of the strong support for it by American Jews, but in the main what the US sees is a reflection of its own image as it looks outwards – except when it looks on its doorstep into Central America. The narrow isthmus which joins the continents of North and South America consists of a chain of tiny countries with fragile governments, many of which are sustained by US martial and material aid. Panama, with its strategically important canal, is a prime example. But top of the list of subjects which have engrossed North American minds in recent years is Nicaragua. Its former dictator, Samoza, was held in power by American aid and the guerrilla army ('freedom fighters', if you are on their side) which fights for his heritage are called the Contras. When the Iran–Contra affair became a national scandal in 1987, two significant factors emerged. The first was that Colonel Oliver North, the man who had masterminded the arms sales to Iran in order to bargain for US hostages and had laundered the money to the Contra cause, became a kind of hero. Gung-ho Americans toasted him and wore badges declaring 'Ollie' to be the kind of person who made America great. Another significant development was that the main issue quickly became Nicaragua and the Contras, not Iran and the hostages. It showed that Central America is not only of strategic importance to the USA but arouses emotions more akin to those of a crusade.

All this emerged in a video I watched on a trip to the USA in 1988. The climax was a sequence in which the Soviet hammer and sickle symbol was superimposed upon a roller caption of countries in the Central American zone. Cuba and Nicaragua had fallen. As the roll unfolded and the ominous music played, the voice-over invited us to consider whether Honduras, Belize or Guatemala would be next and then perhaps Mexico, bringing the red flag to the very borders of God's own country. It was heavy propaganda. The message was thumped home by punchy preaching aimed at the Latin American audience. 'Jesus is the Field Marshall! He is El Presidente!' declaimed Jimmy Swaggart, then still at his zenith of influence as a television evangelist in Latin America. One other sequence is worthy of mention. It showed a US presidential candidate at a Contra camp declaring: 'This is one of the most moving experiences in my life, to be here today.' The speaker was Rev Pat Robertson, founder of Christian Broadcasting Network (CBN) which has given millions of dollars to combat the spread of 'atheism and Marxism'. Common cause among evangelicals of America, who are plentiful and influential, is the downfall of the Sandinista regime. Yet this is the same government which we have just looked at in the context of liberation theology as a reformist movement which came to power in the wake of a corrupt dictator and includes Roman Catholic priests. How can this model of church/state co-operation, which is hailed as God's plan for Nicaragua by one group of Christians, be seen as the work of the Devil by another? The answer lies partly in theology, and partly in the distinct and different way in which the church/state problem has been resolved in the USA.

Let us look first at the unique American solution. It came about when the Founding Fathers of the first American state resolved that the two mighty forces of government and religion must be kept separate for the sake of a free society. They had the examples of religious persecution from the Old World – the impetus which had driven the Pilgrim fathers across to New England. They had brought a 'Nonconformist' conscience from England. But the roots of the religion practised in north-east America in the eighteenth century can also be traced to Dutch emigrants who had brought the Anabaptist tradition with them. This 'third force' of the Reformation era was squeezed out by Lutheranism and Calvinism which made their own accommodations with the states in which they were the predominant church.

Anabaptism stressed the influence of the Holy Spirit and in consequence was less inclined to need church structures and clergy. At its worst it was anarchic – as in the infamous Münster incident where 'King' Jan seized the city – and many of the spirit-filled groups were treated in Reformation times like terrorists who had to be expunged from society. Harried and denied freedom to worship, many found their way to the Low Countries and thence to the New World. Removed from persecution, their anarchy became quietism and many such groups survive in the north-east United States today as Shakers and Mennonites.

Dutch immigrants, coming from a country divided geographically and ecclesiastically between Catholic and Protestant, might also have played a part in the separation theory. But it was Anglo-Saxon Protestants (Anglicans, Congregationalists and Presbyterians) who dominated among the fifty-six signatories of the Declaration of Independence. (Only one was Roman Catholic, Charles Carroll from Maryland who was educated at Jesuit schools in England and France.) They were all too aware of the troubles caused by the Jacobite Roman Catholic contenders for the throne of Great Britain and were determined to start afresh. Half the signatories had received theological education but this was perhaps not unusual since it was part of any university education at the time.

Ten of the signatories were sons of clergy and eight had studied for the ministry. Only John Witherspoon was an active cleric at the time of signing, having served parishes in Scotland as a Presbyterian minister. Indeed eleven of the signatories were Presbyterians and the Bicentennial Presbyterian Survey of June 1988 does not shrink from concluding that the democratic traditions of Presbyterianism were better suited for the making of a democratic style of government. This may indeed be so, but the tradition of all these men was one in which the state religion was established. As indeed was the case for the Anglicans.

The remarkable factor was that these men broke with tradition and created for the first time a system which made religion free from state intervention. In 1779, before the US Constitution was drafted, Thomas Jefferson attempted to pass a law in Virginia, opposed by the church, guaranteeing religious liberty. It took years, but he finally achieved his aim in 1786 with the help of his friend James Madison who warned, 'The same authority which can establish Christianity in exclusion of all other religions, may establish with the same ease any particular sect of Christianity in exclusion of all other sects.' Madison particularly praised Jefferson's third section of the statute which enunciated religious liberty as a fundamental human right. Although written in long subordinate clauses the statute has force when re-read today:

> *Be it enacted by the General Assembly*, That no man shall be compelled to frequent or support any religious worship, place, or ministry whatsoever, nor shall be enforced, restrained, molested, or burthened in his body or goods, nor shall otherwise suffer on account of his religious opinions or belief; but that all men shall be free to profess, and by argument to maintain, their opinion in matters of religion; and that the same shall in no wise diminish, enlarge, or affect their civil capacities.

And though we well know that this assembly, elected by the people, for the ordinary purposes of legislation only, have no power to restrain the acts of succeeding assemblies, constituted with powers equal to our own, and that therefore to declare this act to be irrevocable would be of no effect in law; yet we are free to declare, and do declare, that the rights hereby asserted are of the natural rights of mankind, and that if any act shall be hereafter passed to repeal the present, or to narrow its operation, such act will be an infringement of natural right.

Jefferson's Virginia statute was to have briefer but unequivocal form as the First Amendment to the US Constitution which was signed on 17 September 1787. 'Congress shall make no law respecting an establishment of religion, or prohibiting the exercise thereof.' In 1802 Jefferson was to refer to this provision as 'a wall separating church from state'. It continued through the first half of the nineteenth century, during the WASP ascendancy – when White Anglo-Saxon Protestants were the ruling oligarchy. Social conditions changed with Irish and mid-European immigrations, but this principle prevented any bar against Catholics.

When John F Kennedy campaigned in 1960 to become the first Roman Catholic president of the United States he declared to the Houston Ministers Association:

I believe in an America where the separation of church and state is absolute – where no Catholic prelate would tell the president (should he be a Catholic) how to act and no Protestant minister would tell his parishioners how to vote. I believe in an America that is neither Catholic, Protestant nor Jewish; where no public official either accepts instructions on public policy from the Pope, the National Council of Churches or any other ecclesiastical source.

Kennedy's rhetoric stirred the idealism of the nation at the time, but today it sounds idealistic and unrealistic. The question today is not whether religion and politics should mix, but *how*. The election of a 'born-again' president (Jimmy Carter) in 1976 made religion a high-profile issue in American elections. Despite Carter's failure, religious issues continued to come to the fore. The Moral Majority movement played a significant role in Ronald Reagan's presidential victory in 1980, and in 1984 there was unprecedented involvement by churches in the campaign. The Rev Jesse Jackson's run for the

Democratic nomination was launched, funded and sustained by black churches. Not to be outdone, tens of thousands of white fundamentalist pastors opened their church doors to thinly-veiled campaigns for Reagan. The Roman Catholic hierarchy, which can effectively call upon a quarter of the electorate, weighed in against vice-presidential candidate Geraldine Ferraro who, although Roman Catholic, was pro-choice on the abortion issue. In 1988 Jesse Jackson was back again and the fundamentalists had their own candidate in Pat Robertson, the tele-evangelist.

Despite horrendous scandals which bit deep into the credibility of the tele-evangelists, religion continued to have profound influence on two key issues – abortion and schools. The abortion issue brings together Roman Catholics and evangelical Protestants in a holy alliance which is opposed to abortion as legal murder. The schools issue is partly about the right to have prayers in American schools. Although each day begins with a pledge to the American flag, the involvement of children in state schools in public prayer is forbidden by the First Amendment. Fundamentalists had been in eclipse ever since the celebrated Scopes ('Monkey') trial in 1925, when a state school teacher was put on trial for teaching evolution and won the case, as well as the publicity battle (two million words were filed out of the tiny Tennessee courthouse).

In recent years there were court victories enforcing the right to have Creationist theories taught alongside evolution and when Reagan went into the White House he unashamedly played up to the fundamentalist lobby. It was part of the mythical middle America, small-town, folksy image he cultivated. Despite showing very little interest in attending church, Reagan was given to telling prayer breakfasts that if people sometimes got a busy signal when they were praying, 'it was just me in there ahead (of them)'. In a speech in Dallas he said: 'The truth is, politics and morality are inseparable. And as morality's foundation is religion, religion and politics are necessarily related. The bedrock of the nation's moral order is religion.' In 1984 the president backed a drive to allow prayer in schools. In an address to the National Association of Evangelicals in Columbus he said: 'I firmly believe that the loving God who has blessed our land and made us a good and caring people should never have been expelled from our classrooms.'

The US Congress began considering proposed amendments to the Constitution which would permit voluntary prayer in schools and overturn the Supreme Court decisions of 1962 and 1963 which allegedly 'favoured atheism over Christianity'. The 1984 Supreme

Court upheld the inclusion of a Nativity scene in a Pawtucket Christmas display as a 'passive' symbol and not an endorsement of religion by state funds in contravention of the First Amendment.

These incidents may seem trivial but they were debated furiously in the USA at the time. Evangelicals saw the opportunity to witness for their faith. Liberals and traditionalists were worried that it could cause a breach in the Jefferson wall. When Rev Pat Robertson spoke of a struggle between 'those who believe that Man was created by God and those who believe in the collectivist state', he aroused the fears of many American Jews for whom the separation of church and state is a gut issue. Rabbi Alexander Schindler, President of American Hebrew Congregations, declared, 'Everywhere else in our wanderings we suffered persecution; never here. In all other countries there was an established faith; here there is none. That is why we prize the First Amendment as the very cornerstone of our liberties. And that is why we are worried by the manipulation of theology to serve partisan ends.'

Those in favour of prayer in schools point out that it is voluntary and joke that as long as there are exams, kids will pray hard in school. President Reagan sounds eminently reasonable when he says, 'Hasn't something gone haywire when this great Constitution of ours is invoked to allow Nazis and Ku-Klux Klansmen to march on public property and urge the extermination of Jews and the subjugation of blacks, but it supposedly prevents our children from Bible study or the saying of a simple prayer in their schools?' However, the introduction of school prayer is not imminent. Even if the US Congress passed such a measure it would take years before it obtained enough ratifications by individual states to take effect. But the passion aroused on both sides demonstrates the centrality of the church/state issue in the USA today. Indeed it has become important to understand the power struggles within the world's most powerful nation. For no matter how divergent their philosophies might be, both the fundamentalists and their opponents share a belief in common, a myth which is often referred to as the American Dream, the idea that the most humble immigrant can acquire the blessings of the promised land in a material sense.

It is arguable that the transformation of the North American continent could not have taken place without such a strong unifying ideal. Across a vast tract of land with European settlers in one corner and Red Indian tribes throughout, the states multiplied then unified. Racial, ethnic and language diversity were all there and along with them the potential for sectarian wars and national rivalries. But these

were buried and a single nation welded together which has developed
a distinctive and influential culture in less than two hundred years.
Historically, the achievement of the USA is formidable. It echoes the
story of another nation which went into an alien land to possess it
and forged a single nation from a collection of tribes. The parallels
between Israel and America are too numerous to ignore.

I do not intend to imply, as many neo-fundamentalists do, that
the USA is God's new chosen nation, the agent of His purpose,
but simply to point the parallels between the way in which the two
nations recount their own history and purpose. The Pentateuch, or
first five books of the Bible, tells the story of the giving of the Law.
It is a progression from patriarchs to tribal chiefs known as judges
into kings. In many ways it resembles the conquering of the Wild
West. The sheriffs and US marshals who accomplished the latter
fought for justice and the rule of law, concepts that leap from the
tales of the judges and prophets of the Old Testament. Is the torment
of Marshal Kane in *High Noon* as he struggles between the demands
of his conscience and the love of his wife not the agony of a prophet
obeying Jehovah? Are not the British cast as Philistines and the
Indians as Canaanites? The foundation stone of the Old Testament
is the Law, given to Moses and although developed and modified,
still the permanent unchanging declaration of Jehovah's will for
His people. The US equivalent is the Constitution. Although it is
not held as sacred, in the apparently demythologized world of the
twentieth century, to hear Americans discuss their 'Consti-*too*shun'
is to eavesdrop on holy ground.

The emotional intensity and common respect for the US Constitution is awesome to the outsider. The ideals which the Constitution
represents to the average US citizen are reinforced by stories of the
heroes of the American Dream much as the *Torah* or Law was
taught by retelling the adventures of the patriarchs and prophets.
The myths of the Wild West are preserved on the silver screen
rather than on silver scrolls in the synagogue. The rags to riches tale
which was so often the theme of Hollywood films in the depression
era is like a dream in which a shepherd boy can be anointed king.
Certainly a divinely ordained monarchy is lacking in the Promised
Land of the USA, but perhaps Americans learned the lesson of the
Israelite kings, and the Declaration of Independence sprang from a
protest at unjust exercise of kingly authority. On the other hand,
awe for the office of President of the USA and the zeal which goes
into the seemingly unending presidential election process, make the
US president a mythical figure of quasi-godlike proportions. This

perhaps explains why Watergate was such a trauma for Americans: it exposed the president as a man with feet of clay.

The benefits flowing to the USA from the sense of identity given by such myths are obvious. They have healed the divisions of the Civil War, enabled successive waves of ethnic immigrants to be absorbed into the USA, and have brought prosperity and dynamism to the Western world. But there is a dark side to the dream. This consists of the tendency to see the communist bloc as anti-Christ and to view Marxist interpretations of the world as corrosive heresies. It brings us back to the doorstep on which we began our look at the USA – Nicaragua. I have spoken to a number of visitors to Nicaragua who could not be described as political activists. One was a doctor working in a Sandinista government health centre which was regularly blown apart by the Contras who robbed villages of medical supplies. Others were churchmen who testified to the fact that they had never seen a copy of Karl Marx in a home in Nicaragua but nearly every house now possessed a Bible. The impressions of these independent witnesses do not accord with the suppressed hysteria and propagandizing rhetoric directed at Nicaragua by US government sources. The spectre of McCarthyism has been exorcized but the crusading zeal with which communism is portrayed as the anti-Christ is ironic from a state with no official religion or mention of God in its Constitution. (It was only in 1954 that the words 'under God' were added to the pledge of allegiance.)

Fomenting and sustaining this 'shadow' of communism in the American mind is a type of religion which has arisen in the absence of an official national faith – worship of the state itself. Often called 'civil religion', this has been defined as 'investing American history and destiny with religious significance'. The creed is 'life, liberty and the pursuit of happiness', its scriptures, the Declaration of Independence and the Constitution; the holy festivals would be the inauguration of the president, the fourth of July and Thanksgiving. This view of the nation as a holy city set on a hill as a beacon and model for the world is all too prevalent in American life according to Dr Isobel Rogers, Professor of Applied Christianity at the US Presbyterian School of Christian Education and the Moderator of the Presbyterian Assembly in 1988:

The idea of manifest destiny, that God intended us to civilize this continent, was national policy last century. And we did that – we conquered the continent – and the Indians, the native American, be damned. It was our destiny. At the turn of the century our leaders felt the urge to take American civilization to the world so we took over the Philippines, Cuba, Nicaragua. Our imperialistic tendencies became identified with God's will. Sheer idolatry.

In the interview published in *Presbyterian Survey* of November 1987, Dr Rogers does not catalogue the imperialism of more recent years but goes on to point to racism as a consequence of such thinking, since other peoples do not enjoy the same divine favour. Another consequence is that the nation becomes the source of meaning:

> It says, I am important not because I'm a child of God but because I'm an American. If I'm God's child I don't have to dominate people to establish my identity. The 'my country right or wrong' mind-set hardly ever admits to 'my country' being wrong. Authentic patriotism requires us to support our country and to make it the best country we possibly can. One danger of civil religion, as I see it, is that the church may be silenced. That can happen by edict or more likely by the church being engulfed by government. The church can't allow itself to cuddle up to government, to seek or even accept special privileges. So one of the things the church has to do is maintain a critical freedom at the same time as it is actively involved in the life of the nation. Responsible participation in the political processes is part of the church's task.

That view is representative of white, liberal middle-class congregations. It maintains the Jefferson wall but also keeps the keys to the gate, so that the church can exercise a prophetic role within the city in order to remind the citizens that they owe allegiance to a greater kingdom, one not of this world.[1] This moderate view would seem to be an admirable theory of church/state engagement, preventing the Christian faith from being equated with the nation's way of life or being imposed by legislation, but in dialogue with civil authority 'neither claiming expert knowledge it does not have nor remaining silent when God's Word is clear'[2]. However, those who subscribe to these views in the United States seem to be in a minority, as a quick look at the religious demography of the USA shows.

---

1. Many such American Christians who did not share the jingoism towards Central America became involved in harbouring illegal immigrants through the Sanctuary movement in the 1980s.
2. *A Declaration of Faith*, chapter 7.

Out of a population of 225 million in 1980 an astonishing 88 per cent of Americans were professing Christians; 55 per cent were Protestants which included 26 per cent Baptists; 9 per cent Methodists; 6 per cent Lutherans; 5 per cent Presbyterians. A further 30 per cent were Roman Catholics; 7 per cent non-religious or atheist; 3 per cent Episcopalian; 3 per cent Jews.[3] Although the smaller churches are socially and politically influential, the strength of the evangelical churches cannot be underestimated. In a 1976 Gallup poll 34 per cent of all Americans over eighteen testified to a 'born-again' experience. An astonishing 38 per cent of all Americans count themselves as fundamentalists, i.e. believing the Bible literally, word for word. This group is far less likely to be sympathetic to the Presbyterian moderator's critique of 'civil religion'. Their agenda has arisen because of a need to react against secular trends rather than accommodate them. The biggest group in this category are called the Moral Majority and for many practical purposes they seem to be a majority in their influence.

There is also a small minority who would like the USA to adopt a state religion. They are known as 'Christian Reconstructionists' and send a shudder down liberal spines. They are right-wing libertarians who see a chance to advance their ideas in the period when the television evangelists are keeping a lower profile. They have little chance of succeeding but are significant lobbyists on right-wing issues such as the death penalty, homosexuality and school policy. Reconstructionists like Bishop Paulke, whose church in Atlanta is bursting at the seams and boasts a large multi-racial choir, sees the choice as between 'a humanistic state or God-directed government'. Their guru is the theologian R J Rushdoony whose son-in-law, Dr Gary North, launched the 'Christian Manifesto' on Independence Day 1986. It called for a return to the gold standard and a 10 per cent flat rate income tax. The two men do not see eye to eye personally, perhaps an omen that politically the Reconstructionists are not likely to get sufficient unity to fulfil Rushdoony's aim that 'the saints must take over the world's governments'. What frightens people about the Reconstructionists is the undertone of anger in their theology and their anti-democratic tendency. 'The Constitution cannot save this country,' says Rushdoony. 'Democracy has substituted the will of the majority for the Kingdom of God.'

Far more likely to succeed in becoming the 'national' church of the USA is a coalition of believers from a number of churches

3. AIPO Gallup Opinion Index.

– fundamentalist, conservative Protestant and pro-life; they want greater harmony between public policy and their understanding of Biblical truth. In 1979 a cadre of political operatives of this persuasion formed the Moral Majority and recruited Rev Jerry Falwell, the force behind a tele-evangelism empire based in his home town of Lynchburg, Virginia. Here in Thomas Road Baptist Church, the second biggest in the country, the Old Time Gospel Hour is recorded each Sunday for the 392 stations across the USA which broadcast it that evening. Sixty-two telephone operators are at the ready to receive the cash pledges that are needed to sustain the $100 million annual budget. The apple of Falwell's eye is Liberty University, begun with $30 million in 1984 and still expanding. Its task is to supply a second generation of 'Bible-believing' Christians who will constitute the Moral Majority in the USA. To get that majority, Falwell was prepared to enter coalitions with Roman Catholics (particularly on the abortion issue) and Jews. The Moral Majority targeted various senators with liberal views in the 1980 elections and gained some notable scalps. In 1984 it was solidly behind Reagan and in the 1988 presidential election almost unanimously for Bush.

In a decade Falwell has matured into a sophisticated Moses leading hundreds of thousands of fundamentalists out of the desert into which they had wandered after the Scopes trial of 1925. When the 1960s hit America with liberation theologies for blacks and gays and women, they sat on the sidelines and were appalled. During the 1980s they have fought their way beck to centre stage. With his direct challenge, Falwell resembles a Joshua at Jericho, whose trumpet makes a far from uncertain sound and is directed at the Jefferson wall.

In an article published by *Time* magazine in September 1984 Falwell wrote:

I don't believe that the 'wall' exists in the Constitution. It has been a 'practical' wall that has been a good thing for the US during its history. However, we have never had in this country a separation of church and state. There never was a time in American history when politics and churchmen haven't merged and blurred, including the evangelical ministers of the abolitionist movement who broke the back of slavery and on up through the civil rights movement. The wall is an imaginary wall intended to keep government off the back of the church, to prevent the officialdom of the church from coercing their followers. But it was never intended to keep churchmen from voicing an opinion or asserting moral values.

It is impossible for a person with sincere religious convictions to divorce his daily actions from those convictions. Our personal convictions always translate into our votes, our life-styles, our words. Just as it would be impossible for a labour activist to vote for a right-to-work law, so does a person's private beliefs on the rights of the unborn translate into policy.

All civilized society is governed by legislation of morality by consensus. In America, you can't commit murder or rape or robbery [with impunity] because some time back there Americans decided that that was a good moral way to live. So it is today.

Intelligent men and women who care about each other have to seek what the founders called in their documents 'the general welfare' without oppressing the rights of minorities. Responsible legislation and judicial practice is and always has been morally informed. The general principles of American democracy have always been Judeo-Christian moral principles. That same generation of Americans who came out of the bondage and darkness of the Old World to found this nation, when they framed a Constitution and wrote the Declaration of Independence, referred to their Creator with a capital C, they created a chaplain of Congress, they had prayers in their school from day one. Throughout all these 200-plus years, there has been a commitment to basic values. That's what we're coming back to now.

I could be offended by a president who tried to create a Christian republic, or a Jewish president who tried to create a Judaic republic. But regardless of a president's faith, if he were promoting Judeo-Christian values, I would say amen to him. Yes, there is a sense of secularism in the nation and always will be. But this is also a religious society, always has been and always will be. I applaud that, so long as there is the absolute guarantee of total civil rights for the nonbeliever. I could never be offended at the assertion of those basic values as long as there is a clear commitment to pluralism. It is a fine line, but it is not too great a risk to reassert that we are a nation under God.

In the same issue of *Time*, many of these assumptions were challenged by other Christian leaders in the USA. Claire Randall, General Secretary of the National Council of Churches, denied that church/state separation meant that religious bodies could not speak out on issues on which they had convictions: 'The problem really comes when government officials want to make laws that are based on the more narrow tenets or sectarian positions and try to impose them on the entire society. That is what people are struggling with now ... but it would be a mistake to believe that this country was founded on strict Jewish-Christian principles alone, because the [eighteenth century] Enlightenment influences were broader than that.'

Professor Harvey Cox of Harvard Divinity School is quite glad to see the fundamentalists mixing it in the political arena but warns that they put their credibility as religious leaders on the line when they risk backing particular solutions to problems. His complaint is that they 'overheat' the debate and 'accuse the other people of being in bad faith ... an elected official has the most sensitive kind of responsibility for nurturing the diversity that is the most remarkable thing about American life.'

Rev Richard Neuhaus, a Lutheran and Director of the Center on Religion·and Society, says the new religious right have kicked a trip-wire which has jerked Americans into realizing that they do not, as many imagined, live in a secular society. He warns against fighting the fundamentalists head-on which 'would be disastrous for American society'. Nor is it possible to send them back to the wilderness. He takes refuge in a plea to use the present tensions 'to reconstruct a public philosophy, one that is responsible to and in conversation with, the religious-based values of the American people.' Neo-conservative Neuhaus believes this woolly concept will 'further the American hundred democratic experiment'.

In the *Time* survey, the most balanced assessment of the new religious right came from Fr Joseph O'Hare SJ, former editor of *America* magazine and president of Fordham University:

> The important distinction is not between public policy and private religious beliefs. You can't have politicians who are schizophrenic. The line that must be drawn is what one believes are the moral and human values that should be protected by the law. On abortion for example ... what is the right law is a judgement on which good people who share opposition to abortion can disagree. My quarrel with the new religious right is that they do not simply disagree with their opponents – they want to excommunicate them.

Fr O'Hare does not want compulsory prayer for schools but thinks that the idea of giving different religious groups access to school facilities should not be dismissed out of hand.

The schools issue has persistently surfaced in rulings by the Supreme Court since 1947. This body – which is the arbiter of law and the Constitution – plays a crucial role in deciding between an accommodationist or strict separationist view of church and state. The pendulum has swung both ways and the position of some groups has changed during this period. Hard-line Protestants were not always so keen on religion being extended into schools. When in 1947 the Court held that welfare services could be extended to parochial schools under the general welfare clause of the Constitution, Protestants were horrified, imagining that it would lead to full public support for Roman Catholic schools. A year later, the organization Protestants and Other Americans United for Separation of Church and State (POAU) was formed.

In 1952, school boards were allowed to provide religious instruction off school premises and Justice Douglas' judgement at that time is often quoted:

> We are religious people whose institutions presuppose a Supreme Being. When the state encourages religious instruction or cooperates with religious authorities by adjusting the schedule of public events to sectarian needs, it follows the best of our traditions . . . to hold that it may not, would not be to find in the Constitution a requirement that the government show a callous indifference to religious groups. That would be preferring those who believe in no religion over those who do believe.

In 1962 the Supreme Court ruling in the *Engele v. Vitale* case banned the use of official prayers in schools following the deployment by the New York State Board of Regent of the prayer: 'Almighty God we acknowledge our dependence upon thee and we beg thy blessings upon us, our parents, our teachers and our country.' A storm of protest followed.

Other decisions have extended the freedom of conscience arising from religious belief. Seventh Day Adventists and Orthodox Jews have had their job security protected when they abstain from Saturday work. Black Muslims have been allowed religious literature and pastoral visits when in prison. Jehovah's Witnesses have been exempted from saluting the flag and reciting the Pledge of Allegiance. In 1970 the ruling in the *Welsh v. USA* case helped to establish conscientious objection as a civil right when it legalized a new basis for exemption from military service. Hitherto belief in a Supreme Being was necessary, but afterwards a deeply held and morally consistent repugnance to war and the taking of life was deemed an acceptable ground. These liberal principles were consistent with the doctrine promulgated by Justice Jackson (ironically during a time of war) in 1943:

> To believe that patriotism will not flourish if patriotic ceremonies are voluntary and spontaneous instead of a compulsory routine is to make an unflattering estimate of the appeal of our institutions to free minds. We can have intellectual individualism and the rich cultural diversities that we owe to exceptional minds only at the price of occasional eccentricity and abnormal attitudes . . . If there is any fixed star in our constitutional constellation it is that no official, high or petty, can prescribe what shall be orthodox in politics, nationalism, religion or other matters of opinion or force citizens to confess by word or act their faith therein.

That ruling is an impressive doctrine for the fair treatment of dissenting groups, but when the groups become sizeable minorities and the choice is between sharply polarized positions, the issue is not so simple.

This applied not only to the schools issue but to the other church/state flashpoint – abortion. In the 1973 *Roe v. Wade* case a crucial decision was made by a seven-to-two majority by the Supreme Court, liberalizing abortion law by forbidding states to outlaw it except in the last ten weeks of pregnancy, the period during which the foetus might be able to survive if born. However, they also went further by rejecting the view that the foetus becomes a 'person' upon conception, and the bitter resentment at that decision by Catholic pro-life and conservative Protestant groups is still a campaigning issue.

The Supreme Court has decided at various times that a government agency may legally lend geography books containing maps to religious day schools but may not lend maps alone or films on geography. It may bus students from their homes to such schools, but not from the schools to museums. It may diagnose speech or hearing problems on the school premises but follow-up treatment must take place elsewhere if public money is involved. The Court has held in recent years that the First Amendment forbids incidental aid to parochial schools and religious agencies, and forbids posting the Ten Commandments in classrooms. It has also quashed laws that require the teaching of 'creation' science (i.e. a literal approach to the Genesis story in the Bible) alongside evolution.

The Court has been used by lobby groups to try to stop the

Roman Catholic Church 'politicking over abortion' on pain of losing its tax-exempt status. Influence in the Supreme Court would be central in building a tunnel beneath the church/state wall through which the fundamentalist phalanx could enter the citadels of government. Some argue that the appointment of several conservatives to the court by President Reagan has increased that possibility. The present Chief Justice, William Rehnquist, has declared that the Supreme Court's implementation of strict separation for the past forty years has 'no historical foundation'. The 1947 watershed decision ruled that neither federal nor local government could 'pass laws which aid one religion, aid all religions or prefer one religion over another' and no tax money could support any religious institutions. In 1971 they developed a three-fold test. Laws must avoid excessive government entanglement with religion; have a 'principal effect that neither advances nor inhibits religion'; and have a 'secular' purpose. For example, in 1987 the Court ruled that this test was not violated by the Mormon Church discriminating on religious grounds to fill jobs. In 1985 it threw out an Alabama law authorizing a moment of silence in classrooms because the law specified that this was for time to pray, but the Court hinted that had it not been so explicit it would have fulfilled the criteria of 1971.

That the pendulum is swinging from a strict separationist view to an accommodationist one is also evident from another federal judge's decision in 1986 to ban forty-five textbooks in Alabama because they established 'secular humanism' as a religion and did not give equal treatment to religious and moral absolutes. Many of those seeking a new church/state approach agree with Justice Rehnquist that nothing in the establishment clause requires government to be strictly neutral 'between religion and irreligion'.

Accommodationists point with some glee to the fact that Jefferson allowed the Bible and a hymnal to be used to teach reading when he headed the DC school board and signed a treaty in which the US government paid a missionary's salary and built churches for Indians.

The issue is not peripheral. The largest Protestant denomination, the Southern Baptist Conference (representing 14.6 million people; 36,000 churches, and 3,000 missions), is split over whether or not it wants to move to an accommodationist position. The 11,000 Independent Baptist congregations (smaller but dedicated and hyper-fundamentalist and controlling 8,000 foreign missions mostly to Central America) are behind the new religious right all the way.

In many ways it is the right-wing Protestants who have made the running on the church/state issue. The low profile of the Roman Catholic Church in the USA on this matter is puzzling. Since they amount to 30 per cent of the population we might expect their church to be thinking in terms of establishing a presence in national affairs similar to the role it plays in other countries. It was only during Ronald Reagan's presidency that diplomatic relations were established with the Holy See. This low profile can be partly explained by a ghetto mentality among many of the Catholic immigrant population, reinforced by anti-Catholic sentiment among hard-line Protestant groups. However, much of that situation changed when John F. Kennedy became the first Roman Catholic president of the USA in 1960. Vatican II's decree on ecumenism and religious freedom lessened the sense of isolation from the rest of American society. But it also made it more difficult to maintain the host of ways, from the trivial to the essential, in which Catholic faith and practice were distinctive and kept apart. Now secular pressures are extremely influential upon Catholics and the strong effect of American culture has resulted in a North American Catholicism which is confronting Rome on several fronts (celibacy, women priests, contraception). Recently the pope demoted a bishop for being too liberal on homosexuality and the Vatican suspended a theologian (Curran) for his liberal views. The two papal visits to the USA in the first decade of John Paul II's pontificate can more easily be seen as pastoral duty-calls to pull the faithful back into line rather than the ceremonial visits of a leader of an influential lobby. These internal tensions have not encouraged US Roman Catholics to participate in the church/state debate, except perhaps on the abortion issue.

Another highly significant section of USA society conspicuous by their absence in the church/state debate are the blacks. Although blacks are found in all the USA denominations, the largest group being Catholics (855,000), the majority of all USA blacks are members of 140 separate black churches, mostly in the Baptist or Pentecostalist traditions, accounting for 15 per cent of the whole population. The strength of the witness and worship of this section was felt when Rev. Dr Martin Luther King led the civil rights marches in the 1960s. In what has been a miracle of peaceful transition, in the quarter-century since Alabama was a racial battleground, most of the demands of the civil rights marchers have been met. The assassinated Dr King is now a national hero with 20 January as his commemoration day and one of his lieutenants, Jesse Jackson, a runner-up in presidential primaries. However, this picture is far too optimistic. It ignores the way that presidential candidate Michael Dukakis brushed Jackson aside when he was selecting a running mate in 1988. It ignores the lack of interest in social issues in many black churches which preach wholesome family values and keep their intoxicating, spirit-led worship within the ghetto. The black population has yet to assert itself within American national politics. Whether or not Jackson manages to be a political trailblazer, blacks are unlikely, for the present, to have any effect on church/state relations in the USA.

Not so another group which has made significant strides during the 1980s. In 1987 Falwell's Moral Majority had a budget of $8.4 million, a mailing list of 6 million, a magazine subscription of 2 million, and·a Washington office. Falwell selected as its new leader a man who was ideally placed to wheel and deal the movement into the citadels of government – Jerry Nims, smooth-talking millionaire businessman in his mid-fifties. Nims had seen his pet project of the 'Nimslo' 3D camera go up in flames, but emerged with his bankroll not even scorched. In his youth he rebelled against being the son of a Baptist preacher and dallied with the hippie and pop cultures before going into business. That took him to Switzerland in the late 1970s where he was swayed by Dr Francis Schaeffer, the conservative evangelical guru who co-operated with him in writing the best-selling *Christian Manifesto* in 1981. On his deathbed, Schaeffer cajoled Nims to use his financial strength for a more powerful role as a Christian. The agent for Schaeffer's challenge was Falwell and the two men hit it off right away. Together they were involved in trying to cleanse the stable of tele-evangelist Jim Bakker when he fell from grace in 1987, but soon washed their hands of the affair as the extent of the task emerged. Falwell quit much of his political work to return to preaching and Nims took the driving seat in what promises to be an interesting ride.

When I met Jerry Nims in his sumptuous home in the Atlanta suburbs he was excited by the prospect of succeeding Falwell. A self-confessed news junkie, he talked about the prospects of using the Liberty Broadcasting Network of which he is now chairman as a twenty-four-hour vehicle for Christian ideals. 'It would be a national religious network with a Judaeo-Christian basis. There's nothing wrong with running *Lassie* repeats, but I just did a deal with the Southern Conference in athletics and we'll be the sole station with rights to that. It's not narrow. The idea is that you shouldn't have to throw your body across the television set to protect your eight-year-old. Our AIDS programme is going to be a shocker. We're not bound like the NBC and ABC are. But we don't need to sensationalize to balance the ratings as long as we're in the black.'

As he talked, Nims described impressive series of wheeling and dealing which gave the unmistakable impression that Old Time religion is Big Business. 'Liberty Broadcasting Network is on SATCOM 4, TRANSPONDER 7,' he rattled off. 'Moral Majority is a 5(I) category. It's non-profit and can lobby. Liberty Foundation is a 4(I) category profit organization which can't lobby.' The phone rang in his den/study above the stables block and I studied the framed photographs as he answered it. One of Nims with President Carter, another with singer Pat Boone. An early pre-born-again photo of Nims in an open Cadillac with one of the Kingston trio on his lap and Bobby Kennedy in the rear seat. A signed one from Ronald Reagan. Nims was defining his new philosophy over the phone to recruit more blacks into Moral Majority and was quite happy to let me overhear. 'We're gonna make it zing. I wanna broaden the base and do a strong thing. We are actively recruiting in the black community for solid guys—' he added emphatically, 'we don't want any flakes!'

He admits when he puts down the phone that MM is 'going to be aggressive, develop positions and views that we express and then put into action. We don't believe the First Amendment is there to protect the state from the church. It's there to protect the church from the state. We're going to be involved in legal activism but from a conservative traditional point of view.' Nims is staunchly opposed to abortion and euthanasia and talks at length about sanctity of life (although he supports the death penalty). He believes that creationism deserves equal play with evolution in public school textbooks. And he believes it's perfectly fair to rank candidates on their moral views – in effect a 'Christian ticket'. He said: 'Politics is like Thai boxing. You use your hands, your feet and sometimes hit below the belt.' A pause for a grin. 'I kinda enjoy Thai boxing.'

This is the formidable high priest of the new religious right. He is a layman, a salesman and a politician:

The foundation of our Constitution comes from the Judaeo-Christian frame of reference. 'Inalienable rights' means the intention to have a moral basis. Thomas Jefferson has been revisionized. His position was not to let federal government interfere with state government. We want to return to the original position of the writers of the Constitution which that decision of 1946 reversed. The argument is between those who say that what's moral today is not necessarily moral tomorrow (relativism) and those like us who say that there are absolutes which are not changeable. The opposite view is that we are here through chance and that the individual has no value, or that Man is the answer and not God. That argument has been dominated by liberal views. Now the evangelical conscience has been awakened and we're fighting. It's taxation without representation not to allow a prayer meeting at a school after hours. It's got so outrageous in our schools that you now can't sing a Christmas carol. Yet you have a government forcing a Georgetown RC school to violate its principles and have a homosexual club on its premises. Or forbidding people holding a prayer meeting in their house because of the zoning laws, and they can only have their friends in to pray if they have their home zoned as a church. It's ridiculous. Today the US government is violating the contract it made at the time of the Constitution. The faceless bureaucracy rules. A third-generation family on welfare become slaves because those running the welfare system don't believe they have worth as children of God. The black community don't want bussing to integrate schools. Coretta King doesn't speak for them. They say, 'Just give us equality – the textbooks.' They are gonna split off against bussing. Now if *I'd* said that I'd be hung. But it's gonna happen.

Nims concedes that if the Moral Majority got all that it wanted, it would not be good for the country.

We don't want a national church. Salvation is a personal decision, but the issue here is about whether the world is founded on absolutes. Non-absolutes say that you can embrace homosexuality as an alternative lifestyle. Our position is that we don't ostracize homosexuals, but we don't give them a preference. Slavery was a violation of the absolutes. I'd have been running the underground to get the slaves out. We either have a Constitution founded on absolutes or moral anarchy. The point of having absolutes is obeying the rules. If you don't, some charlatan can come along, mumble a few plausible phrases and the Department of Justice can't tell the difference between the form and the substance. Today the US government is violating the contract made at the time of the Constitution and our aim as Moral Majority is to take the shackles off the First Amendment. There should be competing ideas – we don't want things to swing back radically to the right. The strength of America is a pluralistic society of the saved and the unsaved.

From Jerry Nims's arguments it will be seen that he believes that the moral absolutes can be isolated, identified and agreed upon. Although he talks in moral and legal terms, the 'absolutes' he refers to are, for him, enshrined, not in the Constitution, but in the Bible. Thus the Moral Majority plays the game of holding the Constitution as the supreme authority on human rights, but in reality they have their Bible in their backpocket which they hold as the supreme rule of faith and morals. From their Bible they have assembled a set of beliefs, those 'absolutes' of which Jerry Nims spoke.

The Brazilian Presbyterian theologian Ruben Alves has entitled this view 'Right Doctrine Protestantism' or RDP, and in his study *Protestantism and Repression*[5] he described this mind-set which is found throughout the world. Although conversion is on an individual basis, RDP is a set of collective attitudes, acceptance of which is a precondition of acceptance in the born-again community. RDP teaches that sin consists of specific acts: smoking, gambling, adultery, drinking, etc. Those who abstain attain holiness. Thus morality becomes a matter of conduct rather than conscience and theology is justification by works.

RDP's aversion to the social aspects of the gospel comes about not because of sloth but because Providence/God has already conquered sin through the atonement of Christ and thus it is not so important to act correctly as to have the right attitude. Right belief in right doctrine is supreme. The convert who drinks alcohol does not undermine RDP, but in repenting actually strengthens it as a system. But the man who does not believe that Jonah was swallowed by a whale threatens the whole basis of absolute knowledge. Alves cheekily concludes, 'The magisterium for the Catholic Church and the Confession of Faith for the Protestant Churches perform exactly the same function.' Like the Inquisition, RDP Protestants are concerned with what a person believes.

RDP includes across its religious spectrum Christians from Fundamentalist, Pentecostal and Charismatic churches. From what we have already heard of the Moral Majority we can see that they uphold a form of RDP. But the born-again believer/fundamentalist/RDP adherent has made a selection of the parts of the Bible which

5. Orbis Books, Maryknoll N.Y. 1985.

are to be given the status of absolutes. These are the ones that reinforce the RDP manifesto. Bible texts which enjoin the faithful to burn witches, refrain from eating pork and marry their brother's widow are happily ignored. Erotic poetry in the Song of Solomon is taken as a parable of the relationship of Christ to His Church whereas the Garden of Eden myth is taken literally as is the Virgin Birth saga. Revelation is a prophecy of the End Times and is to be taken literally. There is not necessarily any logical connection between such beliefs in the Bible and right-wing politics and free-market libertarianism, but there is every connection between RDP and both sets of beliefs. It is the linking factor which has selected the Protestant work ethic, capitalism and Providential reward for labour and put them together between the covers of the Bible.

In his book *Domination or Liberation*[6] Alastair Kee identifies Jerry Falwell as the legitimation of the values and policies of the new right. *The New Right*[7] is also the title of a book by Richard Viguerie, one of MM's leaders, in which Falwell writes: 'In the last several years, Americans have literally stood by and watched as godless, spineless leaders have brought our nation floundering to the brink of death.' As a result America is 'depraved, decadent and demoralized.' Falwell does not mince words. But he does mince the Bible, plucking texts to suit his political purposes. Texts are used to oppose the Equal Rights for Women Amendment and to demand continued tax-exempt status for religious organizations, 'this being based on the historical and scriptural concept of church and state separation' (Falwell: 'Christian Bill of Rights' 1980). The proof text invoked is 'Render unto Caesar' (Matt. 22:21) which is about paying taxes to the civil power, not about church/state relations and certainly not about tax exempt status for churches.

The reputation of the Moral Majority was not improved by an incident which Kee recounts. Well known evangelical Mark Hatfield was targeted by MM because of his voting stance on the Panama Canal Treaty. Hatfield commented trenchantly, 'They did not bother to ask my view of Jesus Christ in an effort to reach some determination of my salvation; instead they chose to make some judgement of my salvation on the basis of my position regarding the Panama Canal Treaty. Many evangelicals share my concern that the grievous sins of our society are militarism and materialism, rather that the Taiwan Treaty, the Equal Rights Amendment or the Panama Canal.'

6.   op. cit.
7.   pub. The Virginia Company. VA. 1981.

It is perhaps significant that Dr Billy Graham, who might have been expected to sympathize with the growing influence of the fundamentalist lobby within the country, has moved to disassociate himself from it. There is evidence that Falwell has compromised his deservedly high reputation as an evangelical preacher by colluding with the new right and has been seduced by power. There are others among the RDP community who have been seduced in other ways.

The most influential way is via television and its 'Electronic Church', what is called 'prime time religion'. In the USA it is claimed that 98 per cent of the population believes in some concept of God. That same statistic is the percentage of the population who own a television set. The coincidence does not end there. The average household of these 83 million homes watches six hours forty minutes of television per day. So great is the power of television in reinforcing American culture in the USA that it could be described as akin to the teraphim, the household gods of Canaan. The deregulated approach to radio and television in the USA means that religious movements can mount television programmes and buy time on the networks. Furthermore, they can appeal for money over the air (strictly forbidden in European systems of broadcasting); and are tax exempt in the USA. The absence of an official or national prerogative in the shape of state regulation over religion means that the way is open for broadcast religion to become the unofficial nationwide church of the USA. It has been christened the Electronic Church.

In 1970 the Electronic Church had acquired 10 million viewers across the USA. In 1977 this had risen to 22 million. Six of the top ten evangelists who bought time on US television had over a million viewers. The cost of this exercise had risen from $500 million in 1977 to a possible $2 billion in 1986, and that figure does not include ancillary expenses. Although there is debate about the precise viewing figures, a 1984 survey estimated 13.3 million or 6.7 per cent of the total TV audience were regular viewers, but a 1985 Nielsen survey designed to include cable TV data showed that 21 per cent of households tune in to Christian TV for at least six minutes per week and 40 per cent for at least 6 minutes per month. That amounts to 61 million Americans having minimal exposure. These surveys took the ten biggest among the sixty-two nationally syndicated shows and were able to conclude that Pat Robertson knew in launching his White House bid in 1987–88 that 27 million Americans had already seen him in their homes via television.

Robertson runs CBN, the Christian Broadcasting Network, the third largest cable network in the US, based in Virginia Beach,

VA. The network knows that to keep its audience it is best not to be religious during mid-week, and it has had a few scoops (Rock Hudson's last interview and the interview with the daughter of a spy who shopped her father) of which any TV executive would be proud. But its climax is the '700 Club' on which Robertson markets a mixture of worldly wisdom and biblical texts on global issues combined with a healing ministry. That formula was first successfully applied by Oral Roberts, a patriarch of the Electronic Church whose university with its impressive prayer tower is sited in Tulsa, Oklahoma. Roberts is the high priest of hard sell, and has coined an unlovely faith-speak to market it. God's 'shall-supply promise' means that buying a $50 square foot in which to plant a seed will ensure a miracle in return from God. Like Robertson, Roberts has brought his family into the $250 million annual turnover 'business', but in recent years his takings have slumped and in an embarrassing incident for the Electronic Church in 1987, Roberts mounted his prayer tower promising to fast unto death if the $1.3 million he needed to balance his books was not forthcoming. He got it, but the Chicago dog-track owner who donated it urged him to go and get some psychiatric treatment.

But the dark days for the Electronic Church had only just begun. Jim and Tammy Bakker were another evangelical act which crashed when Jim's adultery with a church secretary was made public. He ran PTL (an offshoot of the 700 Club), which stands for Praise the Lord, although some called it 'pass the loot' or even 'pay the lady' owing to Tammy's habit of weeping copiously on-screen through her flywhisk false eyelashes when money was needed. Bakker had built the PTL network up to reach 13.5 million households when the crash came. His Heritage USA was a kind of Holy Disneyworld with a time-share element built in. Others called it pyramid selling when they found that the facilities were many times oversold – but the empire proved to be less stable than a pyramid.

The astute Falwell saw that if one of the tele-evangelists fell, the others would carry the burden, and he responded to an invitation to try to rehabilitate the PTL empire with Nims as his lieutenant. The two men quit spectacularly, making accusations that it wasn't Bakker's adultery that was the problem so much as another proclivity. 'I felt dirty coming out of that room,' recalls Nims of an encounter with the PTL preacher.

In a January 1988 broadcast Falwell grimly announced, 'In 1987 some great oaks fell.' But worse was to follow. Early in 1988 a redwood crashed. Jimmy Swaggart, the swashbuckling fiery Pentecostalist preacher based in Baton Rouge, Louisiana, and beamed to Latin America with a dubbed voice, who once condemned the Supreme Court and Congress as 'institutions damned by God', and Roman Catholicism as 'a false cult', was revealed to have paid numerous visits to a prostitute in a motel room. His public, breast-beating confession to his family and congregation on live television could have been the greatest stunt yet for getting an audience. But despite the fact that it attracted millions who would not normally watch religious TV, this was more of a public execution than a revival. Assuredly that moment marked the end of the Electronic Church as the unofficial national religion of the USA.

It is worth reflecting for a moment why these tinsel prophets held such sway. Several explanations can be advanced. They endorse the American way of life and values which the viewer already holds. They reinforce beliefs with endorsements by successful personalities. They stress that the individual is important and significant. They supply authority in a personal form. They offer simple solutions to problems readily understood by the audience, e.g. explanations that the devil is behind certain events.

On the 'theology' of the Electronic Church, it is not strictly fair to lump all the preachers together, but they do have a number of factors in common. They agree on the range of RDP issues (especially on seeing as sinful such contemporary concerns as homosexuality, feminism and communism). The Bible is considered infallible. Although they might emphasize different gifts of the Spirit (e.g. healing or ecstatic forms of worship) they all see giving money to them as casting bread on the waters and inevitably gaining a blessing from God. Receiving blessings and atoning for sin can be no more difficult than placing a $10 bill in an envelope and popping it into the mail-box outside the house. The tele-evangelists with phone-in lines for pledges and counselling are well placed to reap this harvest and to sow another through their computerized mailing lists. Since wealth is held out as a sign of God's blessing in this world, the rich man can, by the miracle of television signals, pass through both the cathode ray tube and the eye of the needle at the same time. This is sometimes known as 'Cadillac theology' and while revivalist preachers like Falwell do not indulge in it, he was quite willing initially to be associated with PTL, who did.

Perhaps the most scary thing about the Electronic Church is its use of the concept of the Final Judgement or End Times as a device to persuade through fear. Some employ sleazy theology such as 'rapture' (the idea that God will take true believers into heaven as the elect prior to the fiery Last Judgement). This would not be so worrying if the apocalyptic end of the world were not portrayed as something to be longed for and – what is worse – something believed in by people as powerful as President Reagan who could bring it about by pushing the button marked (appropriately) MAD – Mutually Assured Destruction.

There are hopeful signs that the influence of the Moral Majority and the Electronic Church is on the wane. Not all tele-evangelists are of the Elmer Gantry ilk. In Birmingham, Alabama, where less than 3 per cent of the population are Roman Catholic, a Franciscan nun set up a television network which is pumping out traditional Catholic theology to millions nightly. Mother Angelica and her Eternal Word Television Network are the kind of people who might just get the Electronic Church a good name. However, a standoffish attitude by the RC hierarchy and lack of appetite by the mainstream Protestant Churches to go into the hard-sell market-place means that she is the glorious exception to prove that fundamentalism rules the airwaves.

Even more dangerous than the intolerant absolutism of fundamentalism or the dollar indulgences of born-again theology is another facet of the USA religious scene which flourishes in the church/state vacuum – the Cult. Sometimes known as New Religious Movements, a number of these came into being during the questing period of the 1960s when 'dropping out' from materialist values was increasingly appealing to many idealistic young people. Alas, it became all too clear that many such organizations were both personally and financially exploitative of their converts and deployed mind control techniques.

In *Church/State Relations: Tensions and Transitions*[8] Thos. Robbins explores the circumstances in which church/state separation has enabled churches and clergy to be exempt from duties obligatory upon other community members. As cults diversify their activities, but retain their privileges of tax exemption, they come more into conflict with the state's expanding regulatory mandate. However, the ideal of the Jefferson wall means that what goes on inside a cult is not a matter for state concern. This situation enabled a psychotic monster like Jim Jones free to wreak horrific abuse upon his followers, culminating in their mass suicide. The lying practised by the Moonies (Unification Church) under the doctrine of 'divine deception'; the sexual procurement of converts by evangelistic prostitution, known as 'flirty fishing', of the Children of God;

8. Transaction Books 1987.

the harassment and intimidation by Scientologists of their opponents under the 'Fair Game' doctrine – these are all activities which ought to be under some form of social and legal constraint.

Then there are the various leadership felonies among the cults. The late L Ron Hubbard (Scientology) escaped into hiding after indictment and several leaders of the cult were convicted of a number of crimes. Sun Myung Moon served a prison term for bribery and tax offences. The leadership of Hare Krishna (ISKCON), Rajneesh (Bhagwan) and Divine Light (Guru Maharaji) have all been involved in immoral and illegal activities. Are they then to be exempt from interference because of the First Amendment? They were eventually subject to legal censure, but the freedom from accountability in the first instance makes the crimes all the more difficult to detect and prevent.

Even more difficult is the issue of mind control. Several of the cults practise a form of mind control upon converts. At one end of the spectrum it is difficult to prove coercion, as for instance in the case of the Transcendental Meditation movement. But in ISKCON, Scientology and the Moonies it is much easier to determine what is going on. The casualties of this process often end up isolated from and hostile to their parents, since it is among the younger generation that the cults have found most recruits. Some parents have unwisely resorted to forced 'deprogramming' to rescue their offspring and have thus been accused of reverse brainwashing, coercion and human rights violations.

The last charge is the ground on which the cults have hoped to put up a respectable fight. It is argued that fundamental human rights and freedoms dictate that individuals must be free to believe the earth is flat or bind themselves as a slave to an absurd system. But, as Herbert Rosedale of the American Family Foundation argues,[9] we cannot view conflicts between an individual's constitutional rights and the claims of the cults simply as disputes between parents and their wayward children:

Cult victims are not hippies who are persecuted because they wear their hair long or shave their heads or dress in distinctive clothes. They are not downtrodden victims of majoritarian persecution or impoverished souls lacking the influence and ability to defend their rights without aid from some sensitive benevolent group dedicated to the preservation of civil liberties. All too often

9. The *Cultic Studies* journal, winter 1986,

it is the 'new religion' under the guise of religious discipline which initiates physical brutality or emotional abuse, not the parent.

In a scathing review of *To Secure the Blessing of Liberty: American constitutional law and the new religious movements* by William Shepherd[10], Rosedale pours ridicule upon the author's contention that the rights of 'happy slaves' must be preserved even though society in so doing must put up with a lot of spiritual poison:

> It is absolutely irrelevant whether . . . 'happy slaves' are clamouring for protection of their constitutional right to continue in their condition. Consider in this regard apartheid and religious bigotry and whether these are the kind of 'spiritual poison' we ought to put up with if espoused by a 'new religion'. Still less would one consider a poll of slave owners on the subject . . . These arguments were urged and rejected a generation ago in the attempt to preserve protected individual 'libertarian' rights in the face of a challenge by majoritarian social values related to child factory labour . . . Before concluding that an individual must be free to act without restriction, one must carefully examine the nature of this conduct for which protection is claimed and its effect on the rights of others. Certainly the scales of justice should not be cast aside, without first removing the lady's blindfold.

Those unfamiliar with the pernicious practices of the cults may regard them as harmless eccentricities. Still others may wish to exercise humane tolerance and argue that Christianity itself was a cult in the early days and subject to persecution. This is to ignore the well-documented catalogue of infamy practised by the cults. Scientology is the cult best known to me, but anyone who cares to read the American Family Foundation's *Cult Observer* magazine for a year will be well briefed on the way in which the cults have used their financial strength and the American legal system (where the weak go to the wall), as a buffer to keep responsible oversight at bay. (For example, the way the Church of Scientology used litigation and harassment to prevent former Hubbard aide Gerry Armstrong revealing the patchwork of lies and deception woven by Hubbard around his career record and life.)

A number of the cults have also used their classification as 'religious' movements to gain tax exemption when they could

10. Crossroad.

more properly be classified as psychotherapies. EST and Synanon are two offshoots from the cults in this category. American law makes it an offence to diagnose and treat ailments without proper medical qualifications. This acts as an incentive for cults to make use of the protection of the church/state legislation by claiming to be religions when they are actually forms of therapy. All they need to do is list a few doctrines in their literature and have their quacks wear dog-collars.

The cults are unlikely to reach a significant percentage of American believers. Eventually their kingdoms will be curbed, their tax position made accountable. Like the Anabaptists in Reformation times, the big battalions will unite to squeeze them out. The Electronic Church is on the wane after the sex scandals and financial corruption uncovered during the PTL and Swaggart affairs. But as the church/state tensions resolve themselves in the USA, which big battalion will win out? Will the Moral Majority succeed in changing the separationist stance into an accommodationist one? Another word sometimes applied to American Protestantism is 'transformationist'. This neither advocates a unity of church and state nor complete separation, but an intermediate position which is committed to the sovereignty of God, prophetic witness, a strong social ethic and a realistic view of sin. It is claimed to be 'creative co-operation' and 'benevolent neutrality'.

That is the theory. But in practice who would be the prophets who claimed the ear of the president? Could it be Rushdoony? A Falwell or a Swaggart? The idea is not so silly. With the American president not committed to be the defender of any particular faith and with a system whereby an incoming president fills the White House with hand-picked staffers, it is perfectly possible that another born-again president could thumb his Bible before making a critical decision and believe that God had chosen him as the agent of Armageddon. If you think this is my wild imagination, that fictional scenario is convincingly described in the opening of Charles Colson's book *Kingdoms in Conflict*[11]. As one of Nixon's Watergate staffers, he ought to know.

On the other hand, could the preachers with a social conscience like Rev Jim Wallis of Washington be the new prophets? Wallis accuses the new right of preaching hypocritically in support of a pro-life position while working for political goals such as nuclear armaments or the support of Contra killers in Nicaragua or capital

11. Hodder & Stoughton 1988.

punishment, which are the antithesis of pro-life. 'In place of the gospel of compassion they preach the arrogance of American power; instead of a gospel that is good news to the poor they preach a gospel that honours excessive wealth as a sign of God's favour and leaves the poor to fend for themselves. Theirs is ultimately a religion of the state. They have become like the court prophets of ancient Isreal who were employed by the king to pronounce upon the king's schemes and ambitions.'[12]

From different poles of theology, Wallis and Colson seem to fear the new right and cling to the old separationist stance as the safest way of protecting freedom. Yet, as we have seen, that means giving hostages to fortune in the shape of the Electronic Church and the cults. If the television preachers have proved anything it is that there is a community of faith out there, waiting for a forum in which to express itself. To allow it some constitutional expression need not compromise religious liberty but provide a safety-valve for some of the religious passions which at present are inflicted on the political arena. The other way is perhaps unlikely to appeal to the majority of Americans. It does not involve a state religion or church but the setting up of a forum for all religions in proportion to their numbers to deliberate upon issues of moral and spiritual concern. It need have no power, only influence. The problem is that many Americans believe that they live in God's own country with the best system of government in the world. It means looking in the mirror and admitting that after two hundred years you might not be the most beautiful after all.

12. *Newsweek*, 17 September 1984.

4 Hot Wax and Melted Ice: Russia

Moscow, Trinity Cathedral, 12 June 1988. Cloudless blue skies and a brilliant sun, raising temperatures to over a hundred degrees. Everywhere bells are pealing and the air is full of a new, intoxicating spirit. Mother Church is celebrating a thousand years of existence. Helping, organizing, even prompting through nightly television programmes, are the officials of an atheist state which has for two generations tried to quash and extirpate the same church. Now by a twist of fate – or is it Providence? – *glasnost* and the millenium have coincided. The first has established the basis for the second to be celebrated openly and enthusiastically.

So intent was the Politburo on honouring the occasion that the secular holy of holies, the Bolshoi Theatre, was the site of one of the major celebrations. Its curtains, emblazoned with the symbol of the hammer and sickle, opened to reveal high-ranking churchmen from around the world, state officials and even Mrs Raisa Gorbachev, proving officially to all that religion is no longer the opium of the people. Through a thousand harvests and hot summers and the heat of controversy, the Russian Orthodox Church tended and guarded the soul of Russia. Through the long dark winters of the Soviet republics and the chill isolation of the gulags, its pastors and patriarchs have tried to keep the flickering candles of faith alive.

Amid the stifling heat of a June summer night in 1988, forty miles north-east of Moscow in the fourteenth-century monastery at Zagorsk, the scent of hot wax and incense drifts across a packed congregation chanting in Old Slavonic towards the gilded altar, while outside the overflow crowds mill around the food stalls waiting in long queues to buy religious artefacts, not normally on open sale, which will give the church precious income of which she has been starved for the past two generations. A priest from Odessa assigned to the overseas dignitaries enthuses, 'It's like a honeymoon. We feel drunk and we don't ever wake up. From our TV screens we hear that the church is the heart of our nation and that we need it. Can you imagine?'

For Soviet Christians the events of June 1988 were a milestone in their thousand-year history. For General Secretary Gorbachev they were a platform on which to parade his twin policies of *glasnost* (openness) and *perestroika* (restructuring). If he is to succeed – and the peace of the world may depend on whether or not he does – then it is inevitable that he will want the church to assist him in combating the immense social problems that afflict the USSR. Gorbachev is a practical man and, as more than one visiting dignitary observed, 'he knows the Russians are a deeply pious people and will let the lid off the steaming pot before it blows off.' Before that happens, the USSR will have to go through yet another renegotiation of the church/state arrangement. Laws still forbid religious education and recruitment in the USSR. The church is still in thrall to the state via a bureaucracy operated by non-believers for the protection of atheism. Only older people remember church bells, banned because they disturbed the peace of the countryside. So the silvery sounds of June were more than just a shock to stimulate old memories; they were ushering in a new era. All the Kremlin watchers say it is too early to assess what the political effects will be, but in religious terms the prognosis is good. The Christian Church has usually become stronger and been purified by persecution. Its relatively weak position in Russia today carries none of the temptations of the corrupt days of the tsars. Orthodoxy has remained outside the sterile tit-for-tat battles which Protestants and Catholics have carried on since the Reformation, and the stress on rationalism in Western Christianity which gave rise to the conflicts between science and religion, weakening the latter, have no counterpart in Orthodoxy which would emerge, like African or Latin American Christianity, as spiritually and numerically strong in the twenty-first century.

The cautious cultivation of the church by Gorbachev is in marked contrast to the persecutions of his predecessors during which it remained remarkably strong. Despite the difficulty of obtaining reliable official statistics, it is thought that more than 20 per cent of the 275 million population of the USSR is Christian in the sense of having some church attachment. World Council of Churches and United Bible Society surveys give the Russian Orthodox Church over 50 million adherents with that total swelled by 5 million Georgian Orthodox and 4 million Armenian Orthodox. Later we shall touch on the significant Roman Catholic presence in the USSR, in the Ukraine and Latvia/Estonia; in addition Baptists, both official and unregistered, have a high profile. But the predominant and, for all practical purposes, the national church of the Soviet Union is the Russian Orthodox Church.

Parts of the USSR are predominantly Muslim (11 per cent of the total population) and the shape of world history would have indeed been different if Islam and not Christianity had been adopted as the creed of Russia a thousand years ago. Although the first Christians in all probability were Armenians converted by the Apostle Thaddeus a few days after Pentecost, and Armenia became the first nation in the ancient world to adopt it, Christianity did not at first spread deep into what is today the Soviet Union (apart from early success in Georgia and parts of the Crimea). The fateful moment came in AD 988 when Prince Vladimir followed the example of the Grand Duchess Olga in 955, and was baptised. This might have had something to do with the fact that he wished to marry the sister of the Byzantine emperor. He bade his subjects follow his lead, although they were known as pagans with a penchant for human sacrifice, and in a unique spectacle they waded into the Dnieper River at Kiev to undergo mass baptism. According to another account, Vladimir was looking for a religion to unite the Slavic tribes under his rule and his emissaries visited Santa Sophia (the Church of the Holy Wisdom) in Constantinople and declared, 'We knew not whether we were in heaven or on earth, for on earth there is not such splendour or such beauty and we do not know how to describe it. We only know that God dwells there among men.'

Sanctuaries, icons and liturgy play a central role in the Orthodox faith, and from that moment on, Christianity played a larger role in the history of Russia and the Ukraine, providing a matrix for Slavonic culture, language and literature to develop using the Cyrillic alphabet devised by the missionary monk Cyril in the ninth century and adopted by the church. It is easy to find historical and political reasons why Western Christianity drifted apart from its Eastern version, but when Christendom split finally in 1054 (the Great Schism), it was doctrinal issues that were the final straw. Right from the early days there was a different style to Orthodox Christianity. To the Orthodox the pope is the first Protestant, for it was a pope in AD 589 who thought he had the authority vested in himself to insert the phrase 'and from the Son' after the words 'I believe in the Holy Ghost, the Lord the Giver of Life, who proceedeth from the Father' into the Creed agreed at Nicea in AD 325. It was known as the 'Filioque' clause and caused immense resentment in the East where it was seen as a crass attempt to tamper with the mysterious doctrine of the Holy Trinity, central to Orthodoxy. The Trinity is for them a paradigm for the created order in which matter and humanity are intended to be reflections of the glory of God. The world is a two-way mirror for the Orthodox, while to the Western Christian it is a two-decker dimension. Suffering and sin are imperfections in our grime-stained mirror, but the apex of Orthodox faith is the Resurrection when God transforms humanity into the divinity which he himself possesses. This emphasis explains why Easter is so dear to Orthodox Christians; why they eschew the obsession of the West with original sin and why their monks are not so world-denying.

Another key point in their history emerged at the Council of Chalcedon in AD 451 over the perennially difficult issue of whether the one, united, divine-human nature of Christ should be counted as one or two. In the Nicene Creed the key word is *homo-ousios* (single substance) or *homoi-ousios* (like substance) and the difference of the single Greek letter 'iota' gives us our expression 'it doesn't matter an iota'. It also left its legacy in the form of a church schism between the Oriental Orthodox (largely Asian/African churches) who affirmed one nature and were called monophysites and those of the Hellenic tradition (Greek and eventually Russian Orthodox) who affirmed two natures and were called dyophysites. The Oriental group was reduced by the spread of Islam but today includes the Coptic Church (8 million); Syrians (0.25 million); Armenians (4 million); Indian Orthodox (1.5 million); Ethiopians (15 million). The dyophysites range from the Roumanians (17 million); Bulgarians (8 million); Greeks (8 million); Serbians (5 million); Georgians (2 million); Cypriots (2 million); Americans (2 million) and the Ecumenical patriarchate which takes in almost everyone else from Europe to the Antipodes (5 million). The smallest of the ancient patriarchates is now Antioch in predominantly Muslim Turkey (with 0.25 million) and the largest is in Russia which the Lion *Handbook of Religion* in 1985 credits with 70 million. There are 150 million Orthodox worldwide – a sixth of the world's Christians – 85 per cent of whom live in communist states.

Orthodoxy is a federacy, rather than a pyramid with one church or pontiff at the head. Local churches are 'autocephalous' (self-governing) and a few of the smaller ones are autonomous. The Orientals look to Pope Shenouda of the Coptic Church as their spiritual leader. The Eastern Orthodox group look to Metropolitan Dimitrios I of Constantinople who recently paid a historic visit to

Russia (the first by a Metropolitan since 1589) to meet Patriarch
Pimen of Moscow. Dimitrios' status is low-key in a Muslim country
but he is the first among equals in his church. The word Orthodox
comes from *orthos* (correct) *doxadzein* (to glorify) and thus the form
of worship is very important. The three-chamber church is divided
between sanctuary and nave by an iconostasis, a solid screen with
three symbolic doors, behind which the priest performs the consecration at the Eucharist. Priests are expected to marry but bishops are
drawn from celibate clergy or monastic orders. Although it believes
in apostolic succession and hierarchy, Orthodoxy does not hold its
leaders infallible – only the church (as the mirror through which
the essence of God passes into the world) is infallible and its mind
is expressed through Councils. The church is held together by the
act of communion and while there can be schisms *from* the church,
there can be no schism *within* the church, a tough position which
means that prior agreement in the faith is required before unity can
be achieved.

Union is unlikely to be forthcoming since the consequence of
the Orthodox missing out on many of the intellectual debates
within Western Christendom is that they do not accept many of
the results of modern scholarship upon the Bible, and the tradition
of scholarship among their clergy is low. However, behind the big
beards and the flower-pot hats of the patriarchs there usually lurks
a shrewd and worldly-wise mind. The tradition of Caesaro-papism,
which Constantine started in his New Rome in the East, made the
church a partner of state, not its subordinate. That was to be the role
that Orthodoxy played for several centuries in Russia after Vladimir's
conversion. It became more and more a Russian church particularly
during the 200 years of Tartar rule. In 1448 it became self-governing
(autocephalous).[1] In 1589 Job, Metropolitan of Moscow ('The Third
Rome') became a patriarch, fifth in the order of seniority behind the
Patriarchs of Constantinople, Alexandria, Antioch and Jerusalem (a
pecking order which still prevails, although autocephalous churches
have risen to fourteen in number). The church was involved closely in
the internal struggles of early Russia and in the wars against Catholic
Poland. In 1613–33, Filaret was patriarch while his son Michael was
the first Romanov tsar. But the zenith of the church's influence –
and a catastrophe for church/state influence – came in 1652 when
the twenty-three-year-old Tsar Alexis invited his mentor and former

1. When Constantinople fell to the Turks in 1453 Moscow proclaimed itself
the centre of the Orthodox world.

tutor, the charismatic Metropolitan of Novgorod, Nikon, to become patriarch.

Six foot five in height and awesomely intense, Nikon was determined to reform the Russian church, so he laid down conditions. He demanded that Alexis should follow his leadership 'as your first shepherd and father in all that I shall teach on dogma, discipline and custom'. Nikon's aim was not only the moral rearmament of the church but its supremacy over the state. It would then be the vehicle by which Nikon could assert its pre-eminence over the Orthodox world. These papal pretensions were soon challenged by his own flock when he tried to reform the rituals and liturgy of the church which, due to ignorance of correct forms, had accumulated many deviations and errors through the years. In 1655 Nikon invoked the help of Macarius, Patriarch of Antioch, in his attempts to make changes in such matters as how many loaves were to be consecrated, how many hallelujahs shouted and how many fingers used in making the sign of the cross. This last point caused particular anger. Russians were used to crossing themselves with two fingers (symbolising the dual nature of Christ) and were being asked to use the Trinitarian number of three. Opposition was led by the Archpriest Avvakum who, like Nikon, came from the northern wildernesses and burned with zeal to reform the church.

For a few years Nikon was effective. He successfully constructed the huge Monastery of the Resurrection thirty miles west of Moscow, known as the New Jerusalem (which of course Moscow was, in his eyes). He instituted draconian punishments to get rid of drunkenness among the clergy and humiliated many heads of monasteries. This bizarre autocracy was catalogued by Maccarius's scribe, Paul of Aleppo, who made no secret of his distaste for the Russian climate, food and habits – including that of holding lengthy services in chilly churches with no seats. (Nikon decreed that all believers should be in church for four hours each day.)

But Nikon eventually exasperated his protégé, now his patron, when he forced the tsar to make him regent and constantly interfered in government, treating Alexis's ministers of state with contempt. His enemies fought back and in 1658 the tsar froze him out. Nikon went off in a huff to a monastery, haughtily assuming that his recall was at hand, but the tsar shrewdly deposed him for deserting his duties. At his trial Nikon advanced papal pretensions which echoed those of a medieval pope. 'The highest authority of the priesthood is not received from kings and tsars, but contrariwise it is by the priesthood that rulers are anointed. Therefore it is abundantly clear that the

priesthood is very much greater than royalty.' Ironically, Tsar Alexis
was the most pious of all the tsars; he surrendered more power to
the church than any tsar before or since, yet before the end of his
reign the Russian church was fatally divided and weakened, with
Nikon in exile in a stone monastery cell. Even more ironic was the
struggle between the two reformers, Nikon and Avvakum. The latter
thundered against wicked foreign infiltration into Mother Russia of
such devices as 'bewitched grass' (tobacco) but his particular wrath
was reserved for Nikon's attempts to change the 'Russified' Christ
in the icons of the fiercely nationalist Russian church into the Risen
Christ of the New Testament. 'They paint the image of Immanuel
the Saviour with a plump face, red lips, dimpled fingers and large
fat legs and altogether make him look like a German, fat-bellied,
corpulent, omitting only to paint the sword at his side. All this was
invented by the cur Nikon.'

In 1653 Nikon sent Avvakum to Siberia, but when the patriarch
fell from power Avvakum attempted a return to grace in Moscow,
but his tongue kept getting him into trouble. Although the patriarch's power play had been stymied, Nikon's reforms were allowed
to stand. Avvakum declared that new-born babies knew more about
God than scholars of the Greek church, and proposed, like Donatus
in North Africa a millennium earlier, that traitors to the faith should
be rebaptised if they wished salvation. But it was his bitter assertion
to the young Tsar Fedor that his father Alexis was burning in hell
that resulted in Avvakum being consigned to the flames of a martyr's
pyre in 1682. His fanatical followers were inspired to emulate him
and between 1684–90 some 20,000 schismatics or Old Believers, as
they called themselves, consigned themselves to flames in wooden
stockades in the northern province. Because the state had backed
the church reforms, revolt against the church widened into revolt
against the state and eventually the Regent Sophia, who took over
on Fedor's death, crushed them ruthlessly. They were driven underground and still exist in indeterminate numbers in remote villages,
handing on their peculiarly Russian Christianity from generation to
generation in a heterodox freemasonry which recalls those days of
the Great Schism when church power in Russia reached its zenith.

The reforms which Nikon had hoped would give the Russian
Church the leadership of the Eastern world had shattered it. It
languished from then on, subordinate to the tsar, and when a generation later a patriarch (Adrian) opposed some of the reforms brought
in by Peter the Great, the tsar abolished the patriarchate in 1721,
replacing it with a 'Holy Governing Synod' of bishops, controlled

by a chief procurator subservient to the tsar. The church continued in this subordinate role as an arm of state from 1721 to 1917 when Tsar Nicholas II resigned during the revolution. The revolutionaries saw the church as one of the pillars of the old regime designed for subjugation of the masses, and when the Bolsheviks seized power, they immediately deprived the church of its legal rights including that of owning property.

Struggling to re-establish its independence, the church put forward plans to revive the patriarchate, but when an independent patriarch, Tikhon, was elected and took a strong stand against the Bolsheviks, it had fatal consequences. In 1922 all valuable objects owned by the churches were confiscated and Tikhon was arrested. Another faction sided with the Soviet government. The mini-schism was healed when Tikhon was released and declared support for the government, but by then it was too late. In 1925 Stalin abolished the patriarchate and began a systematic persecution of the church which was rivalled only by the most bloody Roman emperors. An estimated 50,000 clergy, monks and nuns perished, as did countless laity. The first Soviet constitution, introduced by Lenin in July 1918, had recognized the right to disseminate religious propaganda, but this was revoked by Stalin. In 1929 new laws forbade religious instruction for persons under eighteen years; made the registration of religious associations obligatory if consisting of more than twenty persons (whose names were required), the state being being able to refuse registration without giving reasons; all clergy had to be registered before they could exercise their office and the church was limited to holding worship only. With such circumscribed functions and with the climate of persecution it was surprising anyone registered at all, but there were many brave and pious people who did so. Stalin only relented in 1943 when he needed the support of the church to rally the soul of the nation in the life and death struggle with the Nazi invaders. Their reward was the restoration of the patriarchate in 1943 and the re-opening of some 25,000 churches.

Despite the 'destalinisation' programme announced by Nikita Krushchev in his secret speech in 1956, even apologists have to admit that he bought it at the expense of the church by cracking down on it in an attempt to appease hardliners. From 1959–64 Krushchev increased state control. The number of officially registered churches can be read as a barometer of the severity of the persecution during this period. In 1913 there were 80,000; 39,000 in 1925; only 1,000 in 1939; 6,000 in 1945; 20,000 by 1957. The total was down to 5,000 in 1973, owing mainly to the Krushchev crackdown when penalties were increased for infractions of the 1929 laws dealing with religious practice. In 1961 a new law made it possible to remove children from believing parents.

In 1958 the registration of religious acts (sacraments like baptism) was made compulsory and the number of members of religious associations limited to twenty exactly, thus excluding the major part of the worshipping community from any say in the life of a local church. The twenty people were obliged to raise the necessary finance themselves to pay a priest (who until recently was paid much the same as the average worker but taxed at five times greater rate). Effective administration was put in the hands of a lay council of three over whose names the local communist authorities had the right of veto and from whom they must rent the place of worship, since all churches were owned by the state.

The Council for Religious Affairs was created in 1966 by the fusion of the Council dealing with Orthodoxy and one dealing with 'Religious Cults'. All activity of churches, such as opening or closing church buildings or holding conferences, required the sanction of this body. Since Krushchev's fall in 1964, taunting of worshippers at services has stopped and the Council has even intervened on behalf of congregations when zealous officials have tried to prevent Christian communities carrying out their functions. The Council also is concerned to see that priests are of an educated standard, since if they are not, they will diminish the standards of education in the population at large.

The contemporary legal position of religion in the Soviet state has been defined by Article 52 of the 1977 constitution of the USSR. It guarantees citizens freedom of conscience and 'the right to profess any religion or to profess none, to celebrate religious rites or to conduct atheistic propaganda'. It also states that church is separate from state and school – which theoretically gives the church the right of independent operation it has never enjoyed in the USSR. But that is to ignore the suppressing weight of bureaucracy with which religion is burdened, the sanctions imposed when it dares to speak out or exhort people to join it, and the countless incentives and preferments given to the militant atheist whose creed proclaimed is simply another way of advancing in the Party. It has to be remembered that Stalin's 'Seventeen severe Decrees' of 1929 were still in force during the time of the millennium celebrations. Thus the church could not perform social work or welfare services, set up Sunday schools, nor gather in public outside a licensed building; organize study groups, holidays, nor publish materials.

Those who had hoped that the end of the Krushchev era would see a less hostile attitude to religion were to be disappointed. The twenty years after his overthrow saw many more imprisonments in labour camps and deaths through ill-treatment. Reviewing this period, experts on Soviet religious affairs insist on a distinction between Soviet 'religious policy' and Soviet 'dissident policy'. The first concerns the general view of religion and its future (superstition which will wither away) and the latter a particular manifestation of religious beliefs (demands for human rights etc). Brezhnev himself took no interest in religion and there was no evidence of any high-level debate in the communist party about it. It was taken for granted that official stances would continue to oppose it by propaganda and that it would decline, like snuff-taking has in Western society.

The policy towards dissent was uncompromising but rose and fell in intensity partly in reaction to events and partly when the Party thought it had nothing to lose in diplomatic circles (for example, during the cool climate after the invasion of Afghanistan). Brezhnev followed his characteristic path of 'reaction' – a response to events beyond the regime's control. In the mid-1960s there was not only Czechoslovakia to contend with but the rise of dissent within Russia. Writers and human rights activists were linking up with religious dissidents and in many instances were the same people. People in the West were becoming aware of the *samizdat* (underground literature) appeals produced particularly by the *Initsiativniki* (unregistered Baptists).[2]

During the 1970s, over 500 Orthodox priests were suspended from their duties and the dissent movement gathered strength on three fronts. First there were growing links between religion and nationalism in various parts of the Soviet Union, notably in Lithuania (where it is expressed traditionally through the Roman Catholic Church which is strong in the region) but also in Georgia and the Ukraine. Potentially more explosive at present is the situation in the Central Asian Republics which are beginning to feel the influence of the growing Islamic revival that has taken hold in Iran. Muslims are the fastest growing section of the 275 million Soviet population but their forty-four million people remain under-represented in the Politburo and Central Committee. Fears of 'religious terrorism'

2. In 1976, a secret document was published in the West detailing Soviet laws on religion made in 1971 but kept secret from the churches required to obey them.

and 'religious fanaticism' are taken seriously and the débâcle of Afghanistan was undertaken in that context.

In the late 1980s, trouble broke out in the Nagorno-Karabakh region of the republic of Azerbaijan which has administered the region since 1923, although 75 per cent of the people are Armenians. Strikes and demonstrations were held in an attempt by the Armenians to secede to Soviet Armenia, but Moscow vetoed the idea. But whereas Brezhnev might have sent in the tanks, Gorbachev might well favour a solution which would allow Nagorno-Karabakh to become 'autocephalous' (a good Orthodox tradition) and has promised aid to preserve the Armenian linguistic and cultural heritage (the religious heritage is Oriental, not Eastern Orthodox). Under Moscow's rule, Armenia's parishes were reduced from 1,500 to 52 and for 100,000 Armenians in Nagorno-Karabakh not a single church exists.

In Lithuania in 1987, 78,000 citizens signed a petition demanding that their exiled bishop be returned to them. None of the six other bishoprics had a permanent resident bishop. Although this has now happened, the Kremlin is still uneasy about encouraging expressions of solidarity among Roman Catholics which could lead to calls for the Lithuanian Republic to be given greater independence. Roman influence is even stronger in the Ukraine where Eastern rite Catholicism refused to die after it was officially liquidated by the government in 1946 and absorbed into the Russian Orthodox Church. In 1987, two underground bishops and twenty-three Ukrainian priests sought official recognition for their church from Moscow, and there are claims that 1,200 underground priests are holding daily masses in 'forest churches' in the Ukraine. Like Armenia, the country is becoming extremely restive and the dilemma for the Kremlin is whether to restore the Catholic Church and thereby control the nationalist movement or try to absorb it into Orthodoxy.

The former course is more risky taking into account the reign of a Polish pope in Rome who is not slow to excite the aspirations of Catholics in communist lands to affirm their faith more strongly. This is one reason why the invitation to John Paul II to the millennium celebrations went out slightly late. Officially the response of Cardinal Willebrands was that the pope would not consider going unless he could meet Catholics. That is likely to be the truth. For its part, the Kremlin would not wish to see him stirring up the delicate situation in Lithuania and the Ukraine and it is unlikely that the pope, being the man he is, would look favourably on the Orthodox having hegemony over Catholics. The pope takes seriously one of the prophecies of Fatima, in which three children were vouchsafed by a vision of the Virgin at the village of Fatima in Spain in 1917, which predicted that the world would collapse unless Russia embraced Christianity. Increasingly the pope's utterances seem to be concerned with the communist world. On his side there are disadvantages associated with a visit to Russia, since the Ukrainian Catholics might see it as endorsing the Orthodox hegemony and even if he were allowed to go to Lithuania it would pose problems since the Vatican has never recognized the USSR's sovereignty over the republic which has been Catholic for 600 years.

This highlights an irony in church/state matters in the USSR. The Russian Orthodox Church regards itself as the true church of the whole nation and does not wish to sell off bits of its empire. The Kremlin can count on its continued allegiance when it comes to keeping out the Catholics. This less generous face of Orthodoxy is also seen when it comes to relations with Baptists who are regarded as 'poachers' of believers who belong in the Orthodox Church.

The second factor in church/state relations in the USSR in the twenty years prior to *glasnost* was the coming together of religious and secular dissent. Around the time of the Helsinki Accord the West became increasingly aware of dissidents. Solzhenitsyn and Sakharov, Jews, Baptists, humanist writers, poets and artists were all caught up in the network of dissent which tried to keep the leviathan of the state from swallowing the fragile freedoms longed for by ordinary citizens.

Whether devout Orthodox like Solzhenitsyn or atheist like Sakharov, they shared a belief in humanitarian values. Some were exiled and pined for Russia. Others belonging to Russia's 2 million Jews were refused permission to go to an alternative homeland in Israel. Some, like the 'Siberian Seven' Pentecostalists who spent years in the US embassy in Moscow began as religious dissidents and ended up as political footballs.

But the spearhead was launched by a young man who had become a priest at the height of the crackdown in 1962. Father Gleb Yakunin launched a dissent movement in 1965 with a letter to the then Patriarch Alexei: 'It is clear that the Russian Church is seriously and dangerously ill,' and went on to criticize Orthodox leaders who connived with the government's 'illegal control' of the church and 'deviated from their sacred duty before Christ'. Alexei's response was to suspend Yakunin from priestly duties, but he persisted, and in 1975 sent an open letter to the Assembly of the World Council of Churches in Nairobi, detailing religious oppression in the

USSR and inviting help.

This aroused a great deal of interest, but fearing the alienation of the Russian Orthodox delegation who regarded him as a rebel against the authority of the church expressed through the bishops, the WCC applied the double standard it uses when dealing with Marxist or black nations, and urged caution upon the dissenters. In 1976 Yakunin founded the Christian Committee for the Defence of Believers' Rights which included other Christian groups. At the time of the Helsinki accords on Human Rights the group sent hundreds of documents to the West detailing abuses. For this Yakunin was charged with 'anti-Soviet agitation and propaganda' and was sent to a hard labour camp in Siberia. He was released last year and, as a product of *glasnost*, restored to a parish near Moscow, but continues to be a thorn in the flesh of the authorities. Now in his mid-fifties, he called, prior to the millennium celebrations, for the removal of Patriarch Pimen, claiming him to be too ill and senile – 'a symbol of our church as it exists today – very passive'. He told a reporter, 'When it comes to my parish, it is just as it was thirty years ago. If people approach me after I stop leading the prayers, the monitor [state official] makes me leave. The monitor says I can't talk to people privately in the parish house.'

Outside the Soviet Union, the catalogue of heroes and martyrs was kept alive by organizations like that at Keston College in Kent, England, which monitors human rights abuses and produces the influential journal *Religion in Communist Lands*. There is no doubt that this helped to put a spotlight on the activities of the Soviet state when it began to increase arrests of believers (180 arrests in 1979 increasing to 400 in 1982) in the post-Afghanistan clamp-down.

The third factor which contributed to the state suppression of religion throughout the 1970s and 1980s was that worship was becoming increasingly attractive. The old picture of churches being full of old women in shawls, bowed in prayer, was changing. Young people were experiencing a new interest in religion. Even the Soviet anti-religious press was forced to admit that the Baptist *Initsiativniki* attracted many of their adherents from among young industrial workers – the group the Soviet sociologists thought ought to be least susceptible to the 'superstition ' of Christianity. Further embarrassment for the atheists was that those who had begun to question the ideology of the Party were being attracted into the Russian Orthodox Church, allegedly the preserve of the ignorant *babushka*. From this group came the campaigners for religious freedom who formed the Christian Seminar. About half of the *samizdat* reaching the West are religious in content. But the Russian Orthodox Church also benefited from the resurgence of interest in Old Russian culture, the current nostalgia for past glories and the desire to preserve old buildings. Young people are turning to the church as much to discover their roots as Russians as their faith. Officials can joke with a grain of truth when they say, 'I'm an atheist – but I'm an Orthodox atheist!'

A key factor in the growth of any organized religion is its supply of clergy. No doubt realizing this, the Soviet government took early steps to shut down the seminaries that supply them. Stalin closed them all but relented after the war. Three remain, training as many students (900) as were attending seven seminaries before the Kremlin closed four more. There are five applicants for every place and entrants must have completed a secondary education and proved spiritual commitment. Two-thirds of entrants now come from families where there is hostility to religion, a sign that the church is spreading. The syllabus is heavy and the hours long. Twenty-five subjects including Old Church Slavonic and the normal higher education curricula are taught. Students read the Bible and *Pravda*. On the walls hang pictures of patriarchs, Lenin and General Secretary Gorbachev. The three seminaries are in Leningrad, Odessa on the Black Sea (which is the summer residence of the patriarch), and at Zagorsk, the spiritual centre of the church, some thirty miles from Moscow. Students are funded by the church and given a grant of about one-sixth of the average worker's wage.

Although some seminarians have had work experience, the students are mostly young men (Orthodoxy does not even have women priests on the agenda, but there are fifteen convents in the Soviet Union where nuns often work as nurses in tandem with their devotional duties). The cream of the seminaries are sent to Zagorsk for higher study. On graduation the priest has the choice of entering a religious order, in which case he must take vows of chastity, but can then receive promotion in the religious hierarchy (there are seventy-three bishoprics to bid for). Married priests are sent to serve in parishes and are expected to go forth and multiply. But no matter how fecund the priests are, the total number of 10,000 clergy will not be maintained by a yearly output of less than 200 priests. It does not take a prophet to see that high on the agenda of *perestroika* for the Church must be the expansion of its seminaries.

Monasteries do not play as significant a role in the Orthodox Church as they once did. One reason is that the state closed them all down. In the days when the church was rich in property and lands there were 1,100 monasteries, but this declined to three in the Brezhnev era. But the state recently returned to the church the Danilov Monastery, Moscow's oldest, which had become a paint shop. In 1988 the painters began restoring icons and preparing Danilov to house the patriarch's staff. Next on the shopping list was the return of the holiest shrine, the eleventh century Monastery of the Caves at Kiev which had been siezed in 1961 and which was returned to the church as a millennium present from General Secretary Gorbachev. Father Filaret, the abbot, is optimistic that the walled hilltop complex which attracts 15,000 tourists per day during summer will soon have its gold domes repaired to reflect properly the glory of the liturgy from below. But not all monks stay in Russia. Some are now permitted to resume links with the self-governing monastic community at Mount Athos in northern Greece where the Russians had, pre-revolution, one of the finest sites.

If manpower is at a premium, curiously money is not. Although taxed at a higher rate than workers, church officials are not poor. The minimum salary for a deacon in a country parish is only slightly below the average Soviet wage and the rector of a seminary receives double the average wage. A bishop's salary is comparable with that of a leading Soviet official. A parish priest lives free in a furnished house and can expect gifts (mainly of food) from his parishioners. Worshippers pay for rites performed on their behalf, and income comes from offerings and from the religious artefact industry. This is centred on a factory near Moscow which is known for the quality of its glass and metal work. Two thousand tons of candle wax pass out of its doors every year. Eleven million baptismal crosses are made annually at the factory, a pointer to how many Soviet babies are being initiated into the church (one in six is admitted officially). A million funeral garlands (paper strips bearing religious images and texts inserted into the coffin) are made annually, which represents 60 per cent of Soviet funerals. The church also runs its own publishing house and three editions of the Bible have been produced in the past generation. Previously they were restricted to the clergy and could fetch huge sums on the black market, but in the *annus mirabilis* of 1988, 100,000 were allocated to the Orthodox, and the Baptists allowed to import 100,000. However, should the unrestricted sale of Bibles be permitted, then it will obviously not take the Orthodox long to turn that into a profit-making business. Their factory seems a model of capitalist endeavour in a nationalized church which has embraced privatisation and succeeded.

So far we have looked at the ways in which the state has

restricted or suppressed the church. A more sinister note is struck when we come to look at the ways in which the Orthodox Church is an agency of the state. The KGB is not as stupid as Hollywood likes to think and has for years been applying the principle: 'If you can't beat them, join them!' At Assemblies of the World Council of Churches one parlour game is to guess the KGB man in the Russian Orthodox delegation.

A kinder view of one WCC official is that the Orthodox hierarchy consists of 'churchmen who are struggling to safeguard their Christian integrity against great odds'. The attitude of the Orthodox hierarchy is to try to find an accommodation with the state to allow it to operate. This leads them to attract the criticism of 'sycophancy' from the likes of Fr Yakunin and Fr Dmitri Dudko who reiterated the message of Yakunin's letter to the 1983 WCC Assembly but has since recanted and stays at his post.

The hierarchy accuse the dissidents of destroying the harmony they have built up and thus threatening the freedom of the church. Metropolitan Nikodim told *Time* magazine in June 1980: 'Groups that exist or would like to exist around Dudko and others are not for the benefit of the church, since our church finds its own unity. The action of the church is not for sensation or effect.'

Some churchmen even go so far as to present Christianity as Marxism at prayer, a view not reciprocated by the communist party. The church contributes heavily to the Soviet Peace Fund which is loyal to the Politburo line on *détente* and disarmament. Patriarch Pimen has called on the faithful to back the Kremlin's 'policies of peace' and other Orthodox leaders have lent weight to campaigns against the neutron bomb and NATO rearmament. However, this is hardly inconsistent with the gospel or their counterparts in the Western churches. But the problem is that sycophancy can develop into spineless appeasement. In 1975 the Deputy Chairman of the Council for Religious Affairs drew up a report bearing the revealing title 'Cadres of the Church and Legal Measures to Curtail Their Activities'. (Officially, its authenticity was denied when it was leaked to the West, but whether or not it is satire it rang all too true to observers of the Soviet scene.) The report boasted that, 'there is no consecration of a bishop, no transfer, without thorough investigation of the candidate by appropriate officials of the Council.'

Cynically, the author goes on to divide the clerical sheep and goats from an atheist perspective. Seventeen members of the hierarchy including Patriarch Pimen are characterized as 'not personally

involved in spreading the influence of Orthodoxy among the population.' A second group of twenty-three are 'loyal to our state but
all too intent on expanding church influence' and a third group of
seventeen are regarded as subversive of the laws on cults. Even pliant
church leaders, it notes 'have always held and always will hold positions alien to Marxism'. The report applauds one official in Tomsk
who curtailed Lenten celebrations in one village which were creating
a 'sensation'. The picture drawn by the report is borne out by the
dissident groups who say that many of the freedoms accorded the
church in Moscow are window-dressing to impress Western reporters
but that in the provinces local authorities regularly interrupt services
especially at Christmas and Easter.

More serious charges against the leadership of the Russian Orthodox Church were published by the dissident journal *Glasnost* prior
to the millennium celebration. The allegations concern Patriarch
Pimen, who was appointed in 1971 and was scarcely able to get
through the 1988 celebrations because of his diabetes and general
frialty. Prior to his appointment he was noted in the documents
as being only too willing to assist the Religious Affairs Council
with information. Furthermore, in various applications he had lied
about his record between 1937 and 1944 during which time he was
imprisoned twice for desertion. Other details in his personnel record
(in all large organizations in the USSR it is usually KGB *apparatchiks*
who run this department) reveal him to have been a womanizer. Both
these facets would have rendered him open to blackmail by the KGB
for whom he would have been an ideal 'puppet patriarch'. The test
of whether *perestroika* will extend to the church will come with the
appointment of Pimen's successor. Will he be a Gorbachev of the
church, committed to holy *glasnost*? Will he be another grey man
in a black cassock determined to do the will of the Kremlin and
preserve the status quo?

Since *glasnost*, more churches have opened, more detainees have
been released and the churches in Russia are poised for great strides
forward. Rev Michael Bordeaux, founder and general director of
Keston College, which has monitored human rights abuses over
the years, is cautious in his welcome, hoping that *glasnost* will
not prove to be merely another 'Prague Spring'. In the euphoria of
post-millennium celebrations it is difficult, he says, to speculate on
what changes might be made, but certainly there will have to be a
proper basis established for consultations between the church and
the state. 'If there were to be consultation, three of the top points
on the church's agenda would certainly be education, literature and

the right to own property [leading to the opening of church buildings without registration].'

Bordeaux goes on to imagine what might happen if the Soviet state were to permit major concessions in these areas. 'What Christians of the West need to fear is not the abolition of *glasnost* but the advent of a true *perestroika* opening up every avenue to a new era of co-operation and inter-aid. We in the West are simply not adequately prepared for the opportunities and demands which that would bring.' He cites the diocese of Irkutsk, which is roughly the same in area and only slightly smaller in population than Australia but has less than fifty registered churches against the equivalent of 19,000 in Australia. A change in law could mean that the demand for churches would exceed the supply of clergy, Bibles and, most of all, money for building materials. If this opening up were to happen, says Bordeaux, it could lead to one of the greatest opportunities in Christian history. 'Soviet Christians can and will do a great deal. They have already achieved miracles of spiritual regeneration but there is a challenge to all of us to refocus our priorities also.'

That message was echoed at a seminar I attended on church and state in November 1987:

> Because the Russian church is the church of the people, history abounds with evidence of Russian patriotism which invariably presented itself as Christian Church patriotism. During recent decades, in alliance with other peace-loving forces, patriotism has undoubtedly been a political concept according to the results expected, but for the church this originated from a deep Christian essence. The struggle for peace is the Christian undertaking of conscious and responsible realization of virtues of faith, hope and love. It is loathsome to think that any second, every human being – friends, relatives, fellow men of the countries and continents of the whole world – could be destroyed in the apocalyptic flame of nuclear fire. Therefore the contemporary patriotic devotion of the Russian Orthodox Church believer is the struggle for peace.

The speaker was Professor Zabolotsky of the Leningrad Theological Seminary and he was voicing the Orthodox view on *détente* – but it was also an orthodox view, not only in its reliance on Christian theology of peace but in seeing the created world as a canvas on which God's vision must be painted:

> The modern world is so closely related that there is hardly any

place for selfishly orientated ambitions. Therefore the concept of patriotism should be considered not merely in the context of personal concern within the boundaries of our own Motherland. Nowadays patriotism has become global in scope, and therefore regardless of any national, racial, ideological, social or political differences, humankind has come to realize it possesses only a unique common Motherland – the Earth. The Earth was given to people to possess and cultivate (Gen. 28:4). Sovereignty over the planet consists in its preservation until His Last Just Judgement will be done – not by means of human hands, but solely by the omnipotent God's will.

Professor Zabolotsky's ideas are a strong synthesis of Russian Orthodox concern for the nation's soul, and a desire for the spiritualization of the material world which the Orthodox Eucharist proclaims. The themes of *détente* and ecology echo much that is being said by religious leaders in the West as a critique of industrialization and secularization. In short, it gives the Russian Church a role as a peacemaker both with its own state and with the Western Christian Churches. But before we become optimistic about such peacemakers inheriting the Earth, several caveats have to be highlighted. As Professor Hoskins said of religion in Russia in his Reith Lectures in 1988:

> The church has been seriously, perhaps fatally, weakened by the Party's own treatment of it. Decades of active persecution alternating with contemptuous manipulation have left it not only numerically reduced but spiritually debilitated to the extent that it may no longer be able to play the role the Party now envisages for it.

First, there is the difficulty for the Russian Orthodox Church in surrendering its claims to be the one true church of Russia. There might be no question of organic unity among the diversity of Christian Churches in Russia, but would the Orthodox allow the resurgence of Catholic ambitions in the Ukraine without a fight? So far persecution by the state has united the Christian Committee for the Defence of Believers' Rights but would the lifting of restrictions lead to resentment as the various churches competed in the open market-place?

Nor can the role of the West be ignored. I am not persuaded that the inter-aid of which Rev Michael Bordeaux speaks would be readily welcomed by the Russian church, never mind the Soviet state. Russian Christianity has, as history shows, been deeply associated with the national soul and ethnic culture. That same history has been one of isolationism both in theology and in culture. The Napoleonic and Nazi incursions and the Cold War of recent years will not fade from the racial memory overnight. The Russian people may well be able to look forward to a new era of religious revival and a new structure for church/state partnership, but it will, I suspect, prefer to develop its own distinctive continental style of Christianity rather than link up with Western forms, whether they be offered by Rome, Geneva or even Baton Rouge.

It is possible that they might even see the West as needing their missions more than they need its missions. Should that happen, it will create a third revolutionary and evolutionary form of church/state Christianity to exist alongside that of Latin America and the other continent where Christianity is growing fastest in the world – Africa.

5 Black, White and Shades of Grey: South Africa

Imagine a divided country in which two warring groups held sway. A political device was invented to help hold the society together. Each group, or tribe, was allowed to have its own schools paid for by the state, and developed its own newspapers, radio and television stations, and, of course, worshipped in different churches. Although they lived together in the same cities, the tribes lived separate lives in separate compartments and, by ignoring rather than confronting their neighbours from the other tribe, were able to keep tension at a minimum.

No – the country is not South Africa. Nor is it an imaginary state dreamt up to justify apartheid policy. The nation involved is European and in many ways the original home of apartheid – the Netherlands.

It is well known that the Afrikaners were the inventors of the apartheid system. What is perhaps less well known is that they imported it from their home country when they first colonized the southern tip of Africa through the Dutch East India Company in 1652. Today the Netherlands (population 14 million) knows the system as *verzeiling* ('pillaring') and it is now less a feature of Dutch life than before the post-war years of the late 1940s when the predominantly rural Holland of bulb fields and canals underwent a belated version of the industrial revolution which had hit other European countries a century earlier.

The religious history of the Netherlands had been one of tension from the Reformation onwards when it was not only a Spanish colony but a refuge for Protestants. Many of the Anabaptist sects that emigrated to the New World did so through the Low Countries. After the overthrow of Spanish hegemony in the Thirty Years War, the mid-seventeenth century saw the Golden Age of Dutch influence,

preserved in the paintings of its Old Masters, and it was then that
the Dutch Reformed Church became the official religion. Napoleonic
conquest reasserted the place of Roman Catholicism and in 1848
the constitution reaffirmed religious liberty for all and was quickly
followed in 1853 by the restitution of the Catholic hierarchy. The
religious demography of the Netherlands in 1900 was roughly two-
thirds Protestant (concentrated in the north) and one-third Catholic
(mostly in the south). Today it is roughly one-third Protestant, one-
third Catholic and one-third secular. The rigorous Dutch mind is
inclined to follow things to their logical conclusion and this has led
some agnostics to embrace secularism with a fervour just as strong
as the Puritan Protestant's.

Dutch Catholics today are distinctive in the way in which they
have adopted the reforms of Vatican II to such an extent that they
have revolutionized their church and earned it the special attentions
of the Vatican and the pope who has appointed ultra-conservative
bishops to try to keep the lid on this troublesome province. Modern
industrial and secular pressures have forced many holes in the
dykes which *verzeiling* erected between the religious groups in the
Netherlands, but it is worth remembering the cultural pattern out
of which the Dutch came, when we now look at them in the tribal
context of Africa.

The Dutch tribe was ousted by the British in the Cape Colony in
1795 and trekked north, sparking wars with the native Zulu as they
settled in the mineral- and gem-rich land around the Orange River. A
century ago, when the British gained control of Natal and annexed
the Orange Free State and Transvaal, the Dutch Boers went to war
(and lost) in 1902. Two dates this century are important – 1910
and 1948. The first saw the creation of the Union of South Africa
after which, fearing absorption, the Dutch descendants formed the
Broederbond, a secret society which has been called the Afrikaner
mafia. Its influence was partly responsible for the Dutch 'tribe'
establishing itself as the leading force in the new country. They
outnumbered two to one the English 'tribe' who, according to
novelist Alan Paton, 'don't want to rule everything and everybody.
Both Afrikaners and English have a love of the country, but the
Afrikaner's love is in general more fierce, more emotional, more
aggressive. It is his history that has done it to him. We were never
defeated in war, never trekked, never had to pick ourselves out of
the dust.'

That Dutch courage partly accounts for the ascendancy of the
predominantly Afrikaner National Party which has ruled ever since

1948 and which brought in the apartheid laws which have dominated the post-war social and political history of South Africa. It marked the end of British influence which had resulted in up to 50 per cent of blacks in urban areas in the Cape Colony having a vote in the first years of this century. From 1854–1910 blacks and coloured had a vote based on income and occupation which was diluted in its effectiveness with the coming of the Union and taken away altogether in the 1920s. There is no telling what the history of South Africa might have been if the British had reasserted the independence of the Cape and Natal prior to the next milestone in South Africa's history, the creation of a republic in 1961. The previous year saw the atrocity of the Sharpville shootings in which sixty-nine blacks were killed during a protest against the identity documents they were forced to carry. Following this, the African National Congress (ANC) and the Pan African Congress (PAC) were proscribed. Today the banned ANC is joined by the United Democratic Front (UDF) as the main organ of opposition to the South Africa state, but the Christian Church is playing a part in the crisis of southern Africa which will be crucial to its outcome. Before looking at the central figures in that drama, some background is necessary.

Today there are eight different black cultural groups in South Africa and over eight white cultural groups – according to the clergyman who is minister of the church attended by state President P W Botha while parliament is in session in Cape Town. Rev Dr Ernst Van der Walt, visiting Edinburgh in 1988, gave the following figures for South Africa's main ethnic groups. In a total population of 29 million, 22 per cent are Zulu; 18.2 per cent Whites (9 per cent Afrikaner, 6.4 per cent Anglo-Saxon, 1.9 per cent Other); 15 per cent Xhosa; 10.5 per cent Tswana.

There is no special status granted to any religion or confession by the South Africa constitutions of 1961 or 1983. The 1983 Constitution begins:

> In humble submission to Almighty God who controls the destinies of nations and the history of peoples, who gathered our forebears together from many lands and gave them this own land ... we declare that we are conscious of our responsibility towards God and man; and are convinced of the necessity of standing united and of pursuing the following national goals: to uphold Christian values and civilized norms ...

Uniquely among twentieth century documents of a similar kind, the

Constitution does not mention either individual or collective human rights, which perhaps explains the reason it is viewed by the outside world as the illegitimate usurper of the human rights of many of its citizens.

Both the standard bearers of apartheid and those opposed to it within South Africa have been drawn from the Christian Churches. Apart from 20 per cent of the population who follow traditional African religions, 77 per cent of South Africans are nominally Christian. They comprise: 10 per cent Roman Catholics; 40 per cent Protestants; and 30 per cent African independents – some 6–7 million belong to 3,500 different churches many of which are in the Pentecostal tradition. The Protestants sub-divide into 3.4 million Dutch Reformed; 2.1 million Methodists; 1.5 million Anglicans; 0.8 million Lutherans; 0.5 million Presbyterians; 0.5 million Congregationalists.

The Dutch Reformed Church's proper title is the Nederduitse Gerereformeerde Kerk (or NGK) and it comprises the Mother Church of 1.4 million, and 2 million members of daughter missionary churches which include black members and ministers (one of whom is the leading anti-apartheid campaigner Rev Allan Boesak).

In some ways the country is typical of Africa. It is tribal. Since the Afrikaners settled over 300 years ago, they count as an indigenous tribe. The civil strife which categorizes many of the other African countries is present in South Africa, but has not broken into violent conflict as it has in Matebeleland in neighbouring Zimbabwe.

Another facet of African life is the creation of shanty towns around the big cities as a result of the drift of people into the sources of industrial wealth. These burgeoning social problems pose fearful dilemmas to all governments. Kenya has seen settlements grow around Nairobi, and President Daniel Arap Moy has reacted testily to criticism from churches about standards of deprivation. Compared with the rest of Africa, South Africa's Soweto is in the stockbroker belt of slums, a fact which many reports ignore because a comparison with other African countries is not made. This is partly due to good communications systems out of South Africa and relatively free media. I am not being naïve here or ignoring the reporting restrictions imposed by South Africa in recent years, simply noting the fact that it still appears to be a lot easier for television cameras to report state actions there without possible reprisals than in many other parts of Africa. The oppression of immigrant workers by police and military is not only a South African phenomenon. The starving refugees of Sudan and Ethiopia are shovelled away from the

cities by governments which have been lucky to escape the spotlight
of international moral censure.

But if South Africa is judged, it is not usually judged on its
similarities with other African states but on its differences. Despite
the élitist way in which the white races have exploited the system of
apartheid, the number of non-whites receiving secondary education
in South Africa in 1984 was still over a million compared with
454,000 whites. However, while a third of whites and a quarter
of Asians went on to tertiary education less than one in fifteen of
blacks received this. But there are still more black women with professional qualifications in South Africa than in the rest of the African
continent. South Africa also fares well in the prosperity league table.
South of the Sahara it has 10 per cent of the continent's population
and 85 per·cent of the gross product. Its mines employ nearly
three-quarters of a million people and the income they generate
is sent back to neighbouring states by immigrant workers – one of
the reasons why the 'front-line' states are usually exempt from calls
for trade sanctions against South Africa since their economies are
so dependent upon it. As an exporter of many of the industrialized
world's key commodities, South Africa is a prosperous nation. Previous trade sanctions only resulted in it becoming self-sufficient in
the restricted commodities – hence the UN, which once instructed
its members to stop selling arms to South Africa, has now to request
its members to stop buying them from South Africa. The sanctions
issue is vital to the discussion of church/state conflict in South Africa,
since many of the leading churchmen have put their weight behind
a call for sanctions as being the alternative to violent resistance.

The opposition to sanctions is based on two arguments. The first
is that blacks will suffer most, as will the economies of the front-line
black states whose economies are so interwoven with that of South
Africa. The second is a more subtle counter-attack which says that
capitalism and prosperity are the best friends that black Africans
can have. The latter view was advanced by British journalist Paul
Johnson in the January 1988 edition of *South Africa International*.
Capital, he argues, is not interested in colour bars or ideology:

It is the great dissolvent of castes and classes, sweeping away in
its impersonal search for profits the artificial inequalities mankind
creates among itself, whether based on heredity, occupation, caste
or colour. It destroyed the feudal system. Left to itself, it must
destroy apartheid. Capitalism is incompatible with apartheid for
broadly the same reasons that it is incompatible with feudalism

– it cannot co-exist with a social and political system based on inherited racial caste which forbids freedom of movement and a free market in labour and which subordinates all business decisions to the needs of an irrational world-view.

Johnson points out that black demands for better education, citizenship rights and property ownership, less police supervision and the right to a job on merit alone, are backed by the business community. As standards of living rise, he argues, the vote follows and the needs of capitalism and the blacks complement each other. Johnson represents the optimistic view which contends that too many people have too much to lose for a catastrophe to befall South Africa.

That prophecy is not shared by many of the Christian leaders whose names have become household words in the West through media coverage of South Africa. At the enthronement of one of the best known, Desmond Tutu, as Archbishop of Johannesburg, the Archbishop of Canterbury said, 'I cannot escape the sense of history unfolding – the sense that here on what was once the Dark Continent, there is the threat of greater darkness still.' The church's guiding lights amid this encircling gloom are by no means unanimous about the path which should be followed to achieve justice for all races in South Africa and an end to apartheid. With no democratic channel open to them and dissenting organizations banned, the two means to achieve this end which are most often debated are sanctions and violence.

The group best known to the outside world revolves around the South African Council of Churches of which Tutu was formerly Secretary. He succeeded Dr Beyers Naude, a white NGK minister, who earned a banning order for his outright espousal of black rights. The latest secretary of the SACC is Rev Frank Chikane who delivered the Bishop Ambrose Reeves lecture on church and state in South Africa in London in 1988 (Reeves was deported for his criticism of the Sharpeville shootings in 1960). Chikane argued that there was only one way for the church to respond in the South African situation – 'critical involvement'. Non-involvement or neutrality was tantamount to support for the status quo, which was incompatible with the gospel and justice. He highlighted the extensions of the ban on protests in February 1988 which prohibited eighteen organizations 'carrying on or performing any activities and acts whatsoever'. This legislation meant that those who had been detained and put in solitary confinement could not be prayed for publicly.

Here is what Chikane said at that lecture in April 1988:

The Proclamation of the 24 February 1988 prohibited organizations from 'carrying on or performing *any* activities and acts *whatsoever*', closed all possible effective, non-violent and peaceful means of opposition to end apartheid. It is clear from the order that the government is saying, to the voiceless and disenfranchised majority, 'no peaceful, non-violent, political activity and resistance against apartheid is going to be allowed. Instead we want you on the battleground.'

The Minister of Law and Order, Mr Adriaan Vlok, confirmed this interpretation of the Order when he said in parliament that these organizations which claimed to be non-violent realized that they could not succeed militarily against South Africa and thus they used non-violent methods to try and 'overthrow' the state.

It is this clear choice of violence by those in power which moved church leaders in South Africa to hold an emergency meeting to decide on a couple of actions in this regard. The main concern of churches was that they are the ones who have been most vocal against violence in the country. They are the ones who encouraged the liberation movements in South Africa to use non-violent means to end apartheid. The closure, therefore, of all non-violent means to change the system created a crisis for the churches. It raised moral questions as to whether those who made these statements could continue doing so without providing alternative avenues for the victims of apartheid. One of the questions was whether we can still accuse the liberation movement of violence if the government has itself openly resorted to violence.

It was because of this crisis that church leaders decided to march to parliament to deliver a petition which urged the state president to take the following immediate action for the sake of peace to avoid bloodshed and death:

(i) the lifting of the restrictions of the 24 Feb 1988 and the end of the State of Emergency;

(ii) the unbanning of all banned organizations, the release and removal of restrictions on political leaflets, allow exiles to return and free all political detainees;

(iii) then enter into negotiations to evolve a new dispensation in which all can live together in peace, freedom and justice.

This, the church leaders believed, was the only way in which the problems of South Africa can be resolved. Chairperson, you all know what happened afterwards. The church leaders were summarily arrested and later accused of 'choosing violence and communism above Christianity' [Adriaan Vlok] in that lamentably peaceful march. They were accused of hiding behind the 'cloak of sanctimoniousness' and warned that the government would not hesitate to act against the church leaders. Like Bishop Reeves who was called a 'meddling priest', the church leaders were accused of being 'political prisoners'.

Mr P W Botha responded to the actions of the church leaders by attacking the Archbishop Desmond Tutu and thereby the church leaders in a letter to Archbishop Tutu. This started an exchange of letters which heightened the tension between the church and the state in South Africa.

The church leaders nevertheless have re-committed themselves to witness, protest and act to end apartheid, irrespective of the consequences and these attacks against them.

Chairperson, the consequences of the stand of the churches are very serious. The risk has become a physical one. It is a risk in the hands of the official security forces, the risk of church leaders being eliminated or murdered by sophisticated and professional death squads, right-wing units, or crazy individuals motivated by such virulent attacks against specific church leaders as the state president, Mr P W Botha has done.

News may have reached you already that following the intensified church/state conflict in South Africa during February and March, physical threats and actual attacks on church leaders and personnel in the church have increased. Reports of attacks on the home of Dr Allan Boesak and his family have been made public, the intensified raids and summary detentions of SACC staff in various regions in the country may have been brought to your notice.

The traumatic hostage drama on the 11 April 1988 by a gunman who held one of our staff members, and threats by a white gunman after midnight this last Friday at Khotso House to force the night watchman to open the building for him; all these acts, by the forces of darkness in defense of the evil and racist apartheid system, have turned our Christian witness in apartheid South Africa into a *life and death issue*.

Chairperson, to be a Christian in South Africa is no more a luxury or just a matter of tradition of 'civilization' (as those who are victims of the so-called Western civilization would call it), or something that is done because others are doing it, or part of a given social norm. To witness to Christ honestly in an evil and racist South Africa is to put your life at risk, even the risk of a violent death.

As I have said before in other places, I doubt that we have an option. It does not look like we can avoid the pain and suffering on the cross if we have to challenge the evils of the apartheid system. Here there is no 'detour' to avoid the cross.

Under the circumstances, witnessing to the risen Christ might turn to blood-witnessing, turning some to martyrs. That is why church leaders in South Africa said in their petition to the state president: 'We have not undertaken this action lightly. We have no desire to be martyrs. However, the gospel leaves us no choice but to seek ways of witnessing effectively and clearly to the values of our Lord and Saviour Jesus Christ and you [the government] give us virtually no other effective and peaceful means of doing so.'

Ladies and gentlemen, the issue facing church leaders in South Africa is the question of *obedience to God*.

In the face of the order prohibiting peaceful and non-violent anti-apartheid groups in South Africa 'carrying out or performing *any* activities or acts *whatsoever* [own emphasis], outlawing all forms of effective and peaceful, non-violent political activity and resistance to end apartheid, implying thereby that this could only happen at the battleground, at a violent level, the church leaders had no option but to act to prevent an all-out bloody war in South Africa.

As we have said already the church leaders concluded in their statement that it was the apartheid government which was 'deliberately obstructing peace in our country and encouraging violence among our people'. We have also already said that church leaders argued that the prohibited activities of the eighteen organizations were in fact 'central to the proclamation of the Gospel' and thus church leaders were compelled, irrespective of the consequences, to take over these activities insofar as they believed they were mandated by the gospel. The church leaders said in their statement: 'Our mandate to carry out these activities comes from God and no man or government will stop us.'

The statement continues to say that '*if the State wants to act against the Church of God in this country for proclaiming the gospel, then so be it*' [own emphasis].

For the church leaders in South Africa, therefore, the choice is that of obedience to God and obedience to an earthly human power. It is a choice between the proclaiming of the gospel which demands justice, peace and righteousness and the heretic gospel that not only justifies Botha's evil apartheid system but supports it, thereby contributing to the pain and suffering of the victims of this system. In this respect church leaders have chosen to obey 'God rather than men' (Acts 5:29).

The Archbishop Desmond Tutu put it succinctly after our attempted peaceful march in Cape Town which was stopped violently. He said that, 'what we did today is not a negative action of disobeying. It is a positive one of saying [we obey God]. We are witnessing for our Lord and Saviour Jesus Christ. If that action has consequences, such as being arrested, then hard luck. We are going to obey God rather than man.' He ended by saying, 'We are not defying, we are obeying God and we ought to obey God every day. This means that in our obedience to God we are forced to disobey evil and unjust laws.'

One mistake that those in power (particularly the state president) made, was to threaten and warn the church leaders not to continue with their actions of witness and protest, and by launching a vicious and malicious attack on church leaders based on a deliberate distortion of the truth, hoping that by so doing this would deter the church leaders from obeying their God. The mistake of Mr P W Botha is to assume that Archbishop Tutu's statement, that if this 'witness *has consequences, such as being arrested then hard luck*, we are going to obey God rather than man', is just an ordinary human intellectual statement. No, this is no luxurious statement at the level of the intellect only, but it is a statement of faith, a religious statement. It is a matter of obedience to God!

The recent *praxis* of the church in South Africa is a call for the church of Christ in the world to rediscover the evangelical tradition of the early church. In a world where evil abounds, where there is less and less justice for the poor and powerless majority, the church is called to express its witness. And, faced with these enormous and fearful forces of evil, it might, in so doing, be changed from the church, a church of Christ.

It is not just a call for a rediscovery of the evangelical tradition of the early church. We have long standing traditions of servants of God throughout the history of the church who stood in obedience to God. 'Here I stand, I cannot do otherwise' is not a new tradition in the Christian church.[1]"

1. The Ambrose Reeves lecture delivered Westminster Central Hall, London 22 April 1988.

Archbishop Tutu has a talent for capturing the ears of those outside the South Africa imbroglio. A protégé of Bishop Trevor Huddleston, Tutu's mischievous style has won him friends – and enemies. When the South African government renamed the Bantu department that of 'plural affairs' he joked that a black from up-country was now a rural plural, and if an artist, he painted rural plural murals. Tutu jokes are widespread: one Afrikaner policeman says to the other, 'I hear Tutu's dead,' to which the second replies, 'Ach man, I didn't know he was even in jail.' Black humour, indeed. As the leader of the 1.5 million Anglicans, of whom half a million are white, he is limited in his influence and is often criticized as unrepresentative of blacks.

Bishop Isaac Mokoena, the Life President of the Reformed Independent Churches of South Africa, which represents 4.5 million black Christians, is scathing about Tutu's big salary and his chauffeur-driven car. There is bitterness against Tutu in many of the black townships among Pentecostal Christians who resent his forays abroad during which he advocates the trade sanctions which would affect them badly. But there is little doubt that he is winning the propaganda battle. The protest of the petition was the most significant of recent years because it removed the avenue of peaceful protest from the churches and moved them closer to support for violent means to effect change which is espoused by the ANC. It drew this response from the state President P W Botha whose style is typical of the blunt, masterful persona presented by Afrikaners:

> I have gone out of my way to invite leaders of Black communities, and also religious leaders, to co-operate with me in pursuing a just, peaceful and prosperous future for all in South Africa and our region. Many of them already do so.
>
> It is therefore disturbing that you and others, who claim to represent the Church of Christ and the Word of God, act in the irresponsible way that you do.
>
> You do not hesitate to spread malicious untruths about South Africa here and abroad. You should be fully aware of the numerous misleading statements concerning local support for sanctions and for the ANC, alleged atrocities by the security forces, the treatment of youths, and the fabrication of false testimony for especially the overseas media.
>
> You love and praise the ANC/SACP with its Marxist and

atheist ideology, landmines, bombs and necklaces perpetrating
the most horrendous atrocities imaginable; and you embrace and
participate in their call for violence, hatred, sanctions, insurrection
and revolution.

In this regard you may recall Archbishop Tutu's statement
during a lecture in St Paul's Cathedral in 1984 when he said:

'If the Russians were to come to South Africa today, then
most blacks who reject communism as atheistic and materialistic
would welcome them as saviours.'

You may also recall the archbishop saying that the aims of the
SACC and the ANC are similar; and added in Atlanta, Georgia,
in January 1986 that:

'We hope one day to hear the leaders of the Western world
say we side with the ANC which sought to change an unjust
system peacefully, and were sent into the arms of the struggle
because the West abandoned us.'

The SACC, in its support of the Kairos Document, apparently
regards communism as a myth, and in its acceptance of the
Harare Declaration and the Lusaka Statement expressed support
for sanctions, disinvestment and boycotts against South Africa,
and support for the Marxist terrorist movements.

It is alarming that God, and the Church of God which I also
love and serve, can be abused and insulted in this manner; that
individual members of the clergy who claim to be messengers
of God, are in reality messengers of enmity and hatred while
parading in the cloth, and hiding behind the structures of the
Church; and instead of pursuing reformation, they are engaged
in the deformation of religion, through the proclamation of false
so-called 'liberation theology' . . .

I request you urgently not to abuse the freedom of religion
and worship, and the goodwill of the people and the Government
of South Africa for the pursuance of secular and revolutionary
objectives. In the name of God and in the spirit of true Christianity
I call upon you to be messengers of the true Christian religion, and
not of Marxism and atheism.

Religious freedom is the cornerstone of proper human rights. It
is a well known fact that South Africa is a country which cherishes
and safe-guards freedom of religion. Even in the armed forces more
than one hundred different denominations are actively engaged in
the preaching of the Gospel.

In this regard it is ironic that you yourself challenged churches
in South Africa to provide ministry to the terrorist movements;

while at the same time withdrawing chaplains from the SADF!
I am amazed that you as a theologian can compare me and
the Government with immoral and godless people referred to
in Ephesians 5:11–13, while ignoring Ephesians 4:31:

'Let all bitterness, and wrath, and anger and clamour and
evil speaking be put away from you with all malice'; and also
Ephesians 5:9: 'For the fruit of the Spirit is in all goodness and
righteousness and truth.'

In this spirit I call upon the co-operation of all churches and
church leaders towards creating peace and goodwill among the
peoples of our land, for the benefit of the Church of Christ.

In conclusion I want to put a question to the SACC. We are
both confessing that we are followers of Christ in spite of all our
human weaknesses. Christ, as far as we know, openly took part
in the spreading of the gospel during the last three years of his
life on earth. Can you quote one single instance from the Word
of God in which it appears that Christ advocated violence against
the State; or led a demonstration against the State; or broke a law
of the State?[2]

There have been many rivers crossed in the past generation and
many have been hailed as Rubicons or rivers of blood – Sharpville
(1960), Soweto (1976) – but the prophesied bloodbath has never
come. 1988 marked the seventieth birthday of Nelson Mandela,
the jailed ANC leader, and the worldwide celebration of this event
showed how sympathetic international opinion was to the ANC.
President P W Botha was quick to try to defuse the situation by
offering terms for Mandela's release. Mandela's organization, the
ANC, had originally adopted a non-violent stance in the days of
Chief Albert Luthuli, but under Mandela and the current leader
Oliver Tambo it declared that the ANC's violence was the inevitable response to state violence. In an attempt to win the support of
church representatives from South Africa and from the international
community, at a meeting in Lusaka in 4–7 May 1987, Oliver Tambo
said:

The overwhelming majority of the tens of thousands who have
been killed, imprisoned or detained in SA have never carried arms.
Their only crime is that they dared to stand up to oppose racial
tyranny, and that by violent means. The apartheid regime left us

2.   South African Consulate-General, 24 March 1988.

no choice but to take up arms. In the same way, Nazism left the people of the world no choice but to fight ... we would also like to make the point here that to the best of our knowledge the Christian Church has never been pacifist. We understand very well the attempts to seek a peaceful solution to the conflicts of southern Africa. However, it cannot be right that the concept of a just war should be applied selectively and the violence of the oppressed be equated to that of the apartheid state.[3]

Tambo went on to deal with the issue of ANC communist involvement and compared the ANC's funding to Allied co-operation with Stalinist Russia during the last war. The ANC did not want to take sides in the East-West conflict, he claimed. He was successful in persuading the churchmen to back the 'Lusaka Statement' which declared the South African government illegitimate, called for its removal and recognized the ANC and other liberation movements as 'authentic vehicles' of the black people to achieve self determination. The twin pillars on which the thinking of the Lusaka churchmen was based were two influential documents produced by the anti-apartheid campaigners which caused controversy well beyond South Africa when published – the 1985 'Theological Rationale' produced by Boesak and others; and the 1986 'Kairos' document (*kairos* = 'a timely moment'). The former, calling for prayer for the removal 'from power of those who persist in defying God's laws and a corresponding commitment to work for good and legitimate government', created a potential for church/state confrontation not previously seen in South Africa and it was not long after this that Boesak was arrested and held for three weeks in solitary confinement. Many held that the Rationale was moderate, but Kairos went further, identifying three theologies: state theology which justifies apartheid; church theology which addresses the oppressor and not the oppressed; and prophetic theology which it postulates as the only true theology. The introduction says: 'In opposition to tyranny and oppression Christians may be required to take solidarity action or join significant political movements working towards the overthrow of tyranny where clear Christian choices may not be possible or available.' It goes on to talk of the need for spirituality of combat and that 'the time has come for the churches to declare their alliance with the forces of liberation against the apartheid regime'. Although the document does not name the

3. World Council of Churches published text, May 1987.

ANC or the UDF, it is most often interpreted to refer to them and has provided a kind of fudge in which those who favour violence to overthrow the apartheid state can claim a theological basis for their actions.

The Kairos document alienated many of the churchmen outside South Africa who have been pressing for peaceful change. Professor Peter Beyerhaus, dean of the theological faculty at Tübingen University and formerly a Lutheran missionary in South Africa, called it 'a thorough-going endorsement of the Marxist view of class struggle'. Criticizing the distorting and playing down of Scripture, Dr Beyerhaus said that it should not be concluded that all the 150 clergy who had subscribed to the document were Marxist atheist, but 'from the appallingly hateful spirit pervading their paper they have allowed Marxism deeply to penetrate their minds'. He accused the authors of trying to seduce others to the 'synthetic substitution' to their policial religion which was 'a coloured specimen of modern ecumenical theo-political thinking, classified as 'contextual theology'.

At the time of writing, the churches have not yet openly advocated armed struggle but, with growing impatience, have refused to condemn the ANC's deployment of violence, usually shifting the emphasis back on to the violence of the state against people, citing the 700 killed in the Soweto riots of 1976 and the children shot in the 1980s as examples of 'state terrorism'. Not only have the dissenting church leaders in South Africa proved highly effective in mobilizing opposition to the government, but they have persuaded the World Council of Churches to devote funds to help the ANC. In 1985 this led the Transkei to prevent churches being members of the WCC. Other laws prevent foreign funds reaching bodies like the South African Council of Churches.

The Lusaka Statement was a sign that the anti-apartheid churches had international opinion behind them in their relations with the South African state. The Roman Catholic primate, Archbishop Denis Hurley, has been an outspoken critic of the South African government and has been charged with contravening the Defence Act when he alleged misconduct by the South African forces in Namibia. The charges were withdrawn in February 1985 when the prosecutor said the archbishop had been misquoted, but Mgr Hurley stood by the allegations. The archbishop has used his influence to bring pressure from the Roman Catholic Church worldwide. In 1988 after four years of negotiations it was announced that the pope would not be visiting South Africa on his forthcoming Southern Africa visit – on the advice of Hurley. Mr Pik Botha, the South African Foreign Minister, later issued a statement saying effectively, 'this was none of our doing – we would have been glad to have him'. Clearly, in the opinion of the Vatican, the legitimation that a papal visit would have brought to the South African government outweighed the advantages to Roman Catholics of seeing the pope.

The incident illustrates the way in which international opinion has swung behind the churches in their confrontation with the state. With the ANC and PAC banned, it is churchmen who have become the effective opposition to the state. In 1983 they helped form the United Democratic Front from groups opposed to apartheid. It was a response to the new constitution announced that year by President Botha which set up a tricameral parliament for whites, coloureds and Indians, and apportioned homelands to blacks in which they would have a form of independence. It was apartheid at a distance and at the UDF inauguration Rev Allan Boesak spoke of the homelands policy thus:

> Surely the most immoral and objectionable aspect of the apart-heid policies forms the basis for the wilful exclusion of 80 per cent of our nation from the new political deal. In the words of the proposals made by the president's council, the homelands policy is to be regarded as 'irreversible', so our brothers and sisters will be driven further into the wilderness of homeland policies, millions will have to find their political rights in the sham independence of those bush republics; millions more will continue to lose their South African citizenship; and millions more will be removed from their homes into resettlement camps.[4]

Boesak was present at the Tutu petition incident and is a patron of the UDF. In many ways he is the most significant figure on the South African church/state scene. He is part of the Dutch Reformed Church – the Moderator of the NGK Mission Church. He cannot be dismissed by the Afrikaner overlords as unrepresentative or part of the Anglican lobby. He also hit them where it hurt when he was elected Moderator of the World Alliance of Reformed Churches (representing 70 million members) at their Ottawa meeting in 1982

4.   Fount 1987.

which expelled the NGK from membership and declared apartheid a heresy. That blow to the pride of the NGK has been swallowed, for they have now fallen into line by dissociating themselves from apartheid, and the influence of Boesak has been crucial. He was detained in 1985 and charged with subversion, but charges were dropped. His time in solitary confinement gave rise to a moving sermon among the collection published under the title, *If this is Treason – I am Guilty!*

This book illustrates the power of Boesak's oratory. There are echoes of the cadences of Martin Luther King. Both men share a scholarly background to their preaching and a startlingly powerful use of language and biblical imagery. Like Dr King, Dr Boesak's female friendships were the subject of attention from the security police. In 1984 the *Star* published allegations of an affair between Boesak and a white woman church secretary obtained from 'evidence' supplied by the police. Subsequently Boesak was exonerated by his church, and Brigadier Johan Van der Merwe of the security police admitted that in certain circumstances it was in the interest of the police to disseminate false information to discredit leaders of 'subversive' organizations.

Boesak acknowledges a debt to Martin Luther King, who in turn drew upon the inspiration of Ghandi whose early dissent was shaped by his life in the racial context of South Africa. Tutu is better known abroad but Boesak will more likely emerge as anti-apartheid's prophet, preacher and theologian. He is not only an inspiring orator but has a broader power base in the numerically strong black NGK. Reflecting on the ideology of what he is doing in *Black Theology/Black Power*[5], he is anxious like King to avoid the mistakes made by the American Black Power movements whose prominence in the 1960s was short-lived and whose mistakes South Africa could have been tempted to repeat. 'Getting rid of an implanted slave mentality is central to the philosophy of Black consciousness,' he writes but cautions, 'The Black experience provides the framework within which Blacks understand the revelation of God in Jesus Christ. No more, no less.' In other words, black consciousness can assist in preventing distortions of scripture and keeping the cultural goals to the fore, but black power for the sake of black power does not

5.   Mowbrays 1978.

become justifiable by dragging in scriptural allusions after its goals
have been announced.

Thus Boesak is a Christian theologian not a 'Black' theologian,
and his stature is the greater, and his appeal wider, because of that.
Boesak's style moves from biblical and theological bases outwards
rather than putting humanitarian concerns parallel to theological
proclamations. For instance when he deals with the church/state
question in *A Call for an End to Unjust Rule*[6] he begins with an
incident in 1977 when the security police raided his home and the
captain, who was an elder of the white NGK, criticized him for a
statement he had issued recently calling for prayer to remove the
government. Did he not realize that Romans 13:1–7 called for
obedience and respect for the governing powers? Boesak replied:

> To begin with, Romans 13:1, so often understood as the basis
> for unquestioning obedience, is not in fact that at all, but a salient
> point of sharp criticism on governmental power. The words 'for
> there is no authority except that which God has established' do
> not mean that the government which is the government of the day,
> comes from God, but rather that the power, the authority which
> the government represents, is established by God. Even if it had
> been different in Paul's day, Christians in the modern world can
> no longer hold uncritically to that point of view. In democracies,
> governments are elected by the people and they can be thrown
> out of office by the people. It is the voters who are responsible,
> not God. Even more pertinently, in South Africa the Nationalist
> Afrikaner government would never have been in power had black
> people been given the right to vote. It is not God who is responsible
> for the tragic state of affairs in South Africa, it is the voters and
> the people they have put in power.'[7]

He continues the exegesis, drawing on Old Testament references
and Peter's injunction to obey God rather than man, relating his
argument to Calvin's concept of just government, and concluding
that the God of Romans 13 has been turned by the South African
National Party into the beast from the sea of Revelation 13. The
necessity for government to be based on justice leads him to conclude
triumphantly that it is necessary to resist the South African state not
in spite of Romans 13 but *because of* it.

It is love for the neighbour which infuses, shapes and substantiates

6. St Andrews Press 1986.
7. ibid p 141.

Christian action in the world according to Romans 13. Therefore
the critical tension in Romans 13 is not between the Christian and
the state, it is rather between the state and the neighbour. Again
the demand is for the Christian not to be indebted to the state in
any way, but the Christian is obligated to the neighbour, to unrestricted love. Whatever hurts the neighbour, Paul says in effect,
(verses 8–10) is impermissible. Therefore the ultimate question for
the Christian is: when government policy or law clashes with that
demand of unrestricted love, what then?[8]

Boesak argues that the government is not an enemy as a matter of
course nor is confrontation with government its own justification –
that leads to the tyranny of anarchy. It is the unjust acts which give
rise to the moral duty to act. 'A church wanting to confess Christ
will understand that it is not enough to protest against evil, one must
give oneself for the sake of justice and peace; that is overcoming evil
with good. And that is the essential nature of our resistance . . . it is
better to damage our relations with the government than to damage
our relationship with Jesus Christ.' Boesak is not writing black
theology. Nor is he a liberation theologian in the Latin American
mode. His thought system is derived from the Calvin tradition of
biblical theology and applied with devastating effect to the situation
in South Africa. To catch the flavour of his preaching I want to quote
a passage from a sermon delivered at the funeral of three community
leaders at which he accused the police of their murders:

The state president spoke a week ago to hundreds of young white
people. He said to them that it is his duty to stop terrorism, just
as Jesus drove out the money changers from the temple. I would
like to ask the state president whether he knows what he is doing
when he tried to read a theology of violence into the life of the
man whom the Bible calls the Prince of Peace. I would like to
know why those church leaders who are so quick to condemn
us when we ask to pray for the removal of unjust rule and who
say that we want violence – why don't they rise up and tell the
state president: 'You cannot use the name of Jesus to justify your
violence'? Why are they silent? It is their duty to preach not only
to those people who are voiceless but it is even more their duty
to preach to those who have the power to change this country
tomorrow if they want to.

8.   [op. cit. p 153]

And another thing: the state president must think about whether he is right in simply assuming that the terrorists he is talking about are those brothers who have to fight from across the border. The experience of black people in this country is different. We do not think that the terrorists are those who are the freedom fighters of this land. The African National Congress (ANC) did not shoot our people when they were defenceless at Sharpeville twenty-five years ago. The ANC did not kill our children in 1976 when they were walking peacefully on the streets of Soweto. The ANC did not kill our children during the school boycotts in 1980 in Cape Town. It was not the ANC who killed little Thabo Sibeko, who was six years old, last year on the East Rand. It was not the ANC who killed forty-three people at Langa township on 21 March at the massacre of Uitenhage. It was not the ANC who killed our four brothers whom we are burying today. The government did it – and so *they* are the terrorists! It is a most dangerous thing when people in power begin to believe their own propaganda!

And I urge those white people who are serious about the future of South Africa: look a little further than your newspapers, listen a little deeper than to the voices of the commentators on South African television, and come and talk to our people in the townships. There you will hear the truth. There you will see the truth. There you will see what it means to live under apartheid. I know that this funeral will not be the last one. I know that our mourning will not end today. I know that tomorrow and tomorrow and tomorrow and tomorrow there will be more tears that will flow. And there are difficult days ahead. The violence of the South African government knows no end. More of our brothers and sisters will be detained. There will be more whose names will be added to some hit list, and more will be killed by those faceless murderers who hide behind balaclavas and who hide behind their guns and who hide behind the protection that they get.

But this is the price that we have to pay for our freedom. We are here today, but we will do more than just mourn. We have heard it over and over again. We will not simply mourn; we will wake up from mourning, and we will dedicate ourselves anew to the struggle for justice and liberation and freedom and peace.

If I die tomorrow, do not come to my funeral and sing freedom songs if you are not willing to participate today in the struggle for liberation and justice. If I die tomorrow, do not revenge my death with more senseless violence and hatred, but raise up a sign of hope that this country will become what it must become and that we will make our contribution to that. If I die tomorrow, do not give up and do not despair, for I know that our victory is near, and that apartheid and injustice will never endure and that our people shall be free. If I die tomorrow, raise up a sign that the victory of this country is not written in the guns and the violence, and the armies of the South African government, but that the victory and the future of this great country are written in the hearts of our people in our determination to be free and in our willingness to give our lives for struggle that we believe in.

I know that as we have to go from funeral to funeral many of us will become tired. Many of us will become tired of protest, will become tired of knocking at the door, will become tired of seeing our brothers and sisters dying so much. But as long as our people, black and white, are shackled in the chains of oppression and racism, there will be a fight to fight, and we must not give up. As long as our children die needlessly and untimely there will be a fight to fight – do not give up. And as long as injustice still reigns supreme in this land there will be a fight to fight – do not give up. As long as little children are born just to die, too soon, there will be a fight to fight – do not give up. For this country is yours, this land is yours, the future is yours – do not give up.

So while we mourn, let us commit ourselves again to the struggle for justice and freedom and liberation. There are things that we can do. We can begin to ask ourselves what those of us who come from Natal, and those of us who come from the Western Cape, and those of us who come from Transvaal, should ask ourselves: Why it is that the people in the Eastern Cape can have a successful consumer boycott, but we do not do anything about that in the Cape or Natal or Transvaal! One of the things that should come out of this funeral is for the people of this country to go back home and organize for that, and we will lay low those who think they are the powerful. We will keep away from them our buying power. We should begin to do that. We must do it in Cape Town, we must do it in Johannesburg, and we must do it in Durban.

And to our people in the townships who have shops I say, You are part of this struggle too. When we say that we shall boycott the white shops we want your full co-operation. We want you to make it possible for our people to do that. You do not raise your prices, you lower them. You lower them because it is the cause of the struggle. And if you do that you will be known as people who fight with us and who struggle with us for justice.

I must say that if the only thing we do when we go back home is to raise a sign of hope for our people so that we can see, and the world can see, that in spite of what is happening to us we are not a defeated people, we shall have achieved a noble purpose.

Boesak is highly significant for two reasons. First, because his theology of dissent against the state is not tribal or racial, but universal. Certainly it derives from European philosophical systems (Boesak was educated at the Free University of Amsterdam) but it is neither defined by that nor limited in its application of the norms of justice to the African situation. Second, it meets his critics on their own ground. He is a minister of the Dutch Reformed Church, an insider, albeit of a different race from the Afrikaners, and he can take the tradition which they claimed gave them the right to rule and turn their arguments on their head and be elected President of the World Alliance of Reformed Churches.

It is impossible to say how much Boesak contributed to the under-mining of 'apartheid theology' within the NGK. In the closely inter-twined world of the Afrikaners and the NGK, the National Party had a *verligte* (enlightened) group who were anxious to get rid of some of the more restrictive aspects of apartheid, such as the law forbidding inter-racial marriage. Cinemas and sport were desegregated. Blacks could own property in black areas. Their counterparts in the NGK produced a document for the 1986 General Synod entitled '*Kerk en Samelewing*' (Church and society) which declared, 'The Dutch Reformed Church is convinced that apartheid, as a political and social system by which human dignity is adversely affected, and whereby one particular group is detrimentally depressed by anoth-er, cannot be accepted as a Christian ethical principle because it contravenes the very essence of neighbourly love and righteousness and inevitably that of the human dignity of all involved.'

It was a significant climb-down. (In 1982, Rev Nico Smith, a professor at Stellenbosch, the Afrikaners' Oxford, and a for-mer Broederbond member, had quit to become pastor to a black congregation.) But the 1986 Synod shrank from going the whole way. It continued the colour divisions within the NGK itself. It did allow 'open membership', although this was to be at the discretion of local congregations. Furthermore it still sanctioned the Group Areas Act (obliging people of different colour to live in separate areas), and the Race Classification Act which ensures that education remains segregated. Although the new NGK Moderator, Rev Professor Johan Heyns, was in favour of further reforms the conservative wing led by theologian Carel Boshoff, son-in-law of the architect of apartheid, the assassinated Hendrik Verwoerd and a leading Broederbonder, threatened that further reforms would precipitate schisms. The expected schism happened. Thirty ministers out of the NGK's 2,000 seceded, led by Professor Willie Lubbe, but most of them attracted only about a hundred church members each. They joined the right-wing NHK[9] and Dopper Kerk which together have less than 200,000 members. Their basis of secession makes weird reading. Entitled 'Faith and Protest' it quotes the Bible in support of apartheid, the creation of separate nations and churches and rejects open door membership of a church in basis of faith in Jesus Christ. Their numbers are encouragingly low but their act of schism may be used as an argument to stall further reform on the grounds of risking more splits, in the way that the neo-Nazi party of Mr Eugene Terre Blanche is used as a bogeyman to stall political reforms. In an interview following the 1986 Synod – the next will be in 1990 – Moderator Heyns pledged himself to build bridges between his branch of the NGK and the Sendingkerk – Boesak's branch. On the long-term prospects of the Afrikaner's willingness to change, Heyns had this to say:

> Since July 1985 South Africa has been under a State of Emergency for all but three months. Ostensibly, the regulations are aimed at curbing revolt and suppressing violence. However, the vast majority of Afrikaners must eventually perceive that the true significance of the State of Emergency is more than that.
>
> At its deepest level it signifies the birth-pangs of a new South Africa, and thus also the birth of a new Afrikaner. The changes against which people protested – even with violence – and which necessitated the proclamation of the State of Emergency have brought the Afrikaner face to face with one of the greatest crises in his history.
>
> Certainly, in Afrikanerdom's far right group there are already disturbing signs of political extremism. There groups show no appreciation of the legitimate aspirations of the non-white peoples, neither do they have any idea of the necessity for a new political

9.   Nederduitse Hervormde Kerke.

dispensation in South Africa and the demands such a new political order will make on the Afrikaner. Part of the far right has little if any contribution to offer: these people concentrate on a policy of restoration which actually amounts to nothing more than a kind of reiteration of the past. Their views, then, need not be taken too seriously.

Another segment of the far right has a clearer vision of the future. They believe the principle of partition must be universally applied as this offers the Afrikaner his only defence and protection. Here, the ideal is an Afrikaner national state situated in its own geographical area, governed by white Afrikaners, with no power-sharing of any kind. Thus the current reforms are a serious threat to the Afrikaner's white exclusiveness and so he is urgently summoned to fight for his freedom.

This fight for freedom is to be waged, not with military weapons, but by subtle methods of infiltration and indoctrination. To this end, true Afrikaners are called on to penetrate existing cultural organizations to gain control of them and to influence their members. The control of schools and parents' organizations is particularly important, to ensure that the children are educated in the right political climate and idiom.

This counter-reformation is not restricted to adults – the youth is regarded as a vital sphere of concentration which involves a lengthy process of preparation and indoctrination. In every town and every region spiritual forces will have to be united while there must be a clear realization that the Afrikaner economy must not be controlled by alien groups or constructed on foreign labour.

Clearly, this section of the Afrikaner right-wing will not disappear. Without doubt it will continue and, dependent upon the dogged persistence of its members and the success they may achieve, perpetuate restlessness, tension, and internecine conflict among Afrikaners.

Naturally, the question is what influence this will have on the nature and tempo of reform. To my mind it would be fatal if these people were to determine either the type or pace of reform. Nonetheless, their very presence and the way they operate will cause wide divergence of opinion in the ranks of those responsible for reform. Some will want to ignore them; others will feel they ought to be heard, which will seriously inhibit the reform process. Yet I believe that the impulse for fundamental reform will be so strong that the right's political influence will not adversely affect its progress to any great extent.

From the Afrikaner's history it may be deduced that he wants to live, and if survival means re-casting basic political ideology he will do so. He is not a slave to his policy, for he realizes that there are values greater and more important than political policy. Nor is he enmeshed in a static pattern of social existence, for he knows that Afrikanerdom is a living, dynamically developing organism. It is not a building which is repaired and restored as the years pass, but a tree which grows new branches, flowers and fruit, yet remains essentially the same.

We are now witnessing the most exciting event in the history of the Afrikaner: the birth of the new Afrikaner.

The new Afrikaner is engaged in conquering his exclusivism. Political power is increasingly being shared with people of other cultures; protective legislation is being repealed, and patterns of social co-existence changed. The ward is emancipated, and the guardian becomes the partner of the liberated. The age-old guardian-relationship is being transformed without traumatic upheaval into a relationship of partners. In political, economic, and social spheres this is evident every day.

But will the Afrikaner survive as an independent group in such an integrated society? At present, whites comprise about 16 per cent of the population. By the year 2000 this percentage may dwindle to 12 per cent or even less, of which the Afrikaans-speaking section will probably amount to half or a little more. Seen against those statistics, can the Afrikaner survive? Undoubtedly, because his history has demonstrated a will to survive.

Yet, he must find a cultural home that will unite him as a people. By 'culture' I mean all the material and mental creations, the language, the songs, the art, the games, the politics and the social institutions that distinguish one community from another. It is in these cultural creations that the Afrikaner will have to find his home if he wishes to remain independent and make his contribution to the development of South Africa.

There are already signs that the Afrikaner understands thoroughly the truth that he must have a substantial cultural home. Only once he has discovered his strength and power there, will he face the challenges of the new dispensation. Then this new Afrikaner will not only speak his own language, but the other's language as well. He will listen to the other's music, play with him, admire his art, worship with him and work with him towards a new future.

In all this he will not merely make his own contribution. He will himself be enriched, without losing anything of his own identity as a person, an Afrikaner or a Christian. The new Afrikaner will seek a future South Africa where a variety of people enjoy their own cultures within an all-embracing nation with a common national culture.[10]

It is tempting to see the South African situation literally in terms of black and white. Viewed that way it is a simple matter of the minority oppressing the majority and fixing the agenda so that the latter cannot avail themselves of the fruits of power. In many ways that is an accurate picture of the situation. The white tribe *is* ruling the black tribe. But it is not the full picture. Africa is full of instances of tribal rule in which democracy goes out of the window. The distinctiveness of the South African situation can be seen by comparing it to the other countries around it which are post-colonial but demographically different. There the white tribes were European and tiny in number. The changes of government which have taken place in Kenya, Tanzania, Uganda, Zambia and Malawi have established states which owe much in their genesis and development to Christian missionaries. President Kaunda of Zambia was brought up in a mission school. Dr Banda of Malawi was a Presbyterian elder educated in Edinburgh. There are strong Christian churches in all these states but they are not established in a European model. They are expected to be loyal to the leader and there is perhaps an irony in the fact that while many of these states were helped in achieving their independence by the agitation of the church against the colonial state, such criticism of the state is not appreciated by the more authoritarian leaders of these countries in the post-colonial era.

KENYA

A good illustration of this is Kenya where 73 per cent of the country's 16 million population is Christian. In the serious rift which developed in 1969 between the dominant Kikuyu tribe and the Luo tribe to which the assassinated politician Tom Mboya belonged, secret oath takings were ordered by President Jomo Kenyatta to obtain loyalty. When these were criticized by Presbyterian Church leaders, beatings and deaths followed. Bishop Henry Okullu was bitterly criticized by the powerful attorney-general Charles Njonjo for preaching politics

10. *Leadership* magazine, Vol 5. No 5, 1986.

from the pulpit and was blocked as the new leader of his church in Kenya. When Njonjo himself was suspended for plotting, there were other churchmen who spoke on his behalf and they too were told by President Moi's ministers to cease dabbling in politics. Although Kenya's constitution guarantees freedom of worship, in 1984 Bishop Alexander Muge of the Anglican CPK[11] had to remind the government, 'Freedom of worship is not a privilege as some politicians assume. It is a right. And it is the duty of every government to recognize and safeguard that right ... the church must fulfil the role of watchdog over the state and remain in principle critical of every state and ready to warn it against transgression of its legitimate limits.'

The acrimonious relations between the government and churchmen who have been exercising a mild version of Tutu tactics in Kenya in recent years remind us that Pretoria does not have the only authoritarian government in southern Africa.

UGANDA AND MALAWI

Far worse than any of the SA excesses was the tyranny exerted by Idi Amin in Uganda (population 13.2 million of whom 78 per cent are Christian). Amin was a Muslim but introduced a ministry of religious affairs in 1971 to control the activities of the churches. The strong Christian Church in Uganda provided a martyr in the Anglican Primate, Archbishop Janani Luwum, allegedly killed by Amin personally at the height of his atrocities. Uganda, one of the gems in the British post-colonial crown, has still to recover from the ravages of that era.

While he can in no way be accused of the same degree of tyranny, Dr Hastings Banda of Malawi (population 5.6 million, of whom two-thirds are Christian) has a one-party state in which religious sects such as the Jehovah's Witnesses have been brutally persecuted and, when he first assumed the reins of power, Church of Scotland missionaries who protested against human rights violations were summarily deported, despite the fact that Banda was an elder of their church.

ZAMBIA

Perhaps the state with the least authoritarian attitude towards the

11. Church of Province of Kenya (Anglican)

church is Zambia (population 5.9 million, of which 72 per cent are Christian). It provided a recent example of religious persecution which was not the fault of the state when the charismatic Roman Catholic Archbishop of Lusaka, Emmanuel Milingo, was deposed from his see and disciplined in Rome because of the turmoil caused by the thousands of Africans who were flooding to healing services at which he performed exorcisms and healing 'miracles'. Hailed a great healer by some and a witch doctor by others, Milingo was an authentic bridge between the spiritist tribal beliefs and the Western Catholicism in which so many Zambians had been baptised. Apolitical and popular, he was recalled to Rome without a proper case being stated against him and still languishes there as a reminder perhaps that it is not only states which deny religious freedom, but churches too.

MOZAMBIQUE AND ZIMBABWE

The aforementioned East African countries are examples of colonial countries with strong Christian churches founded by missionaries but now African and indigenous. There are two other states in East Africa which are also the products of colonial and missionary effort but which could actually be said to have an ideology of the state. Mozambique and Zimbabwe are Marxist states in which one-party rule renders church criticism of the state somewhat muted. In Zimbabwe (population 7.5 million, of whom 40 per cent belong to tribal religions and 58 per cent to Christian churches), the one-party state was introduced by Premier Robert Mugabe before the ink had faded on the Lancaster House agreement. Churches and missionaries who give advice which the government does not want to hear are given short shrift.

The first President of Zimbabwe was a Christian minister, Rev Canaan Banana, but his liberation theology is a long way from that of Boesak. Despite admiring references to Martin Luther King, Banana outlines a basis of church/state thinking which does not spring from the European model or the American experience of the 1960s. It is Marxist Christianity. 'Only a genuine form of Christianity which springs from the people's experience would find room in Zimbabwe ... our revolution is people-centred and every activity has to start from the people, for the people and by the people.' Continuing in this sloganizing way, the former president of Zimbabwe continues his study *Theology of Promise*[12] with such headings as 'Christianity is Socialism' and 'Wealth Comes from Rapine and Spoil' and 'Towards a Proletarian Church'. Rejecting Western theology as an élitist process, he sees the task of the church to 'identify itself with the cause of social justice, equality and the development of the poor, not through pious evangelical pronouncements from the pulpit but through joint, purposeful action with the state'. The definition is Robert Mugabe's and is stated in the foreword to Banana's book. He goes on, 'When we talk of socialism versus capitalism we are actually talking of morality versus immorality, of equity versus inequity of humanity versus inhumanity and dare I say it, of Christianity versus un-Christianity.' With a definition like that, it is not surprising that there is only room for 'Marxist-Christianity' in Zimbabwe. Whites are understandably fearful that if that kind of theology gains ground there will not be a free church in a free state at all. Not long after Mugabe took power he put under house arrest the black Methodist Bishop, Abel Muzorewa, who had led an interim government prior to independence. Pastor N B Musa, a former terrorist who had undergone conversion and formed the Apostolic Revival Movement to evangelize former combatants, was arrested in 1983 and accused of using Christian meetings as a front to organize subversion and link up with Muzorewa. He was released in 1983 and now lives abroad. The white RC Bishop of Umtali, Donal Lamont, was exiled by Ian Smith's regime for helping guerrillas but returned in 1981 to a hero's welcome. However, Pastor Musa says that he left Zimbabwe a year later with a broken jaw, having run foul of the revolutionaries who now run the country. There are still civil disorders in the south of Zimbabwe where former rivals of the Mugabe guerrillas and former Smith regime 'scouts' are not under control. That would explain security measures by the state, but it is clear from the way that Mugabe has reacted to criticism that there will be no role for a church which criticized the way in which the state carries out these measures. In other words, churches will not be permitted to assume the kind of prophetic role of the former colonial missionary churches whose activities ironically were instrumental in bringing about the independence which gave power to Mugabe's party ZANU (PF). Pastor Musa made the prediction[13] that Rev Canaan Banana (who once said, 'If you see a guerrilla you see Jesus Christ') would be deposed by Mugabe as soon as he ceased to be useful as a figurehead. This is indeed what has happened. Mugabe is now the

12.   College Press 1982.
13.   In *Marxism v. The Church*, Cleveland Press 1985.

only head of state.

The other front-line state which borders South Africa is Mozambique, the former Portugese colony which became a Marxist state in 1975 and contains some 11 million people, half tribal religionists and one-third Christians, the bulk of whom are Roman Catholic. President Samora Machel, although from a Free Methodist background, said on assuming power, 'There will be no privileges for any church here in Mozambique. The privileged will be the Mozambican people, and only Frelimo will organize them – no one else!' He has also said, 'Religion, and especially Roman Catholicism, contributed to the cultural and human alienation of Mozambicans, making them into submissive instruments and objects of exploitation by appealing to the Christian doctrine of abnegation.' On yet another occasion before 100,000 people he chided the churches for allowing themselves to be ruled from outside – Catholics from Rome, Presbyterians from Switzerland and Methodists from America. Many missionaries have left or been expelled and their property expropriated by the state. There are also hundreds of thousands of refugees who have made their way into neighbouring Malawi. Mozambique harbours ANC bases which induces South Africa to give aid to subversive forces within the country, adding to the continuing unrest.

While there are a small number of gung-ho anti-communist fundamentalist American missions in Africa who cause trouble in the newly independent states, these hardly outweigh the human rights violations perpetrated against churches who try to fulfil the role of independent moral arbiter in African Marxist states.

One of the puzzling factors in this situation is the selective reporting and high-intensity spotlight that is turned on South Africa. It is treated differently. The front-line Marxist states do not practise the sin of apartheid. They do not have a denial of human rights written into their constitution. But it would be naïve – or a kind of inverted racism – to ignore the human rights violations in the African countries around South Africa. None are what Europeans would call 'free'. The removal of colonial power has been beneficial to the dominant tribe but not always to those who have surrendered power. It is not surprising therefore that the white tribes of South Africa, which now count as indigenous and have nowhere else to go, are paranoid about a one-man-one-vote solution in South Africa. Conscious that time is not on their side, they have been anxious to decant some of the black tribes into homelands.

The situation is further complicated by the fact that the dominant black tribe, the seven million Zulus, is opposed to the ANC and has its own tribal system of Kwazulu government. Their leader, Chief M G Buthelezi, an Anglican, is deeply critical of Archbishop Tutu. The Zulu organization Inkatha which has 1.3 million members exists 'to foster the spirit of unity among black people throughout South Africa . . . and the development of the black people spiritually, economically, educationally and politically . . .' Buthelezi asks the churches, 'Is there a black group in South Africa which is more democratic than Inkatha?' He criticizes the churches for their support of the ANC and is joined by his nephew, Zulu King Goodwill Bhekuzulu, in warning that the stances of Archbishop Hurley and Tutu and Dr Boesak are leading to anarchy and murder. The notorious 'necklace' killing (in which a rubber tyre filled with petrol is put round a victim's neck and set alight) has been used against Inkatha members by ANC supporters. It has been supported by Mrs Winnie Mandela in speeches and is used as retribution against Inkatha who are seen as collaborators with the South African government security forces. The ANC counter-charge that Inkatha have used bullying tactics and violence in an attempt to maintain a feudalistic type of power.

Many of the black independent Christians, who outnumber the members of the RC, Anglican and NGK considerably, are supporters of a live-and-let-live policy in the black homelands which is seen as a sell-out by the ANC. Bishop Isaac Mokoena of the Independents says the ANC are the real oppressors of the blacks. 'The war in South Africa is not black versus white, or white versus black, but black versus black. The necklaces are not condemned by the ANC or Mrs Mandela. The majority of blacks who have died in the violence in the townships have died at the hands of their so-called liberators – the ANC.' The bishop calls the ANC leadership in exile, a 'faceless elephant sitting in Lusaka' and is reminded by the death of his chaplain who was gunned down outside his church that he may be signing his own death warrant by speaking out against the ANC.

Neither the Zulu nor the independent church stances in South Africa are widely reported. They are more representative in numbers, but not as influential with international opinion which is firmly on the side of the UDF which has so far taken a non-violent stance and has yet openly to back the ANC campaign of violence. The dogs of war are barking but no one has yet dared to let them off the leash. With such a draconian and efficient military and police system, the SA government would have the upper hand in such a conflict. This makes the role of the church in the situation all the more crucial. If they simply become the chaplains of one battalion or another, offering encouragement and moral justification for violence, then they will harm rather than help the situation. The hopeful sign is that they are doing more than that. Theologian Rev. Professor James Torrance was struck by an encounter in 1988 with a millionaire South African businessman who was an Orthodox Jew and who told him, 'The Dutch Reformed Church is the one body that can save this country from disaster.' Professor Torrance visited Stellenbosch in the wake of the NGK 1986 Synod when the NGK Moderator Johan Heyns was addressing students on the key theological issue of church and state. The church, he argued, derives its structure from Christ and therefore has no prescribed form of authority or relationship with states. In a hall packed with young students he was cheered to the echo. The more conservative speakers stressed that the church derived its structure from ethnicity, pluriformity, and natural law. No one applauded. That gave Professor Torrance hope that the next generation of Afrikaner youth will not be content to repeat the sins of their forefathers.

The church which tries to open dialogue with Afrikaners on the redistribution of power in society, clutching a copy of Canaan Banana's *Theology of Promise* or by putting forward Latin American liberation ideas of base communities in the black townships is not likely to get very far. That kind of approach will end in tears — and tear-gas grenades. The concept of 'revolution' may be terrifying to the Afrikaner because he sees it in terms of guillotines and Bolsheviks and the bibles of Marxist-Leninism. But there is within the European Reformed tradition a positive view of 'revolution' which is non-violent and can be applied to the South Africa situation. This is the legacy of Calvin in Geneva, of the Puritans in England, of the Covenanters in Scotland, and of the Founding Fathers in the USA. It is the kind of revolution which laid the basis of modern democracy in these countries. It justified the switch from the idea that authority to rule resided in kings. The twin principles it evolved became the basis of true democratic society: right not might and human consent not force.

Applied to South Africa, these ideas challenge the whites who feel they have a God-given 'right' as the king felt he had a right to impose his authority. Now that the NGK have admitted that 'right' is no longer behind apartheid, all that remains is might. But to continue to exert might without right is tyranny. That is the revolution in liberty and justice which must take place.

The other principle outlined by Calvin is that there is no divorce between personal holiness and social holiness. Thus when the black people received the dignity of their humanity as fulfilled in Jesus Christ there was no way that this could be limited or modified, nor could they be told to go away and accept partial dignity and rights. Thus the revolution is inevitable. The only question is whether it will be by consent or by force. If the hard-headed Afrikaners are to be convinced, it is unlikely to be by softening their hearts. It may be a coloured minister of one of their own churches who will convince them, in their heads, by using the arguments of the Calvinist theology mastered by Boesak, learned in Amsterdam, the city that first saw apartheid founded and which maintained partitions between Catholics and Protestants in a divided kingdom. Today it is a city that is renowned for its relaxed attitude to races and creeds while the countryside around it has undergone an industrial revolution in less than a generation. It is to be hoped that Amsterdam will export that kind of peaceful revolution to South Africa for the second time in history.

6 Capitalism, Communism and Christendom: Europe

Held together by the Roman Empire and then by a common faith, a thousand years ago Christendom was approximately equal to Europe. Schisms, wars, treaties and enmities have changed that picture through the years, but no European state except Albania has expunged Christianity. From the Baltic to the Mediterranean, from the Mountains of Mourne to Moldavia, through a spectrum of climates, a variety of terrain and a babel of languages and cultures, Christianity struck a variety of deals with the Caesars and commissars which have guaranteed its survival as a significant presence. So varied are these forms of church/state co-existence that to consider them together in a single chapter seems to invite contradictions. What does the state-embraced Catholicism of Spain have in common with the dissenting Protestant Church of East Germany? What do the Swedes have in common with the Serbs other than an initial letter? At first sight very little. Even the crude division of Europe into East and West by the 'iron curtain' does not sufficiently reflect the diversity of church/state relationships in Eastern bloc societies, some of which have more significant church presence than those in the West.

Yet on a global scale, European Christianity is now in a minority, and geographically Europe fits inside the southern tip of Africa where, as we have seen, there is much debate about church and state relationships. Partly to stress the scale and perspective of European Christianity on the world scale, and partly to illustrate the variety of forms of church/state relationship within Europe, I propose to give only short sketches of the most significant types and of the countries where church/state interaction is a live issue.

Possibly the most significant event in post-war Europe has been the creation and growth of the EEC. In 1992 this evolution will take a further step when trade barriers between nations come down. Already agreed are laws permitting movement of labour between EEC countries and hopes are high that a common currency may be agreed before the end of the century. However, it does not take a prophet to predict that one of the last things that will occur in Europe is a common market in religion. Not only have the Catholic and Protestant Churches dug themselves in deep constitutionally through arrangements with the various EEC states, but some states actually have laws which prohibit the activities of other Christian churches.

GREECE

One of the newer EEC members, Greece is the only country in the world that is officially Eastern Orthodox. Church/state relations are extremely complex owing partly to the Byzantine heritage, and the Greek Orthodox Church is so closely woven into the fabric of Greek life that even atheist communists do not consider themselves properly married if they do not have their nuptials solemnized by it. The *World Christian Encyclopaedia* lists 98.2 per cent of Greece's nine million population as Christian and 97.6 per cent of them as Greek Orthodox. First the cradle of Christianity, and then the citadel to which Orthodoxy withdrew after the crowning of Charlemagne by the Pope of Rome in 800 until finally the Great Schism of 1054, Greek Christianity was eclipsed during the Ottoman Empire. But after the Greeks had asserted their independence in the war of 1821, the Patriarch of Constantinople agreed to let them have self-governing status in 1850. Not much disturbed this entrenched establishment, but its status was spelt out in modern times by the constitution of 1952 which began: 'In the name of the Holy, Consubstantial and Indivisible Trinity . . . the established religion in Greece is that of the Eastern Orthodox Church of Christ . . .' In 1968, when King Constantine was deposed, another constitution (incorporated into the 1973 constitution installing the presidential republic after the reign of the colonels) stated: 'The dominant religion is that of the Eastern Orthodox Church of Christ . . . she is autocephalous, exercises her sovereign rights independent of every other church and is administered by a Holy Synod of Bishops.'

In practice, the Greek Orthodox Church is granted privileges which prohibit proselytizing for any other church. This is no paper law. In 1985 three Britons on a Youth With a Mission ship were sentenced to three and a half years in prison for converting a young Greek man and giving him a copy of the New Testament (only the Orthodox Bible is permitted by law in Greece Art 1. Par 4 1973). There is clearly no common market in religion here.

The Holy Synod has the right to be consulted on any changes affecting its administration. During the colonels' reign (1967–74) there was a period when the church under Archbishop Hieronymous collaborated openly with General Papadopoulos and for his quisling service the Holy Synod was given the use of the state seal to pass binding legislation on church matters. Since this was rescinded in 1975, the new primate, Archbishop Seraphim, has done his best to undo the effects of those years and in 1975 a new constitution was proposed with freedom of conscience allowed. However, other churches and religions must still seek a licence to operate from the Office for Non-Orthodox Religions and the Orthodox have the right of surveillance of any ecclesiastical acts and must give permission for an non-Orthodox building to be erected. Mixed marriages must be celebrated before an Orthodox priest after a bishop has given permission.

The Greek Orthodox Church is not poor. In 1952 it transferred 80 per cent of its lands to the state in return for considerable wealth and more recently it decided to part with the remaining 325,000 rural acres worth $1 billion. However, this has sparked off a church/state confrontation, with the church claiming it had not been consulted over how the land should be used and that the education and religion minister who masterminded the sale is 'ignorant of church matters.' The minister, part of the Papandreou Socialist administration, wanted to hand over the land to large state-owned co-operatives ('It is the only modern way of farming. The EEC supports it and we all know how uneconomical it is to cut up land into small bits and pieces'). The church wants its holdings divided between landless and poor farmers and points to the losses made by the state co-operatives. The new bill would also cede control of the land to elected laymen whom the church fear could turn out to be Marxist nominees. There have been threats that the Greek Church will secede to the authority of the Ecumenical patriarchate in Constantinople, sometimes known as the Phanar, which still administers parts of Greece under an act of 1928 (e.g. Crete on a semi-autonomous basis and the monastic state of the Holy Mount of Athos). This is unlikely, but much heat has been generated (in one 1987 demonstration outside parliament 50,000 people joined placard-waving priests and nuns, and Archbishop Seraphim boycotted the National Day service in Athens Cathedral). It shows that Papandreou's 1981 election pledge to loosen the church/state bond will prove no easy task.

As yet there are plenty of EEC regulations governing bread and wine, but none governing Holy Communion. It would be a foolish person who would wish for such developments, but clearly the future in Greece must involve some kind of loosening of the restrictive monopoly of the Greek Orthodox Church. It would clearly be a breach of more than the Treaty of Rome if an Irish priest took a holiday in Greece and invited the neighbours round to his holiday cottage for Mass and was promptly arrested. That such a bizarre incident would be theoretically possible highlights how difficult it will be for the Orthodox Churches to preserve their Byzantine heritage in a modern state.

Ironically, the two nations immediately north of Greece both have an Orthodox Church as the predominant religious institution and despite the fact that they are members of the communist bloc, church/state relationships are improving. In Bulgaria, the Orthodox Church enjoys a good deal of toleration partly because of its championing of Bulgarian freedom against the Turks. In Romania the Orthodox Church is similarly identified with the aspirations of the state and under the strongly nationalist regime of Ceaucesçu, which came to power in 1965, persecution has been relaxed and it has been able to maintain a higher profile. However, in both countries the authorities use the church to discipline religious dissenters and during the 1970s there was a spate of arrests.

ROMANIA

In Romania (population 22 million) two-thirds of the population are Eastern Orthodox. The state supervises the church through the Department of Cults and pays part of the salary of priests and theological professors. Under the constitution there is freedom of religion, and Patriarch Justinian found no difficulty in reaching accommodation with Ceaucesçu nor has his successor Justin since 1977. In return, concessions for publications and theological education have been gained, but the believer is still disadvantaged in career prospects. 'The Lord's Army', a wing of the Orthodox Church which engages in evangelistic and worship activities outside church premises, is illegal and its leader Traian Dors has spent time in prison. In 1981 five priests addressed a 'testimony of Faith' to the patriarch criticizing the 'prostitution of the church' and its sterility, materialism and hypocrisy. They called for the right to educate children about religion, freedom for pilgrimages, access to the media and the legalization of 'the Lord's Army'. All five were disciplined and two unfrocked.

BULGARIA

Bulgaria (population 9 million) is the East European country ideologically closest to the Soviet Union. Bulgarians seem to have an affection for the Russians, not always shared in Eastern Europe, as their liberators from 500 years of Turkish yoke. A national Orthodox Church was permitted by the sultan in 1870 but excommunicated by a Greek council and only restored in 1945, by which time they had had to make their peace with another master. The Orthodox Church has been given limited financial grants in return for the lands which the communist state expropriated. The constitution of 1947 declares, 'The Bulgarian Orthodox Church is the traditional faith of the Bulgarian people. It is bound up with their history and as such can be considered a church of the popular democracy.' In 1953 the legal status of the Bulgarian Orthodox Church (which accounts for about 60 per cent of the nation) was enhanced compared with other churches, although freedom is guaranteed to all religious rites. In the new Constitution of 1971, 'hating and humiliating a man' on account of his religion is forbidden and all citizens are equal before the law (Art. 35). However, the same document warns, 'abusive acts which tend to place the church at the service of political organizations of a religious background are forbidden. Religion may not be used to justify refusing to carry out duties under the law (Art 53:4–5).'

In 1981, patriarch Maksim was involved prominently in the celebrations of 1,300 years of the Bulgar nation and, as in Russia, the Orthodox Church sometimes acts as the mouthpiece of the state in promoting peace policies. It is worth comparing church/state coexistence in some of the satellite nations of the Soviet empire which have a strong national culture. As we have seen, where the predominant church is Orthodox, it seems to ally itself with the state along the old Caesaro-papist model. Where it is Roman Catholic (e.g. in Lithuania, Poland, Czechoslovakia) the church becomes a focus for dissent.

HUNGARY

For many years dissent was nowhere more apparent than in Hungary (population 11 million). Situated as they are right in the centre of Europe, Hungarians can trace their Christian origins back to the third century and throughout their history have felt the ebb and flow of religious currents in Europe. Threatened by Islam for centuries, they absorbed the Lutheran Reformation but eventually the Roman Catholic faith emerged triumphant as the state religion of the Austro-Hungarian Empire at the end of the last century. Roman Catholicism is still the predominant church (nearly 60 per cent affiliated). One-quarter of Hungarians are Protestant with the Reformed Church of Hungary (Presbyterian) accounting for 19 per cent, and evangelical Lutherans for 4 per cent. When the state was declared atheist in 1949 and Roman Catholic property expropriated, public protests against the regime were orchestrated by the primate, Cardinal Mindszenty, who was arrested and sentenced to life imprisonment. He became a symbol of defiance against the regime. After the uprising of 1956 he lived in the American embassy until papal pressure forced him to go to Vienna in 1971. He regarded priests who co-operated with the regime as candidates for excommunication and the regime itself as illegal and himself as the representative of the monarchy.

As long as this redoubtable character lived, the pope could not appoint a successor, nor did he wish to humiliate the man who had become a national hero and symbol of resistance to communism. But the pope did reach a historic agreement with Hungary in 1964 (the first of its kind with a communist country) enabling the Vatican to appoint bishops approved by the government. Thus a partial thaw had taken place over the years while Mindszenty stayed 'on ice' as primate.

Meanwhile the Protestants had made their own accommodations with the state. When Cardinal Lekai took over as primate in 1976 he made various accommodations, and diplomatic relations were established with the Holy See in 1978. Other gains were in the field of theological education, religious publishing and church building. But in the past decade this appeasement policy has come under criticism from within Hungary in the emergence of 'basis communities' on a liberation theology model, led by Fr Bulanyi who preaches poverty and non-violence and who was condemned by the Hungarian bishops' conference in 1982. The other significant critic of such appeasement lives in Vatican City. The Bishop of Rome,

Karol Wojtyla, the pope from Poland, is more inclined to look on Mindszenty as a hero of the faith than as a pig-headed old man. Pope John Paul II is more inclined to see Hungary as a failure and the more militant stances of Poland as the model. But, as we shall see later, Poland is probably the exception to the general rule that most concessions won by the churches in Eastern Europe have been at the price of endorsement of the political strategies of the secular authorities.

CZECHOSLOVAKIA

In Czechoslovakia (population 15 million) the churches are firmly under the control of the state and a system of licences for clergy to operate is in force. The Roman Catholic Church is predominant and two-thirds of the population have allegiance to it. After the communist coup of 1948 church property was seized and the state took over the purse strings and the payment of clergy. There followed twenty years of cold war during which church freedoms were curtailed despite the guarantees of freedom of religion by the Constitutions of 1948 and 1960 ('Religious practices may be observed inasmuch as they do not transgress the law' par. 1). The Prague Spring of 1969 ended the Dubcek year of *glasnost*.

The next twenty years were a difficult and fraught period for the Czech people. Some activists formed the Charter 77 human rights group and saw their conscientious religious duty as campaigning outside Czechoslovakia for international public opinion to pressure change. Others thought the way forward lay in co-operation with the state and change from within. State sponsored organizations like Pacem in Terris were used to shunt clergy into dummy reform organizations who toed the line on state policy, and eventually the Vatican called the bluff by banning its priests from taking part in them. 1988 was a salutary year for the church to re-assert itself (forty years after the communists seized power, fifty after the Nazis and twenty after Dubcek). 10,000 attended a Mass within sight of President Husak's office and others chanted freedom slogans outside the home of eighty-eight-year-old Cardinal Tomasek, who had emerged as a tough and courageous leader.

At their centre was a thirty-one point petition calling for the separation of church and state; the appointment of more priests and the observance of basic political rights. The petition is the most outspoken act since 1968 and has been signed by 300,000 Catholics. Its core is the long-running row with the authorities over the country's bishoprics – only three out of thirteen are occupied. Because the government insisted on politically acceptable candidates, the Vatican left the vacancies unfilled, but thereby deprived the Czech church of a hierarchy. Fortunately the Soviet *glasnost* era has dawned to take the heat out of what might have proved to be a repeat of the 1968 crackdown.

Religion has not proved a rallying point for nationalist aspirations among Czechs or Slovaks (although the predominant Protestant church (which is Lutheran) is centred on Slovakia, the majority faith of Catholicism is fairly evenly spread).

YUGOSLAVIA

In Yugoslavia (population 22 million), by contrast, where religion and nationality are closely identified, religious fervour is usually interpreted as a cloak for unacceptable nationalist sentiments. The various republics which constitute the Yugoslav federation have a distinctive divide: Croatia and Slovenia are mainly Catholic (just under one-third of total population); Kosovo is Muslim (one tenth of total population) and in Bosnia and Hercegovina, all three religions live side by side.

The more liberal communism of Tito was partly the reason that religion was not persecuted; but there was also the more cynical reason that the state was wary of turning the churches into rallying points for nationalist factions. While religious education and the training of priests are all permissible, teachers may not be believers and it is impossible for believers to hold positions of responsibility in the state or armed forces under laws enacted in 1980. The lack of solidarity among the churches can be explained by the age-old rivalry of the Catholic and Orthodox Churches exacerbated by the grim events of the last war when Catholic Croatia was a fascist puppet state which assisted anti-Serbian and Orthodox atrocities.

POLAND

Solidarity has become synonymous with the name of Poland. So much has been written about Poland during the Solidarity era and the decade of the Polish pope that it seems presumptuous to attempt a summary. But in a way it can be summed up by two bare statistics: communist Poland has 35 million people – 90 per cent of them are still Roman Catholics. This goes a little way to explaining the success of the Roman Church in post-war Poland which is based solidly on the support of the majority of the people who treat their Polish pope as a king in exile and rely on the church to defend human and national rights. But, as Neal Ascherson has shrewdly pointed out, the most forceful strand in Polish nationalism was socialist and its leaders were suspicious of the reactionary attitudes of the church and 'when it comes to morality, Poles suit themselves. Marriage is no more stable in Poland than anywhere else, sex is a national sport and I have never noticed a boycott of the "atheist state's" offer of abortion and contraception.'[1]

Poland was Christianized in AD 966. The fifteenth century was the 'century of saints' and the sixteenth the 'golden age' when scholars like Copernicus flourished. After the Reformation, a significant Protestant presence appeared and factions of nobles gathered round the various faiths (Catholic, Lutheran, Calvinist) which gave an excuse to Russia, Prussia and Austria to step in and carve up Poland in the late eighteenth century, and it was not until after the First World War that Poland again became a national state. It made its own concordat with the Vatican in 1925 and religious education was required in schools. During the Nazi era, Poland descended into hell when one fifth of its population was liquidated (half of them Jews) and then another 2 million were deported or 'disappeared' when Stalin's troops arrived in 1945. The new communist state unilaterally renounced the concordat with the Vatican.

The extraordinary fact is that more than forty years later the Roman Catholic Church in Poland is more ebullient and confident than in any other part of the world and has truly risen from the grave to which it had been consigned. Several key events stand out in this process. By 1950 the state found that it had been unsuccessful in its attempt to freeze out Rome and create a national church which it could manipulate along the Eastern Orthodox models. It then struck a compromise deal with the church in which it recognized the pope as head of the church in return for the church agreeing to support foreign policies such as Poland's claim to sovereignty over former German territories. The church was then able to name bishops to replace temporary apostolic administrators. Events soured, however, in 1953 with the arrest of the Polish primate, Cardinal Wyszinski, and although he was released in 1956 at the start of the Gomulka regime, the experience baptised him as the prophet of his people, a role he held until he relinquished it in 1978 to Karol Wojtyla. The cardinal used this role to be a thorn in the flesh of the Polish state.

1. *Struggles for Poland*, Michael Joseph 1988.

During the 1970s, several further advances were made in church/state relations. In 1971, the beatification of Maximilian Kolbe, who died a martyr's death at the Auschwitz concentration camp, proved to be a day of national significance (and the pope would not have forgotten this when he prompted the canonization in 1985). In the same year the state transferred property rights in the former German territory to the church and excused it from registration of its other properties. Although the Polish church receives no subsidy from the government this was of considerable advantage. In 1971 new church buildings were also permitted and by 1974 the Vatican was involved in talks directed towards the normalization of relations between church and state, whereas previously this had been a matter for the primate to hammer out with the state.

Thus when the Solidarity uprisings took place the church was well placed to make use of its role as a spiritual leader and force for reconciliation. The international pressure created by the pope's constant attention to events in his native land and his three return visits, helped Cardinal Glemp, the new primate, to go with a mandate to the state. For his part, General Jaruzelski, the Polish leader, was keen to achieve a broad compromise with the church and win its backing for his reform proposals. In May 1989 a concordat between Poland and the Vatican established diplomatic relations with the Holy See and included a law granting the Roman Catholic Church legal status in Poland for the first time since the war. 68,000 clergy became part of the social security system. However, church officials want the government to make concessions on human rights, e.g. the granting of freedom of association and trade union pluralism and legalization of the banned union Solidarity. The church is involved in talks between the authorities and the opposition which could bring the inclusion of an opposition group in parliament, a startlingly novel development in a one-party state. Church-backed intellectuals are also co-operating with the authorities in drafting a law of associations. This is *glasnost* with a Polish accent.

If further proof were needed that the Polish church has won a significant place for itself in the Polish state as well as victories for human rights, was provided in 1988 by the 'papal' visit-in-reverse of Mikhail Gorbachev to Poland when he stood in awe at the altar of St Mary's Church of the Assumption in Krakow as a fifteenth-century wooden triptych depicting biblical scenes was unfolded before him. Impressed by the 'frank and productive' church/state relationship in Poland, Mr Gorbachev is not likely to fear problems from the Russian Orthodox Church which is attended by his own mother in a car with motor-cycle escort every Sunday.

With such predominant presence in Poland, the Roman Catholic Church is in a good position to effect a deal with the state which would give it certain advantages. That situation prevails in a number of other European countries where the cultural and constitutional role of Roman Catholicism is a major factor in national life. These are the countries which have church/state concordats granting it a privileged position. If the Eastern Orthodox operates a 'Caesaro-papist' model of church/state relations, then these countries inherited a 'Papo-Caesarist' way of doing things.

They are Italy, Spain and Eire, all different in their history but similar in one thing – the overwhelming influence of the Catholic Church. In turn, the contribution of these countries to the growth of Catholicism has been crucial. Spain has been a conservative force throughout history, from the infamous days of the Inquisition through the formation of the Jesuits in the period of the Counter-Reformation. Today one of the most conservative forces within Catholicism is the organization Opus Dei and that too has Spanish origins. Ireland was, and still is, a prime source of missionary priests and nuns and, aided by the Irish habit of emigration, has exercised influence far from its own shores upon the development of Catholicism. Italy is, of course, the home of the Roman Catholic Church and the Vatican, an independent state created when the papal states became part of Italy in 1870. Although since the Second Vatican Council the curia of cardinals has become more cosmopolitan, it was from Italy that the leadership (popes and cardinals) was drawn and the old saying is still true that the real level of power in the Vatican is the first Italian you meet on the way down the hierarchy.

Spain has a population of 37 million of whom 97 per cent are professed Roman Catholics. However, only one in four is a regular churchgoer and a few have moved on to other religions, the most popular being Islam with 300,000 members. There are two schools of Catholicism, the traditional and the optional, which has been termed 'diet-Coke Catholicism, low on starchy dogma and fizzing with sentimentality about peace and brotherhood'. (*The Economist*, 3 Oct 1987)

Spain was Christianized early in the first century and when the Arian Visigoths overran the Iberian peninsula, they too embraced Christianity. During the Muslim Berber rule, which began in the eighth century and reached its zenith in the tenth, Islam was the dominant religion. Crusades to re-establish Christianity succeeded gradually and by the fourteenth century it was firmly entrenched. Probably the attempts to force Moors and Jews to convert or leave, plus the allocation of land to military orders and feudal estates, helped to develop the authoritarian character of Spanish Catholicism. During Spain's Golden Age the colonies became areas for missionary thrust and at home the Counter-Reformation and the Inquisition effectively prevented religious movements outside the established church. As the monarchy declined, it interfered more in the church and in 1753 a concordat gave the king the right to appoint bishops. It was not until 1868 that religious toleration for non-Catholics was granted. Following the triumph of General Franco's fascists in the Civil War in 1939, a new concordat was worked out. In many ways it took over the dispensations of the 1851 concordat which acknowledged the Roman Church as the only religion of the Spanish nation and granted rights and privileges to it. The state still enjoyed the patronage of bishops and the new 1953 concordat agreed to give tax exemption to the church and pay salaries of clergy who were exempt from military service and could not be prosecuted without their bishops' approval. Civil recognition of marriages and annulment decisions and the obligatory teaching of the Catholic faith in all educational establishments was also provided for.

In 1967 a revision of the Constitution took place and a law on religious liberty was introduced. The head of state was still, however, compelled to profess the Catholic faith and although religious liberty was recognized, it was 'conceived according to Catholic doctrine . . . and must in every case be compatible with the religion of the Spanish state as it is proclaimed in its fundamental laws' (Art. 1.3.)[2] Further restriction on those in holy orders from contracting a marriage without canonical dispensation (now virtually unavailable in practice under Pope John Paul II) and the requirement that non-Catholic religious confessions must register with the Ministry of Justice who assessed them on the basis of their Constitutions, made this law on

2.   As quoted in *World Christian Encyclopaedia*.

religious freedom something of a bad joke. It hardly accorded with the spirit of Vatican II. After Franco's death in 1975, revisions to the power of the ruler to nominate or veto bishops and for clergy exemption from prosecution were introduced. In 1978 Spain decided no longer to have an official religion and proper toleration of religion was granted, for example, discrimination over burial places and restrictions on establishment of new churches ended, while freedom of marriage and to change beliefs was granted. The Roman Catholic Church still has a leading role: 'The public authorities will keep in mind the religious beliefs of Spanish society and will maintain co-operation with the Catholic Church and other confessions.' There have been tensions between church and state and between the liberal/radical and conservative wings of Spanish Catholicism. Politically active left-wing priests and priests sympathetic to Basque separatists are more than balanced out by Opus Dei activists. The latter belong to the society founded in 1928 by Spanish Mgr Escriva to Christianize leading figures in society, and whose right-wing influence in key posts in Spanish life is still profound, earning it the nickname of the 'Holy Mafia' and 'Octopus Dei'. With the changes in church/state bonds, the state funding of the church has gradually been phased out. Spanish taxpayers now have the choice of whether to give 0.52 per cent of their income tax to the church or allocate it to the state's culture and welfare programmes. After 1990 the church will have to fend for itself, but until then the state will top up the level to the $110 million which the church has received. However, its land and property will continue to be exempt from rates and the church schools (attended by one in four children) will continue to receive subsidy $330 million in 1987, plus teachers' salaries).

It was inevitable that as secularizing trends and external influences from membership of the EEC gathered force, Spain's Catholic conformity would begin to change. Today the church is still the focus of the rites of passage for the vast majority of Spaniards but the old days of supremacy are over. More Spaniards are turning to contraception and divorce. Tourism and holiday homes have destroyed the religious hegemony of Roman Catholicism enshrined in the Constitution, but it is hard to see a nation that bred the Inquisition giving up 'official' religion without a struggle.

IRELAND

Ireland (population 3.3 million) has, like Spain, given up the special constitutional position once accorded to the Roman Catholic Church. However, like everything to do with Ireland, matters are never that simple. In 1972, the Irish electorate voted by more than five to one in a referendum to delete from their Constitution special concessions to the position of the Roman Catholic Church. But ironically in referendums held since then, the same church has left little doubt that it has a crucial effect on the outcome. The bishops of the Roman Catholic Church in 1973 played a key role in the Irish parliament's rejection of new laws which would have allowed contraceptives to be sold to married couples by pharmacists. Stronger anti-abortion laws and a veto on divorce law reform were all credited to the church's influence in this bastion of traditional Catholicism.

Ireland was the fertile ground for a mission by Palladius and Patrick in the fifth century and in the next hundred years had itself become a missionary centre through which Columba and others evangelized Britain with Celtic Christianity. While this form was eclipsed after the Synod of Whitby in AD 664, and power lay in Roman and English hands, Ireland remained staunchly religious. Like the Poles, the Irish clung to their Catholic faith through centuries of foreign domination. After 1537, the English king was declared head of the Church of Ireland, which has been identified ever since with colonialism. In the north 350 years ago a migration from Scotland set up a Presbyterian presence which survives today in the form of the conservative Presbyterian Church and the breakaway fundamentalist Free Presbyterians led by the uncompromising figure of Rev Ian Paisley. Since the partition of Ireland in 1921 into Northern Ireland and Eire, the unification of Ireland has remained the overshadowing issue in Irish politics, and religion is one of the major factors in this intractable problem. It is further complicated by the fact that all three influential religious traditions (Roman Catholic, Anglican and Presbyterian) are 'all-Ireland' churches and do not recognize the border within their denominational organization.

For all practical purposes, the Presbyterians are concentrated in the north (27 per cent of the total population in the north compared with 15 per cent to the Anglicans and 33 per cent to the Roman Catholics). In the south (Eire) they number a mere 13,000. The Church of Ireland, the Anglican church, prior to partition in Eire had a tenth of the population but has sunk now to less than 3 per cent and is still declining owing to the 'ecclesiastical genocide' caused by the insistence of the Roman Catholic Church that in mixed marriages the couple bring up any children as Catholics.

In the Irish context the Roman Catholic faith has been synonymous with Irish nationalism. Its clergy have always been drawn from all social classes and its influence felt in every aspect of Irish life. It provided a cohesive force during the years of British rule and many of its priests were and are involved in politics. The present Primate of All Ireland, Cardinal Tomás O'Fiaich, is a Gaelic-speaking Irish nationalist and under him Irish Catholicism has remained tradition-alist, nationalist, and isolationist. That combination has meant that Ireland has kept the character of its religion despite the upheavals caused by the reforms of Vatican II. Indeed, it is said that the Irish caution about Vatican II was not so much conservatism asserting itself as a natural Irish characteristic, since they were still assessing whether they should fully embrace Vatican I (which occurred in 1870)!

Although the Irish Constitution of 1921 recognizes and mentions specifically the churches (in addition to the 'special position' of the Roman Catholic Church abolished by the 1972 referendum), they have no existence in law. Parishes and bishoprics are not considered to be entities in civil law and thus church properties are held through trustees. Indeed, there is no legal relationship between church and state. Unlike other European 'concordat' countries, the Irish state does not subsidize churches, nor give them the right to levy taxes. No assistance or salary is paid to clergy. There is no ministry for religious affairs or department of government for dealing with religious bodies.

However, church/state separation is not so clean cut as that. In the matter of marriage, two kinds are recognized in law – civil and religious. In mixed marriages, spouses are bound before the law by pre-nuptial written promises even though they be given before a priest, while Article 41 of the 1921 Constitution states: 'No law shall be enacted providing for the grant of a dissolution of a marriage.' The paradox in this is that two atheists may marry but cannot divorce. Two Catholics may marry, part, and in time receive an annulment, and then may marry again in church outside Ireland. To complete this uniquely Irish situation it is worth considering an example of a couple from a mixed marriage effected in church. The Catholic partner obtains an annulment and goes to Britain where he marries again. His non-Catholic spouse becomes pregnant but cannot marry her new partner without obtaining a divorce abroad. It is cases like these which would have been addressed by the divorce law reform which was rejected in the 1986 referendum. As long as such laws remain in force together with the ban on the sale of contraceptives and the prohibition of abortion, Protestants in the north will claim them as examples of unacceptable restraints upon them in a united Ireland.

The 'Irish problem' is the recurring nightmare of British politicians. There is no question that the majority of citizens of Northern Ireland wish to remain outside the Republic of Eire. However, the majority of people from Eire take the view that it is logical, historical and desirable that Ireland should be one seamless island. Even joint membership of the EEC does nothing to dim this desire. Preying on this situation like a cancerous cell is the Irish Republican Army and its more respectable face, the political organization, Sinn Fein. The atrocities of the former have never been supported, and often condemned, by the Irish Roman Catholic hierarchy, which is constantly being asked to excommunicate members of the IRA and condemn those who vote for Sinn Fein. That they fail to do either is one of the most touchy church/state issues – in Britain, if not in Eire.

It is worth dwelling on this point. It is of overriding importance since, in the political jungle created by the Irish border, the wood and the trees are difficult to separate. Cardinal O'Fiaich spoke out in sympathy for the 'Dirty Protest' in the Maze prison during the internment introduced by the British to combat paramilitary terrorism and was accused of IRA sympathies. His statements on Sinn Fein are worth examination. In a television interview shown on RTE on Sunday 15 January 1987 the cardinal said, 'If a person joins Sinn Fein as an act of support for violence and the violent activities of the IRA, then that is morally wrong . . . It is not for me to judge a person's conscience. It depends very much on the purpose for which he joins.'

Here is a dark wood of closely planted trees. There is a distinction between the criminally violent IRA and the politically active Sinn Fein and then again between those who join the latter for acceptable reasons and unacceptable reasons. But in practice the daylight does not show between the various options and the act of joining becomes solidarity beyond the individual's control. The point is well made by the cardinal himself: 'I think that what the church has to make clear is that, in voting for Sinn Fein, you are voting for a group very closely associated with violent people and people who are guilty of crimes. Therefore before you vote for them you have to weigh this and that consideration and you have to take into account that your vote may be misinterpreted.'

The same argument could be applied to cardinals who do not seek to see that their comments on the IRA are incapable of misinterpretation. The RTE interviewer brought out the point when he said, 'So, essentially, there is a position where people with moral justification can vote for Sinn Fein?'

Cardinal: 'I haven't said that. I have said it depends on their motives—'

Q: 'But if their motives are right, they can morally support Sinn Fein?'

Cardinal: 'There may be a case where they might. I would have to hear the exact situation with regard to any particular person – why are you a member of Sinn Fein or why do you vote for Sinn Fein – before I could give any moral judgement on his or her situations.'

A writer to the *Irish Times* asked rather pertinently whether the cardinal could offer consolation to those who were seeking a divorce for 'the best of motives'. The quotes above illustrate how difficult it is to get an Irish churchman to quell the suspicions of the Protestants in the north that the Irish Roman Catholic hierarchy is hesitant to condemn terrorists who are on the 'right' side of a united Ireland.

The irony is that the 275,000 Northern Irish Presbyterians and 153,000 Anglicans would, no doubt, make a significant impact on the Irish political scene in a united Ireland and force the kind of changes in the Eire church/state situation which have proved impossible to achieve in the past. But this option seems to be the last one which will be acceptable to Protestants since it seems to be yielding to the IRA demands.

If the goal of the Irish hierarchy has been to uphold traditional Catholic teaching on abortion, divorce and contraception, then they have been remarkably successful. Mass attendance is still high compared to Spain and Italy (up to 80 per cent was claimed by surveys done twenty years ago, although this has since fallen considerably). Although there has been a drop in vocations to the priesthood in recent years, the Irish still send an enormous number of priests abroad and ordinations are split into those for an Irish diocese and those for abroad. Figures for 1970 showed 6,000 foreign missionaries supported by the Irish church and 7,000 in 1965. The other traditional Irish habit during lean times – emigration – has also meant that countries like the USA have a significant number of their clergy who are of Irish descent. Thus at home and abroad, Ireland looms much larger than its offshore position and low population might suggest. It continues to draw strength from its traditional source, nationalist spirit, and while secular influences may weaken it slightly, it thrives, like Poland, in confronting the Goliath on its doorstep.

ITALY

When it comes to the church/state relationship between Italy and the Vatican, it is difficult to know which is David and which is Goliath. Italy is a thousand miles long and has a population of 57 million. The Vatican City state within the city of Rome has just over 700 permanent residents in 0.44 km sq. St Peter's Basilica in the Vatican is the spiritual home for 840 million believers worldwide and in terms of influence per square kilometre the city state of the Vatican is as concentrated an instance of church/state power as it is possible to imagine. Relations between the two are governed by a concordat. In 1870, when the various states making up Italy were unified under a new kingdom with Rome as the capital, the papal states were incorporated and there began a wrangle between the Holy See and the Italian state about compensation, the papal states having been the church's preserve since the days of Charlemagne. The dispute went on for a generation and, ironically, was solved by the fascist dictatorship of Mussolini in 1929 when he granted the church various privileges in the hope of winning its support for his regime.

But Mussolini also gave the Vatican $83 million for the lands seized in 1870 and this was invested in Italian companies like Societa Generale Immobiliare, the construction giant which, years later, was to win the contract to build Washington's Watergate complex – a tiny irony since those funds were managed by an institution called the IOR (Institute per l'Opere di Religione) founded in 1942 to protect the Vatican's finances in war-torn Europe. It is better known by a title which was to become as infamous as Watergate – the Vatican Bank. It may seem unfair to highlight this somewhat shady episode in the Vatican's recent history, but it serves as a recent illustration of the way in which the Vatican operates and why it is known to some Roman journalists of my acquaintance as the Kremlin of the Western world.

During the later 1960s, the Italian state began to tax the vast investments of the Vatican. The Vatican was well placed to use its immunity from Italian tax law, protected by its independent sovereignty as a state, plus its own diplomatic corps serving in countries all over the world in which the Roman Catholic Church had an interest. There was also criticism of some of the Vatican's investments in firms like an Italian firearms factory and a Canadian pharmaceutical company which manufactured contraceptives. Pope

Paul VI was well versed in the diplomatic machinery and enlisted the help of a loyal Italian banker with transatlantic interests, Michele Sindona, to liquidate the investments and transfer the money into the IOR. However, Sindona's New York Franklin Bank collapsed in 1974 with the IOR losing an estimated $70 million. Sindona was sent to prison in the USA for a twenty-five year term. His protégé, the Milan banker Roberto Calvi, took over the role of 'God's banker', although that title perhaps also belongs to the Chicago-born, six foot three former papal bodyguard who ran the bank from 1969–89, Archbishop Paul Marcinkus.

Sindona was later slipped cyanide in prison to stop him opening a can of worms which would have caught some very big fish deep inside the Italian establishment. He had declared Marcinkus to be 'greedy but honest' in his dealings with Calvi who wove a tangled web in using his bank and the IOR to make a vast killing. Calvi used his Banco Ambrosiano to export illegally millions of dollars in what is known as the 'shell game', a means of passing funds to overseas havens. Through the Milan headquarters, he borrowed $1.2 billion on the Eurodollar market which he shuttled to an Ambrosiano holding in Luxembourg and on to Central American affiliate companies. The most important of these was the Banco Ambrosiano of Nassau on whose board of directors Archbishop Marcinkus sat. This movement of money was against Italian law and in 1981 Calvi was fined $13.5 million. The alliance was threatened and the IOR moved in with letters of credit to guarantee the loans. Subsequently, in 1982, when Calvi was found hanging beneath Blackfriars Bridge in London in extremely suspicious circumstances, the Vatican said that he had relieved them of responsibilities, but Marcinkus's signature was on the letters of credit and he owed more than dumb silence. At first sight it may seem that the Vatican was naïve, tricked by Calvi into supporting him, but the letters of credit go back to 1974 and all through the 1970s the IOR was increasing its support for Calvi, and it was only three days before Calvi's death that Marcinkus resigned from the board of the Nassau bank.[3]

The way in which the Vatican dealt with this *cause célèbre* is a parable of the way the Vatican operates. In 1981, Pope John Paul II said that he wanted to make the Vatican's financial affairs 'clear and in the light of the sun'. Hitherto they had been one of the world's best kept secrets. No accounts were ever published and

3. The tangled web of financial double dealing is described in Rupert Cornwell's excellent book *God's Banker*.

once, when Marcinkus was asked for IOR's books, he is reputed to have thrown a dusty leather-bound volume on the table of the bank's office inside the Vatican and said, 'These are the only books.' At the very least Marcinkus stands convicted of incompetence and most organizations would have moved him out of the post after the Sindona débâcle. Pope John Paul II promoted him and, as Administrator of the Vatican state, he is still number three in the Vatican hierarchy. Despite warrants being issued for his arrest on two occasions he sweated it out and remained, astonishingly, in his post until 1989. Normally the Bank of Italy would have stepped in to help the creditors of a bank collapse, but in this case the IOR's letters of credit and its exemption from Italian jurisdiction made this impossible.

In 1984, the Vatican paid $244 million to the Ambrosiano creditors, but at the same time denied any wrongdoing on its part. It seemed a lot of money for an innocent party to pay and encouraged speculation as to whether the Vatican's sin was one of omission, or commission (in dollars). Senior Italian politicians called for the IOR to open a branch on Italian soil so that it would then be subject to Italian banking law, but it has so far refused to do so. A commission, appointed by the pope to look into the soaring cost of running the Vatican since the Second Vatican Council, was made public in 1987 and revealed a huge deficit. It showed that in 1986 Rome had an income of $57 million and expenses of $114 million. The biggest cost was $50 million to pay 2,315 employees. Vatican Radio and publishing accounted for another $21.5 million. Rome was able to cover the shortfall by using the $35 million from 'Peter's Pence', the annual collection taken in parishes around the world to support the papacy. A glaring omission from the report was any details about the investments save a figure of $29 million. No details were given about the holdings of the IOR. When a religious institution deals less straightforwardly than the disciples of Mammon, dumb silence becomes dumb arrogance.

The affair has had serious consequences for church/state relations. It acted as a catalyst for the Italian state to reach agreement over a new concordat with the Vatican which had been outstanding since the mid-1970s. The original church/state agreement was governed by the Lateran Agreements of 1929 and confirmed by the 1948 constitution. These incorporated a guarantee towards Rome as a city of religious significance, and buildings such as the Gregorian University which were outstanding Vatican territory had special protection and exemption from taxes. It was the sacral character of

Rome which enabled the authorities in 1965 to ban performances of Hochhut's play *The Representative* which portrayed Pope Pius XII as a collaborator with the Nazis.

Under the concordat, Italian clergy were paid a wage supplement in addition to their ecclesiastical allowance. But the most controversial clause was Article 34 concerning marriage, effectively the Eire situation. In 1970 civil divorce was introduced in Italy. The Roman Catholic Church broke off discussions on a new concordat and campaigned vigorously to have the law repealed in the 1974 referendum, but lost, even in staunch Catholic areas. Prior to the 1970 law, non-Catholics were unable to obtain annulments since these were the preserve of ecclesiastical courts. Protestant clergy were required to seek civil authority for all marriages they celebrated.

Religion has played a shadow role in Italian politics. Broadly speaking, the Christian Democrats are the party 'approved' by the church, and the growing communist party is regarded with hostility. But in the shifting sands of Italian coalition government, many deals are struck by the successors of Machiavelli and Medici.

When the new concordat emerged in February 1984, the repayment to the 120 Ambrosiano creditors was still outstanding (it was paid in May 1984). Undoubtedly the Italian government used the IOR affair to extract concessions from the Vatican. When the text was published, many of the Mussolini concessions had disappeared and safety fences on issues like divorce, contraception and abortion were missing, leaving room for increased secularization in the future. The requirement to teach the Catholic faith in schools was still there but in 1987 a row erupted when the Vatican accused the Italian state of weakening in its commitment by allowing those opting out to do so more easily at the beginning or end of the day's lesson. A compromise was negotiated by the Vatican Secretary of State Cardinal Casaroli, which left the actual timing of the weekly hour of religion to the discretion of headteachers.

Rome has always been a centre for the world church, but it is only in recent years that the curia has become more internationally based, and the style of the Vatican remains authoritarian. Its press office operates on the defensive principle and when Pope John Paul I was found dead in his room by a nun, the PR machine decided it would look bad and they invented a story that he had been found clutching a devotional book, thus, by failing to tell the truth, enabling all kinds of false rumours to be spread about assassination. The Vatican is the world's only church/state which is a state as well as a church. The head of state is believed by millions of Christians to be infallible in matters of dogma but has shown that in temporal matters the church is all too fallible.

FRANCE

One instance of a leading European nation which once had a concordat with Rome is France (population 55 million, of whom 80 per cent are baptised into the Roman Catholic Church). The concordat persists in the requirement that Rome must consult before appointing bishops, but for all other purposes, church and state have been separated since 1905. The exception is Alsace-Lorraine which formed part of the pre-war German kingdom and retains the system set up by Napoleon in 1801 in which clergy are civil servants paid by the state. A restructuring of the French Roman Catholic Church since the Second Vatican Council has made the church more responsive to the needs of the people, but the centuries of anti-clerical resentment focused by Richelieu-style prelates and fomented by Robespierre's successors have meant that the French church is not a people's church. The decline in church attendance is sharp, especially in the middle-age group and among young people. There are signs that a second stage of church/state relationship may develop with the church becoming more outspoken about government policy on nuclear issues.

SCANDINAVIA

An afternoon drive through Jutland on a particular Sunday in May will reveal an uncommon number of flags flying. There are Danish flags on every flagpole in the rural villages which occur every few miles as the long straight road unfolds across the flat countryside. Clumps of parked cars surround the restaurants and hotels from which the sound of singing can be heard. The Danes are celebrating 'confirmations day' when their adolescent sons and daughters are received into membership of the state Lutheran church.

The girls in white dresses and their families sit earnestly around the table taking turns to propose toasts which are washed down with aquavit/schnapps to cries of '*Skol!*' Song sheets are produced and ditties recalling the character of the neophyte are sung to traditional melodies. Sometimes the whole village will be there. The custom is that all those who give a confirmation day gift to the young boy or girl will be invited to the feast. In recent years, many Danish teenagers have been opting to spend their gift money on a holiday, but this folk custom is still widespread. It has Christianized the old fertility rites and illustrates the way that the state religions of Scandinavia are deeply ingrained in the folk memory and culture of their countries.

If Sweden is turned through 180 degrees on the map of Europe it stretches down to Italy. Yet climatically and ecclesiastically the two countries are very different indeed. Sweden, the dominant country in the Nordic alliance which also comprises Norway, Denmark and Finland, is Lutheran. It was Luther who coined the phrase, the 'powers that be are ordained of God' and Lutheranism has evolved a form of church/state bond which at first sight may resemble the Catholic concordats or the Orthodox Caesaro-papism, but is distinctively coloured by Nordic character.

Although it is not well known, Lutherans are the largest part of the Protestant confession with 69 million members worldwide. Although their numbers are declining in the heartland of Germany (see below p165), there are 9 million in the USA; and India, Brazil and Tanzania have a million each. They often prefer the title 'Evangelical' for their church since they do not venerate Luther as saint. Many of his writings were pessimistic and dictated by the feudalism of Christendom and do not reflect the character of the church which he founded, almost reluctantly. Lutheranism preserves the three-fold ministry (bishops, ministers and laity) but sees Christ as the central agent of salvation − not the church or its canons and traditions − reflecting the classic doctrine of 'Justification by faith alone'. Other doctrines such as 'the Word alone' emphasize the central place of the scriptures as a source of authority. 'Grace alone' and 'the Cross alone' express the idea that salvation comes not from good works but from God's grace bestowing it. The sacraments and the worship of the church (with liturgy playing an important role) are meaningful in that the church exists to proclaim the promise of salvation, and the ministry is a response to this need. Therefore Lutherans are not committed to any particular form of ministry, for example some churches have women priests. Sometimes criticized for allowing 'grace over works' to blind them to prophetic witness against the rulers with whom they have reached an accommodation, Lutherans point to the place given in their theology to Luther's doctrine of Christian vocation − that each believer within his work or role acts as Christian agent. Thus the state churches created by Lutheranism are pragmatic arrangements, not sacred systems which cannot permit alternatives.

For practical purposes, the Scandinavian model can be considered as a whole because of similarities between the systems: namely, the head of state (monarch in all but Finland) appoints bishops; the parliament regulates changes in church constitution and levies a tax to pay clergy and church expenses upon all citizens, who are therefore members of the state church from birth unless they choose to opt out. Although secularization is widespread and church attendance well below 10 per cent, over 90 per cent are members of the state churches. In all the countries there are proposals to loosen the church/state bond but owing to the close identification of the state churches with culture, 'folk religion' and rites of passage for the population, these changes have been in most cases shelved in the countless committees which make up the democratic/consensus politics of Scandinavia. For the record, the facts and figures are as follows:

DENMARK

Denmark (population 5.1 million) is 95.9 per cent nominally Christian with 4.7 million affiliated to the Lutheran Church of Denmark which became the state church in 1536 under King Christian III. (Catholicism was proscribed from 1569 until toleration in 1849.) No restrictions are placed on other religious confessions whose members can be buried in state cemeteries (1975 law). Taxes pay for clergy and the state church is responsible to parliament through a Kirkeminister, at present a smiling widow, called Mette Madsen who is a practising Christian and rules with a light touch.

FINLAND

Finland (population 4.7 million) was annexed to Sweden at the time of the Reformation and gradually followed King Gustavus Adolphus into accepting Lutheranism which remains the predominant affiliation (4.4 million). However, the Orthodox Church is also allowed to benefit from taxes as a 'state' church, but its 54,000 membership is gradually being eroded, both on inter-marriage with Lutherans and by dispersals following the annexation of Karelia by the USSR after the Second World War. Toleration is practised and other confessions can register and tax their members.

NORWAY

Norway (population 4.1 million, of which 3.7 million are members of the Church of Norway) introduced a state church system in 1537 when ruled by Denmark with the king as head of the church. On independence in 1814 the King of Norway was pledged to uphold the state religion, as were at least half the cabinet. In 1973 some controversy was occasioned when a Roman Catholic was elected President of the Commission for Religion and Education which was responsible for drawing up new canons for the state church. Norway is moving gradually to loosen the link. State funding for pastors of the Church of Norway only was extended by a law in 1969 which permitted other churches to receive state subsidy and children to follow automatically the religion of their parents (or their mother when illegitimate). This law also ensured complete freedom of religion provided believers did not enter a religious order before the age of twenty and belonged to only one religion at a time.

SWEDEN

Sweden (population 8.5 million) considers anyone born a Swedish citizen *de facto* a member of the Church of Sweden, i.e. without baptism. Since 1951, citizens may request to be released from membership and need only pay 40 per cent of the church tax levied to pay for the social services performed by the Church of Sweden. The King of Sweden is head of the state church but Swedes prefer to use the term '*folkskirche*'. In 1972 a commission which had been sitting since 1958 recommended disestablishment, but despite a majority of clergy in favour neither laity nor political parties were prepared to implement it. Pending reconsideration of the issue, state control has been loosened. Formerly, hymn and prayer books were authorized by parliament, now only the appointment of bishops and deans is done by the state and, in the case of bishops, they have only a choice of the top three names from a diocesan poll. The Synod of the Church of Sweden can overturn parliamentary rulings.

From 1604 to 1873 Roman Catholicism was proscribed and today the 'non-conformists' tend to be Evangelical or Pentecostal Protestants. These 'Free Churches' make up about 10 per cent of the population although nominally 95 per cent are still registered as Church of Sweden and 3 per cent of the population attend church. The only statistic which comes anywhere near confirming this high membership is the number of religious burial ceremonies. Baptisms run at around 70 per cent and confirmations 60 per cent of those eligible.

This somewhat anomalous gap between fact and faith in the

Lutheran Churches of Scandinavia and particularly that of Sweden does not dismay Dr Krister Stendahl, Bishop of Stockholm, whom I interviewed for this book. 'The Established Church is like a post office,' said the bishop. 'People don't rush to it when it opens, to show their support. They are just happy it's there. Our primate, Archbishop Soderblom, used to say, 'Remember there is always a supporter in the hearts of the people.'

Bishop Stendahl, who spent some years as a professor in the USA before returning to Sweden, supports the status quo on two grounds: first, the church acts as a custodian of the 'folk religion' which the average Swede finds necessary; second, the church system acts in a trustee role to promote moral issues such as aid to underdeveloped countries by the state.

Stendahl identifies two stages in the secularization of Sweden. The first came during the boom years of industrial prosperity between the 1940s and the 1960s when the social climate was consciously eroding the Christian hegemony. 'Morning devotions disappeared in the schools as a regular item and the social activities of the church were starved and transferred to the state. This was a time when old Christian values were violently done away with. People thought they knew what the church was and said "It's a private matter." There was a conscious line drawn between the Christian past and the present. People would say, "I'm not Christian but . . ." Then came the second stage of secularization which we are still in today. There is nothing to fight against. No memory of bad, arid devotions at school assembly. In the 1950s people showed glee at the church's failures. Now they show sadness. Arguments from tradition have very little force in Sweden and that makes each swing of the pendulum that much sharper. For instance, in the 1960s there was a lot of co-habitation – not because of promiscuity or lack of moral standards – but as a revulsion against the secular use of marriage, which was honoured in the breach. It had a moral motivation and now the number of marriages is going up. Even before AIDS, the trend had started.'

The bishop offered another example of how Swedes support their 'folk religion'. 'We are a shy country. The day after Olof Palme (Swedish premier) was assassinated Swedish television called me and said they didn't know how to end the day. These highly secular people grabbed the prayer I had intended sending out to churches. We gave these shy people a language. More of them pray than believe – because we have intellectualized belief. After the prayer, they came up and said "Thank you for that *poem*."

They knew it was a prayer. God knew it was a prayer. But what it was for them was a language.

'The second point is that there is a growing wish to see the church have an effective role. They see that role in terms of activity. They want to supply the church with resources to do a task. That is laid often on to the parish structure – where we have a trustee role. The largest budget is for the young and the old.'

The key to this influential role is the church tax and the motivation it provides for both church and state to stay wed to one another. The bishop admits that there are contradictions in a church which claims 95 per cent of the population as members and yet well below 10 per cent ever set foot in it. 'That is why the church/state issue usually comes down to the church tax and the old principle of "no taxation without representation". Sweden is the only country in the world where the parish council is elected along party-political lines. When I meet with the diocesan council they sit in party lines on either side of the table with the major party in the chair. Swedes tend to say, "How else could we do it?" '

Part of the reason that the secular Swedes have been so reluctant to do away with their system is that there is no great pressure for a pluralistic society. It boils down to the Lutherans plus a tiny minority. So their privileged position provides a ready-made matrix on which to dispense welfare on humanitarian terms.

The Church of Sweden has grown to like its new role and feels it is fulfilling a spiritual function. One could be cynical and say that it can also count on juicy stipends while the church tax is being collected. But there is some movement towards changing church tax to the German model, i.e. a voluntary tax easily collected with the aid of computers which can readily be extended to allow other religious confessions to share in the church/state wedding cake. Before assessing the justification of the church tax system, let us look at the two other areas of Europe in which it operates – West Germany and Switzerland.

WEST GERMANY

West Germany (population 62 million and 93 per cent nominally Christian) was a regrouping after the Second World War of provinces which had begun life as part of the Holy Roman Empire and divided on religious lines after the Reformation. The Peace of Westphalia in 1638 gave the princes the right to determine the religion of their subjects and thus the religious demography of Germany was a federation of small states espousing Protestantism or Catholicism. The partition of Germany in 1945 altered that mix slightly, so that West Germany now has an increased proportion of Catholics (44 per cent) to Protestants (47 per cent) than in the 1919 Weimar Republic. Its church/state provisions were more or less incorporated into the 1949 Constitution which guaranteed a 'free church in a free state'. There is no state religion, nor state department for religious affairs, but religion is taught in state schools and the churches are entities in public law and may levy taxes (*Kirchensteuer*) through the state apparatus which represents between 8 and 9 per cent of all revenue in the provinces. All taxpayers are liable to pay unless they register for exemption, and although the political forces of youth, liberalism, humanism and socialism are making an impact in deregistration, the main political parties and the churches (not surprisingly) are in favour of retaining it.

There is also a state fund for social work projects, administered by a board of six organizations on which the Catholic and main Protestant Church are represented. The Roman Catholic Church signed a concordat with Hitler's Third Reich in 1933 (which was held by a 1957 ruling to be constitutional) and which provides for the legal rights of bishoprics (some of which straddle the East/West border) and church independence from the state. The Protestant Church, which was divided in the 1930s over attitudes of collaboration or confrontation with the Nazis, tried after the war to forge a conglomerate church to heal the divisions of previous years. The Evangelische Kirche in Deutschland (EKD) is a grouping of twenty territorial churches (*Landeskirchen*), reduced to seventeen in 1977 which still remains more a federation of autonomous churches than a single church, although it is predominantly Lutheran in character. Regular church attendance can be as low as 6 per cent in the EKD but only 20 per cent of the population say they never attend and church weddings still account for 85 per cent of marriages.

German Catholics have taken a more progressive line on divorce and laity participation and this has led to tensions with Rome, as did the well-publicized removal of the licence of Professor Hans Küng of Tübingen to teach Roman Catholics. The problems of immigrant workers (the state is obliged by law to admit refugees) has created social tensions in West Germany but these immigrants are mostly Turkish Muslims and have not affected Protestant-Catholic co-operation in recent years. Both churches are rich because of the *Kirchensteuer* and can maintain huge administration apparatus and fund overseas and aid projects beyond the dreams of other non-state

aided churches in Europe – especially their estranged brethern in the
GDR across the West-East border. It would seem that the German
system gives the churches the best of all worlds – freedom from the
state, riches and influence based on a nominal membership of 92
per cent of the population. Some would argue that it is more likely
to breed complacency than converts, but there is little doubt that it
is a system which is the envy of many of the state churches of Europe.

SWITZERLAND

Switzerland has features of both the Roman and the Lutheran
systems. It is not so much one system as a diversity of church/state
concordats, contained within the borders of one of Europe's smallest
countries. Switzerland (population 6.7 million) is not so much a
country as a confederation of cantons, each with their own distinctive church/state bond. Many of them are built on the city state
model which the Swiss reformers (Calvin, Zwingli, Beza) promoted
in line with the idea of a 'City of God' as conceived by Augustine.
However, the different way in which the Swiss reformers developed
the idea points up the radical disjunction between Protestant and
Catholic theology on church/state matters which we have seen illustrated so far. The Catholic concordat countries were dealing with a
church which believed itself to be the sacred ordained repository of
salvation and therefore deserving of special privilege. The Protestant
countries saw the church as one institution among the organizing
forces of society which God had inspired and through which His
grace could act. Christian duty was seen in the wider context of
citizenship. This is the thinking behind church tax and it is worth
recording here the arguments for it used by Calvin:

> The Bible tells us of the existence of several sorts of offering
> in the Israelite religion. All serve to illustrate one of the aspects
> of this essential act by which the believer gives evidence of his
> consecration to God.
>   There is first the personal church tax. This tax, which is equal
> for all, is a reminder of the unmerited redemption of each one.
> In paying it, the believer acknowledges himself to be the object
> of the sovereign grace of God, to whom he owes his redemption
> without having earned it. God 'taxed them all for the same sum, so
> that from the greatest to the least, everyone of whatever estate or
> quality would know that he belonged entirely to Him. We should
> not be surprised at this. It was a matter of a personal right, as the

saying goes. Ability to pay was not taken into account, and the rich man did not pay more than the poor. The tribute was paid as an equal amount per head.' (Commentary on Moses, Exodus, 30:15.) 'We know that the law imposed on each of them a tax of a demi-stater a year, and that God, who had redeemed them, was their sovereign King.' (Commentary on the New Testament, Matthew, 17:24.)

This tribute was paid by Jesus Christ himself. He handed it over as a Roman coin, in order to declare to the Jews that they had been subjected to a foreign power because they had not availed themselves of the unmerited redemption offered to them. Though himself the King to whom every offering returns, Jesus submitted voluntarily to this tax in order to show his fellowship with the sinful people which he was freeing, and whose deliverance is symbolized by this coin. 'For it might seem absurd that Christ, who had come to be the Redeemer of the people, should not have been exempt from paying tribute. To get round the anomaly, he showed from Scripture and also proved by miracle that he was bound by nothing but his own will; because he who had dominion over the sea and its creatures could of course, if he had wanted, have exempted himself from subjection to earthly princes.[4]

Today both Catholic and Protestant churches benefit from the church tax which is differently determined in each canton but usually runs at about 8 per cent. Catholic strength was concentrated in the south and traditional Protestant ascendancy centred in the cities of Geneva, Basle, Bern and Zurich. But in recent years, the expatriate population has tipped the religious demography 53:43 in favour of Catholicism within the 97 per cent of the Swiss population which claims Christian affiliation. At the time of confirmation, state schools allow the pupils day release to receive the instruction which will make them adult members of their respective churches.

There are numerous anomalies in this small country which maintains neutrality but requires that its citizens bear arms; pays clergymen enviable salaries out of the taxes, but in some cities insists that the poor must have the price of a night's lodging in their pocket; and which is the cradle of Calvinism as well as the recruiting ground for the pope's bodyguard. To guide me through these complexities I sought the help of Professor Lukas Vischer of Bern, formerly General Secretary of the World Council of Churches in Geneva, and a leading

4. *Economic and Social Thought of Calvin* A Bieler, Geneva 1959 (pp. 359–60)

figure in the World Alliance of Reformed Churches. He told me:

The Reformation – especially Zwingli in Zurich – had the conception of reforming society also. That gave rise to our Christian city-states, but in 1874 when we adopted the new Confederation it didn't deal with the religious issue except to introduce clauses into the Constitution to ensure the confessional peace. That left the church/state laws at canton level and not at federal level and allowed each canton to keep its traditions. That explains the variety in Switzerland. Some pay their pastors (e.g. Vaud, Berne and Zurich) and are associated in the ordination service. In others (Geneva and Basel) there is separation of church and state. In Basel, taxes are collected by the church not the state, but in Geneva the state does the collecting as a service to the church and only Protestants pay. The state then publishes a list of those who have paid – but not how much they have paid, so you don't know if very rich people have paid half or less. In one canton in the north (Schaffhausen) there is church/state separation and no church tax, but all the monastery property at the Reformation was reserved for the church by the state which administers it but the income is used for church salaries, although this means that the number of clergy posts to be funded is frozen.

Professor Vischer distinguishes one facet of church/state interplay in Switzerland which has become increasingly important in recent years – the role of the church in establishing consensus in social issues:

The democratic self-understanding of the Swiss invaded the church. There was a strong emphasis on local autonomy. The political community equalled the church community, so the same people came together for two different activities and there was bound to be interpenetration. The consequence was that the average Swiss said that something would please God if it had been democratically agreed. Now that is changing. A debate which began back in the 1960s has sharpened into focus the question of whether there is church teaching which cannot be compromised with the democratic process. It began with the question of whether it was morally right to export arms and whether there was a right of conscientious objection to conscription (Swiss have to serve three weeks per year as conscripts until fifty or pay a higher tax in lieu). Then there was the more recent question of whether political refugees ought to be able to claim asylum in Switzerland (the Swiss have strict laws about residency which is not easily granted). In all three areas the church was on the losing side of the democratic vote (i.e. to allow the export of arms, outlaw conscientious objection and require the refugees to leave) and the assumption was that it would go along with the consensus. Three examples of non-conformity brought this issue to a head and represent an important juncture for church/state relations not only in Switzerland but in any society.

The first example was when Pastor Peter Wals of Zurich Seebach gave asylum to twenty expelled Chileans and received a vote of no confidence from his congregation for advocating illegal actions. Secondly in Berne, twenty Tamils were refused permission to stay by the federal authorities, so some congregations hid them with the tacit support of the Berne canton, precipitating a church/state conflict with the upshot that the pastors appeared in court and were admonished, while a doctor was sentenced to two months in prison. But the third, and most dramatic case, concerned the expulsion of Mathieu Musey, a member of the government-in-exile of Zaire, who was hidden by a Mennonite family in the Jura Mountains before being discovered and sent by a chartered aircraft to Zaire. All this caused the Swiss churches to reflect on their right to dissent within a democratic state. Normally that moral right of resistance is only invoked in repressive countries, but that can't apply to Switzerland where the government has a mandate to do these things.

This led to a movement in Switzerland to desist from paying the church tax in protest against the church dissent. In the mid-1980s there was a referendum promoted by militant secularists to separate church and state which was defeated by a three to two majority. Many people interpreted this as solid support for the church. But Lukas Vischer points out that many votes came from those who voted for the churches to remain as cantonal bodies and who resented a federal solution being imposed. Thus the position may not be as secure as the churches would like to think. In Basel canton there are now about equal proportions of Protestants, Catholics and Secularists. This has alarmed church leaders who see their base dwindling. If believers were to fall to such a low proportion that the church tax was no longer justifiable, it would be like taking an already severely ill patient off a life-support machine. The church-tax nations of Europe fear the necessity of relying on income from voluntary givings since it would make them dependent on the combined will of those who pay. That, they say, can be more stifling than establishment when it comes to championing the rights of the underdog who may not be popular with the bourgeois church members who pay the organist and call the hymn tune. The state's money is more anonymous and enables them to be more independent to fulfil the role demanded of its pastors in Berne 'to combat all social evils and denounce their cause'.

The Swiss examples of dissent against the state laws cited by Dr Vischer can be paralleled in other European countries where some churches are calling for civil disobedience and non-payment of taxes over issues such as nuclear weapons. But where does it stop? Do we have a right to desist from paying our television licence if the programmes disgust us morally? Lukas Vischer has given much thought to the way in which church/state issues will develop and argues that attention ought to be devoted to the way in which power is exerted in a society rather than concentrate on the church/state interface:

> The political authority is only one among many powers. Large areas of decision-making are not touched by politics. I think it is exceedingly important to maintain the integrity of democratic decision-making – I'm not in agreement with certain leftist groups who call into question its effectiveness – but if the churches want to take a moral stand on issues then they have to deal with other powers. For example, here in Switzerland on the question of sanctions against South Africa, it's clear that the government doesn't want sanctions and has vested interests. So it is with the bankers that we must deal. Industrial power tries to escape from the debate by hiding behind the result of the democratic debate, but the church must confront it. So far we are not yet up to it. Another example is in Brazil where the government has not proved itself capable of dealing with the vested interests of the landowners and the military, or in Columbia where the cocaine mafia are known by name but where law and politics has failed to control them.

If churches develop as prophet/priest not only to kings and premiers but to presidents of multinationals and international financiers, then church/state models will have to develop with this. The multinational corporation poses a new kind of Caesar which cannot so easily be dealt with by national churches. Roman Catholicism is better equipped for this task, where the worldwide nature of the church is taken for granted. It has greater independence because it can always refer to an authority outside the national boundary. It is also less affected by the gains and losses of establishment or disestablishment because the point of reference is outside the nation state. So far the Protestant Churches have not given juridicial expression to their worldwide *oikumene*. Ecumenical bodies like the World Alliance of Reformed Churches are amorphous and the World Council of Churches too diverse to provide the vehicle for this process. Lukas Vischer is convinced that the future role of the church will be by identification with alternative movements:

> I have more and more the impression that Western Europe fosters an ideology of technological prowess. All developments are measured by this. Can we go on with economic growth – and how? People are preoccupied with where money goes for research and only afterwards do the religious questions come up. But the church has a strong element of identification with international conservation groups, Third World movements, peace and ecology campaigns. The church then becomes the place where alternatives are being discussed. I see the possibility that the alternative movements begin to organize internationally and create a forum that states have to deal with. The point of this would be that technological developments are also international and the organization can provide the shadow for these. In Eastern Europe the church has become the focus of non-political dissent. In Western Europe it is the focus of alternative movements.

Professor Vischer cites the example of the black-market in plutonium which was spotted and challenged in the home countries of the companies which were contributing to it, by threatening them with exposure, boycotts, shareholder challenges etc. It was lobbying of the sort that organizations like Friends of the Earth and Greenpeace have also adopted. But if churches are to become the Ecology Party at prayer and forsake their established role within states in which religious profession is increasingly nominal, then it surely spells the collapse of the traditional church/state concordats, to say nothing of church tax. The historical cycle that began with Constantine and reached its zenith in the medieval popes and theocracies of the Reformation will have come full circle and returned Christianity to its initial role as a minority faith, wondering whether to render respect or rebuke to Caesar.

7 The Naked Empress: England

There is an England where bees hum through English country gardens, where apple trees lean down low in Linden Lea, where ladies in twin-sets and pearls have tea and crumpets in the afternoon, while through the french windows looking on to the lawn wafts the sound of choral evensong from a cathedral whose spire is framed against an autumn sky scattered with starlings startled into flight by a ploughman wearily plodding his homeward way . . .

More accurately there *was* such an England. Preserved in the Barchester Chronicles, perhaps it still exists in the minds of those who listen to choral evensong on Radio Three in the afternoons, but otherwise it lies buried with Rupert Brooke in some corner of a foreign field which does not have sight of modern England. Today, the starlings have settled in the hot-air ducts of a concrete-and-glass office block. The skyline is punctuated not by cathedral spires but by pylons. The homeward-bound ploughman roars his tractor across the flyover linking two fields bisected by a motorway and the twin-set ladies are drinking instant coffee.

Such changes in the landscape and culture of England have occurred in the half-century since the day war broke out, and are as profound as any previous reformation. Immigrations have changed the character of London and England. A new generation of citizens has arrived whose cultural and religious heritage has no connection with Constable and Tallis, Becket and Gore. The Indians, Pakistanis, Greeks, Chinese and Afro-Caribbeans are as British as the man on the Clapham omnibus (one of them is likely to be driving it). But they have nothing in common with the religious heritage of England.

Another force undermining the national religion is secularization, which television has accelerated and promoted just as the newly invented printing press spread the Reformation in the 1520s faster than a preacher on horseback could ride the country. The average Englishman, who was not excessively religious, but was quite happy to have his religion put down as 'C of E' on conscription forms and toddle along to church for the great family festivals, is now not bothering. There are plenty of counter-attractions, and if he went to church he would feel uncomfortable and alien. Toleration has given way to apathy. Nothing so spiteful as rejection of the church, just complete ignorance of it. At the upper-middle end of the class system which has maintained continuity with England's feudal past, there is no longer the need to keep up appearances. The weary commuter who has to rise at six or seven during the week and returns home twelve hours later, is too exhausted on Sundays to go rushing off to church. His faith is not that frenetic. His children watch a video. His wife prepares Sunday lunch for the family while he washes the car and repairs to the pub.

It is hardly the picture of a religious revolution but its effect has been as devastating. On the twin horns of multi-culturalism and secularism, the Church of England has been gored and is slowly bleeding to death. Several factors have prevented the terminal condition of the established church being seen as a crisis. The first is the effort by Anglican churchmen to make their church relevant to the social problems of Britain, particularly among the disadvantaged, and to provide a bridge to the immigrant communities. Coupled with this is the laid-back way in which matters theological are treated in England. Vicars may make the headlines for running off with page-three girls or for making political statements from the pulpit, but when it comes to the decline of faith, bad news is no news. Another reason for complacency is the comforting fact that unless the constitutional position is threatened, the status quo will prevail and the vast investments of the Church of England in property and shares will prevent the decline from developing into a financial crisis. Thus in many of the other countries considered in this book, a combination of conservatism and complacency results in the Established Church of England retaining its position with regard to the state.

But England is different. In the Catholic concordat countries, or in Scandinavia where there are constitutionally established churches, one church is predominant and is democratically unchallenged as the national church. (In Germany and Switzerland, where there are mixed nations with no church predominant, tax revenue is distributed to the churches on the basis of their membership strength or by devolving 'establishment' to different churches in different cantons.) History and statistics decide the matter beyond dispute. In England it is different. As part of the United Kingdom of Great Britain and Northern Ireland, the Established Church of England is effectively the national church of Britain, yet historically and statistically that situation cannot be justified. Before looking at the historical aspect it is worth investigating the bare bones of the skeleton that is left of the Established Church of England. Examining separately the nations within the UK, membership of a church among the population in 1985 was as follows: England 13 per cent; Wales 23 per cent; Scotland 37 per cent; Northern Ireland 80 per cent.

Between 1970 and 1985 there was a 20 per cent decline in the membership of the Church of England, leaving it with 39 per cent of the church members in England compared with 33 per cent owing allegiance to the Roman Catholic Church and 10 per cent to the Methodist Church. When you add the Presbyterians and Baptists (3 per cent each) and the 12 per cent figure for Protestant Church members who are not in one of the above categories (mainly accounted for by the rapid growth of groups who gather to pray in their homes and often called the house church movement), then the minority position of the Church of England becomes abundantly clear. Less than 8 per cent of the population of the United Kingdom (4.5 million out of 56.5 million) is a member of the Church of England and when it is considered that not all members attend church (only two-thirds, according to the survey), then the weak mandate of the Church of England in the UK context is made clear. Of course there are millions more who were baptised into the C of E and have never darkened its portals since then. Because they have opted out of it, they cannot be counted in any way towards statistics in its favour when it comes to a choice of options for a national church.

Furthermore, the high figures for belief in God which tend to appear in polls on religious belief (usually around 80 per cent profess to believe in God, with 70 per cent believing in Jesus Christ) cannot be interpreted as positive support for the Church of England, since they indicate preference for church expression of faith rather than an ecclesiastical one. In the above paragraph, I have taken all British statistics from the UK *Christian Handbook* published by MARC. Other figures used throughout the book are, unless otherwise stated, from David Barrett's *World Christian Encyclopaedia*. Its figures tend to be higher because it includes nominal Christians in the figures for churches. When there is one church which predominates in a country this is a useful broad brush approach, but where there are several Christian traditions it is more accurate to determine actual involvement, i.e. membership.

I wish to argue that the established status of the Church of England is an anachronism and that the claim to be Britannia of the churches of the United Kingdom is statistically threadbare. She is an Empress without clothes. But for all kinds of reasons – some respectable – there has long been a tacit acceptance of Anglican supremacy.

A number of factors, not least the safeguarding of the future of Christian influence, demand a re-assessment of the role of the Established Church in national life. A Gallup survey at the end of October 1984 found public opinion three to one in favour of ending parliament's 'final say' over church affairs. In the poll, 23 per cent were in favour of parliament's veto continuing, 64 per cent against. Among regular Anglican churchgoers it was 29 per cent to 66 per cent. (*The Times*, 6 December 1984).

There is a certain irony in the fact that the Church of England came into being as a result of King Henry VIII's requiring a divorce, when to this day it will not marry divorcees in church nor permit divorcees to be clergymen. Until Henry's Supremacy Act of 1534, which made him head of the church and repudiated the authority of the pope, England had been a thoroughly Christian country. Having pushed back the dominant Celtic Church influence in the seventh century, England was a loyal province of Rome in the era of the crusades, and in 1154 even produced a pope (Hadrian IV). In the Middle Ages, it produced John Wyclif who espoused ideas about the authority of Scripture over church canons more than a century before such concepts were to divide Europe in the Reformation and symbolized a free-thinking tradition in theological scholarship which, in more recent years, has produced John Robinson, Don Cupitt and David Jenkins. Following in the Lollard tradition, at the time of the English Reformation in 1534, Bibles in English were placed in every church, and a century later the King James (authorized version) Bible was to become the touchstone of translations throughout the English speaking world, and exercise profound influence on its language and culture.

When the British Empire came into being, the Anglican Church became a worldwide communion of 60 million believers which, although self-governing in most countries, has spread the influence of the Church of England far beyond its own shores to a total of twenty-seven branches in 164 countries. At the Lambeth Conference held each decade, simultaneous translation is now provided in

French, Spanish, Japanese and Swahili. The British Constitution has never been formulated as a single written document, but the bond of the Church of England with the Crown and parliament of England is clearly spelt out, first by the Acts of 1532 and 1534 which separated the church from Rome and put it under the governorship of the Sovereign under God. For a few years the Catholic Queen, Mary Tudor, reversed this, but in 1558 the Act of Supremacy passed by Elizabeth reaffirmed it. Elizabeth also confirmed in 1563 articles of faith (originally set out by Cranmer under Henry VII to check the growth of Reformed Church theology and practice and which evolved into the Thirty-Nine Articles) which became the document governing church doctrine and practice. They chiefly cover scriptural authority (declaring this to be greater than church tradition or canon); the triune nature of God; salvation; and the church's sacraments and ministry. They are not so much a midway position between Rome and Geneva as an English answer to Roman and Anabaptist excesses. Elizabeth added an opening clause to Article Twenty which declared the church's authority to decree rites and ceremonies, but the interesting difference between the English and the continental Reformation models was that in England the monarch was laying down the doctrinal charter for the church.

This was something Cromwell never dared to do. It was the Stuart kings who, claiming their divine right to pronounce like a medieval pope, foisted their opinions upon the church: Charles I through his Anglo-Catholic Archbishop Laud and then Charles II, who introduced the other standard of C of E orthodoxy, the 1662 Prayer Book, under the Act of Uniformity. Since that day the Church of England has never been able to lay claim to the popular allegiance of the people. Ironically it might have done had history been kinder to the much-maligned Oliver Cromwell. Although an authoritarian, he did not try to enforce one 'true' church on the people. Religious principles dominated his thinking, including the notion of Providence and the vision of Moses leading his people to liberation in a Godly commonwealth. He did not want to change society so much as change the men within it and was willing to subordinate human liberties to further this vision. 'Government is for people's good – not what pleases them,' he said, and likened the Protectorate to a period of initiation. 'You are a people under circumcision – raw!' He believed God wanted the Crown overthrown ('I would not build Jericho again!'), yet he might have granted more liberties to the church had he accepted it. As it was, the return of the Stuarts in 1660 meant that while religion remained a significant force in

English life, the attempts to build Jerusalem never recurred. The king was both emperor and pope.

Parliament became the effective arbiter of Church of England doctrine, although since 1965 the church may authorize services which do not conform to the 1662 pattern. Through the Submission of the Clergy Act of 1533, the ancient Convocations of Canterbury and York received permission to pass canons, subject to certain restrictions. Then in 1919 the newly created Church Assembly was given the power to pass and amend measures having the force of Acts of Parliament, but these still had to go to parliament for a simple yes/no assent and still required the royal assent. In 1969 the General Synod was brought into being. It superseded the Convocations and the Assembly in dealing with measures and canons but its decisions still require parliamentary assent. The General Synod is modelled on parliament and has three Houses (Bishops, Clergy and Laity). A 'no' vote in any one of these three can block major proposals, which require the assent of all three Houses.

In 1533 the Appointment of Bishops Act gave the sovereign power to choose bishops after consultation with the prime minister and the church. In 1974 the Church of England moved for a greater say in this matter and in 1977 the Crown Appointments Commission came into being. It consists of six elected members from the General Synod (three clergy, three lay), four members elected by the vacant diocese, the two archbishops (York and Canterbury) and the appointment secretaries of both the prime minister and the Archbishop of Canterbury. All members can submit (anonymously) suggestions which fall into two categories: mandatory (which must be considered by all) and discretionary (only if deemed appropriate by the secretary). After a secret ballot, two names are submitted in order of precedence to the prime minister who is expected to choose the first. However, despite this complicated procedure, it is widely believed that twice during the first decade of Mrs Thatcher's premiership she has opted for the second names because those names were more to her taste.[1] Thus it would be inaccurate to say that the process has effectively devolved the choice of bishops to the church itself.

The Church of England has been good at producing prophets. Some, like Wyclif, were before their time. It could not contain

1. The instances are: London (when Graham Leonard was preferred to John Habgood), and Birmingham (when allegedly the leftist Bishop of Stepney, Jim Thompson, was passed over for the Bishop of Kensington, Mark Santer).

the Quaker George Fox or the eighteenth century, non-conformist, revivalist Wesleys, and these were forced to found their own denominations which also spread worldwide through the English colonies. Others, like John Henry Newman, went over to Rome. But the 'broad church' has always been a feature of Anglican spirituality and this has held together a spectrum of churchmanship from the low Church, sometimes called Conservative Evangelical, which favours simplicity of ritual and scriptural emphasis, to the High Church or Anglo-Catholic wing, which stresses sacraments and ritual and favours unity with Roman Catholicism. In a poll of church members taken in 1970, 14 per cent said they were High Church, 70 per cent Low or Broad Church and 16 per cent of no particular view. The epitome of this attitude is expressed by the character Coggan (not the former primate) in Hardy's *Far From the Madding Crowd* who declares, 'There's this to be said for the Church [of England]: a man can belong to the Church and bide in his cheerful old inn, and never trouble or worry his mind about doctrine at all.' The shadow side of this live-and-let-live attitude is that the Anglican Church has always been dogged by the problem of authority. Unlike Rome, it does not have an infallible primate.

The role of the Archbishop of Canterbury is a dual one. He is the Archbishop of the See of Canterbury in Kent, and Primate of All England and lives in Lambeth Palace on the Thames in London. But he is also leader of the world's 65 million Anglicans, a body as wide as the C of E is broad. Since 1980 the primate who has presided over a period of church/state tension has been Dr Robert Runcie, a tall ex-Guards officer who earned the nickname 'Killer Runcie' as a tank commander in the war, but whose manner on first meeting can give the impression of feyness. He was expected to be the friend of the Anglo-Catholics but has resolutely maintained a middle stance, particularly on the question of women's ordination, claiming to be in favour in principle but urging delay in implementation. It brought the jibe of 'nailing his colours to the fence' in the infamous and anonymous preface to *Crockford's Clerical Directory*, whose author Canon Gareth Bennett (an Oxford don who later committed suicide when his identity was discovered) expressed the bitterness of the Anglo-Catholics in accusations that the primate picked appointments with 'élitist liberal' thinkalikes of the trendy left. That picture of Dr Runcie which was echoed by the right-wing tabloid the *Sun* as the 'Archwimp of Canterbury' contrasts vividly with Runcie's high standing in the Anglican communion. But in settling questions of authority, the Anglican communion does not have a hierarchical pyramid. As the 1988 Lambeth Conference showed, there are wide differences between its members. With classic Anglican compromise, resolutions were reached in 1988 which allowed converts in polygamous societies to keep their extra wives if they forswore further marriages and expressed understanding as to why some movements chose the armed struggle to achieve justice (South Africa), while condemning Irish terrorism. However it was on the subject of sex that the gulfs opened up between the liberal Americans (who tolerate divorce among the clergy as well as homosexual lifestyles) and the more conservative Africans. Opinion was deeply divided, too, on the question of the ordination of women. Although free to practise in their own provinces, Anglican women priests are debarred from celebrating the Eucharist in England. The USA, Canada and New Zealand had ordained 1,257 women by 1988 while Mother Church in England is still waiting to make up her mind. That simple fact shows that in many ways the Anglican communion is federal and autocephalous since even when it comes to church/state arrangements these churches and the Church of England go their separate ways, without reference to one another. The insularity of the C of E in relation to its daughter churches was brought home to me during the 1986 debate in the General Synod on the ordination of women when the principle was discussed in detail. Those against said it was 'impossible', and that it would destroy the church. Not one speaker – even those in favour – drew upon the evidence and experience of those parts of the Anglican communion that had implemented the measure years previously.

The Anglican churches have no constitutional or canonical authority one over the other, so it is misleading to consider that disestablishment in England would affect the wider Anglican communion or authority within it.

When it comes to doctrine, the C of E tolerates amazing latitude in its priests. Although technically bound at ordination to the somewhat anachronistic and intolerant formulations of the Thirty-Nine Articles, Church of England clergyman now have a get-out clause, thanks to a form of assent introduced in 1975 to replace the 1865 version. Now they simply have to promise to 'declare my belief in the faith which is revealed in the Holy Scriptures and set forth in the catholic creeds and to which the historic formularies of the Church of England bear witness; and in public prayer and sacraments I will use only the forms of service which are authorized or allowed by Canon.' The words *'bear witness'* are a looser form, and the Thirty-Nine Articles need not have the same hold over today's priest, but the parliament-authorized canons are still the rules to which he must adhere. Although in 1965 it became lawful for vicars to use alternative services which have been prepared by the church, previously uniformity of worship was the unifying factor in the C of E which replaced a doctrinal standard. That is the view of Professor Stephen Sykes who contends that reports of Doctrine Commissions have more often dealt with doctrine *in* the Church of England, not doctrine *of* that church.[2] Sykes argues for a more explicit version of what the Church of England believes, which could then be subject to constructive debate. He wrote before David Jenkins, the newly appointed Bishop of Durham, opened a Pandora's box of conflicts on Virgin Birth and Resurrection in 1984, which brought into focus the wide diversity of thinking on these matters within the C of E. Less well known but rather more radical than Dr Jenkins is Rev Don Cupitt, Dean of Emmanuel College, Cambridge. Jenkins typifies the Anglican who is happy to repudiate doctrines about the Deity which many would claim are central and essential, but regards the liturgy of his church as an icon which renders some meaning to existence.

The net result of such controversies has been to convey the image of a church which is uncertain about its beliefs. Although this is unfair to the intentions and opinions of both David Jenkins and Rev Don Cupitt, it points up the difficulty of reconciling beliefs when it is not the church itself but parliament which is the ultimate arbiter. When there is so much fluidity and disparity among bishops on doctrinal matters and because consensus is difficult to achieve in the present climate, it would be a bold person who would advocate that the Church of England should have as arbiters those who are positively hostile to its professed faith.

The irreconcilable differences within the C of E over doctrine are nowhere more vehemently expressed than in the debate over the issue of the ordination of women to the priesthood. Those who argue, like the Bishop of London, that the church is bound to the conception of priesthood exemplified by Christ not only in his manhood but in his deliberate choice of male disciples, are threatening schism over the issue. Others who do not see the church as bound to the culture of past ages and feel acutely the injustice of excluding women from a central part of ministry are probably in the majority, but will most certainly be stymied by the voting procedures in the General Synod (which will require a two-thirds majority in favour in all three Houses for the measure to be passed). Even if it is passed, then, faced with the

2. *The Integrity of Anglicanism*, Mowbrays 1978.

threat of schism, parliament might delay implementation in order to avoid responsibility for such a consequence. That would spark off a serious escalation of the church/state hostility which has been smouldering throughout Mrs Thatcher's decade as prime minister.

The conflict has been gleefully monitored by the press. The major milestones are probably 'The Church and the Bomb' report in 1982 which recommended a phased unilateralism which was contrary to government policy; the 1984 Falklands War Thanksgiving Service in St Paul's Cathedral at which the Archbishop of Canterbury's sermon was said to have annoyed Mrs Thatcher by its apologetic tone; the 1985 attacks by the Bishop of Durham on government economic policies which led to such severe poverty that one family in Sunderland was sharing a pair of shoes; the 1985 report 'Faith in the City' which criticized government neglect of the human problems of inner cities. There have also been outspoken attacks by C of E clergy and critical reports from the British Council of Churches on government immigration policy. The Home Secretary, Mr Douglas Hurd, tried to repair some of the broken bridges when he addressed a fringe meeting of the General Synod in February 1988 at which he said, 'I believe that the government should welcome the church as a partner in our efforts to lift the cloud of discouragement which has settled over parts of our society – especially in the inner cities.' Unfortunately for the Home Secretary, remarks he made to a meeting of the Peel Society at Tamworth the same month about churchmen dabbling in politics gained a wider currency and an accusation from the Church of Scotland's Moderator of the General Assembly, Dr Duncan Shaw, that Mr Hurd was 'conspicuously ignorant about theology and was treating the churches like punchbags . . . while ethics are conspicuously absent from government policies.' The C of E leadership kept quiet during that exchange, but the incident showed how far relations had deteriorated.

Amid all the brouhaha, the significance of the closing sentences of Mr Hurd's speech to the Synod may not have got the attention it deserved:

We need to work together in church and state, to rebuild the moral standards and values which should form the sure foundations of a cohesive and united nation. We shall sometimes differ on individual issues ... but if we are to restore cohesion and acceptable standards of behaviour we need to look to the churches – and here I include religious leaders of other faiths in Britain – to speak and insist and insist again on the individual standards which are the foundations of a healthy society.[3]

There is nothing here that suggests a special or exclusive relationship between the Church of England – which Mr Hurd was addressing – and the state. Indeed it specifically includes the role of other religious leaders. What must have occurred to the most vehement free-marketeers within the Conservative Party is that after selling off the large and unprofitable nationalized industries, could the state not privatize religion? At a stroke Mrs Thatcher could rid herself of the established platform upon which stood the church, berating her performance.

The three pegs upon which establishment still hangs are the appointment of bishops, parliamentary oversight of the Prayer Book; and the position of the sovereign. The sovereign has retained Henry's imperial authority over the Church of England, despite two fundamental changes in the British constitution. The Union of the Crowns in 1603 brought Scotland into the British monarchy with a quite different form of established church, and the 1688 Revolution Settlement disposed of pretensions to a 'divine right' residing in the monarch. However, one consequence of the latter was to block Roman Catholic participation in affairs of state. The Act of Succession forbids anyone with a claim to the throne embracing the Catholic faith – a logical move perhaps when the monarch is head of the Church of England, but one no longer defensible in a liberal democracy. The matter is further complicated by the difficulties which would attend a 'mixed marriage' by an heir to the throne and which were discussed when Prince Charles was rumoured to be about to marry Princess Marie Astrid of Luxembourg. The attitude of the Roman Catholic Church is not helpful either, as was shown when Prince Michael of Kent married the divorcée Baroness Von Reibnitz (now Princess Michael). Apart from bigots or historical pedants with romantic leanings, few would insist that the beliefs of the Royal Family be prescribed by law. In other words, whether or not the Church of England remains the national church of England, it is necessary to remove the shackles of headship from the sovereign.

This would have immediate consequences for the coronation ceremony. The awesome splendour of this event in 1953 in which Queen Elizabeth II of England and I of Scotland was anointed and invested with orb and sceptre, and the impeccable Christian life

3. Mr Douglas Hurd, Home Secretary, 10 February 1988,

and witness of the present Royal Family, should not deflect us from the fact that their descendants might profess no faith at all. This would create not so much a constitutional crisis as an absurd situation which ought to be anticipated if at all possible. There is no reason why the senior clergyman of Britain's churches (the Archbishop of Canterbury) should not bless and pray for the new sovereign and, on behalf of parliament, administer such oaths as may be appropriate, but forgo installing the monarch as head of the Church of England and omit promises which are offensive to Roman Catholics.

The 1688 Bill of Rights 'preserved the king's person by disabling papists from sitting in either House of parliament'. Catholic Emancipation was not granted until 1829 and the influx of Irish Catholics in the last century benefited from this extension of suffrage. But one Act which has gone unrepealed is the 1801 Disqualification of the Clergy Act which debars clergymen of the Roman Catholic Church, Orthodox Church, and Churches of England and Scotland, from becoming parliamentary candidates. The 1801 Act came about as a check against undue representation by the C of E in the legislature since, in addition to the entitlement of the twenty-seven senior bishops to sit in the House of Lords, the Convocations of York and Canterbury were entitled to seats in parliament. Before we come to the House of Lords/bishops issue, let us look at the anomalies of this situation. Rev Ian Paisley can sit in parliament as can Jewish rabbis, but Roman Catholic priests and Church of Scotland ministers cannot. Methodists, Sikhs and Rastafarian ministers can, but vicars cannot. Yet all those prohibited can become regional or district councillors, or members of the European parliament. They cannot wait until the result of their parliamentary election before resigning their ordained status, since their candidature would be null and void. An attempt by the Archdeacon of Derby to get the General Synod to debate the matter failed. Coupled with the necessity of getting majorities in all three Houses and then depending on the government to introduce a Bill on the matter, there is not much chance of this anachronistic law being changed, except in the wake of a wholesale disestablishment measure.

The House of Lords is another matter. In 1970 the Church and State Commission of the General Synod recommended that, on the whole, establishment was a good thing but that perhaps other denominations might be given representation in the House of Lords. (The Reverend Lords Macleod and Soper, Church of Scotland and Methodist respectively, are there personally not *ex officio*.) This idea might seem appealing, but unless it were accompanied by full-scale reform of the second chamber, it is simply introducing a few new deckchairs to the promenade deck of the *Titanic*. If liberation theology, ecumenism, involvement of the laity and democracy have taught us anything, it is that popping a few hierarchical heads on committees is not the way to promote constructive change and release the Christian Church for its most creative and healing role in society.

When the disestablishment of the church in Wales (Anglican in a predominantly nonconformist country) was debated in 1913, the then Archbishop of Canterbury, Cosmo Lang (who established a rare record by having a brother who was Moderator of the General Assembly of the Church of Scotland), defended the establishment of the C of E in a much-quoted speech in the House of Lords. Arguing that there is a subconscious continuity in matters spiritual he held:

> The question before us is whether just there in that inward region of the national life where anything that can be called its unity and character is expressed, there is not to be this witness to some ultimate sanction to which the nation looks, some ultimate ideal it proposes. It is in our judgement a very serious thing for a state to take out of that corporate heart of its life any acknowledgement at all of its concern with religion.

The present Archbishop of York, Dr John Hapgood, in *Church and Nation in a Secular Age*[4] echoes that case for the continuance of an established church for the sake of the nation. It is a plea that relies on the idea that the church must be engaged on a horizontal as well as a vertical dimension, giving glory to God in the High Street as well as on the highest altar. The great English churchman, Archbishop William Temple, was in favour of disestablishment in 1913, but had reversed his views by 1941 when he wrote *Citizen and Churchman*. Seeing the church as not only having a social and humanitarian role to play, he believed that it had also to provide a reconciling role within the state – and this was brought home acutely by the need to preserve unity between Christians at a time when some of them took a pacifist view of the Second World War. Temple also wrote, 'The office of the state is to give effect to public opinion; the office of the church is to mould it.'

4.   Darban, Longman and Todd 1990.

Those who claim that there is 'in this country a general, diffused, inarticulate assent to Christianity as an ideal in the body of the nation ... on the whole the British people like it to be so'[5] are probably correct. But when they extend this folk-faith into an argument for the establishment of the Church of England, their logic fails to match their impeccable academic credentials. One such is the now retired Bishop of Birmingham, Dr Hugh Montefiore, who contends that the essential English character is Church of England, a statement which, when made by someone with experience of the pluralistic city of Birmingham, can only rank as paternalistic. The matter is better stated by the new Bishop of Birmingham, Mark Santer, when he writes, 'The worst thing about the special status of the Church of England is the corruption of spirit that it encourages. We collude implicitly with the notion that 'Anglican' equals 'really English', thereby reducing our fellow Christians to the status of inferior citizens. We may not feel it; they do.'[6]

An example of this élitist attitude is certainly found within the Royal Navy Chaplains Section. Although there is no rank for chaplains (they may adopt the rank of the person they are addressing, but are paid as lieutenants) there are denominational categories: Roman Catholic; Free Churches/Church of Scotland; and the Chaplain, who is Church of England. Six destroyers may go on patrol and may request a chaplain. The non-Anglicans may only go if there is already an Anglican chaplain on board. The argument for this is that while the Anglican may admit nonconformists to his Eucharist, their Eucharist is not valid for his flock and they are barred from the Roman Eucharist anyway. Thus the non-Anglicans in the Navy are, in that maritime term, supernumerary.

Many Royal Navy Anglican chaplains belong to the Anglo-Catholic wing of the C of E and enjoy all that establishment entails. They like the 1662 Prayer Book and so are not bothered about needing parliamentary approval to change it, since they would not wish to do so. They would, however, like some form of rapprochement with Rome and take the line that going ahead with the ordination of women would 'seriously damage the good relationship between the Vatican and the Church of England' as Britain's Ambassador to the Holy See, Wykehamist John Broadley, told an English Catholic reporter in August 1988. The Anglo-Catholic wing of the C of E was responsible for sinking the unity covenant between

5. Rev Professor Owen Chadwick.
6. *The Church and the State*, Hodder 1983, p 41.

the C of E and the United Reformed Church and Methodists, after the latter had agreed to the introduction of episcopacy. This unity would have created a national church with a much broader Protestant base. In rejecting it the Anglo-Catholics were simply exercising their right, but only as a denomination and not as people who aspire to be trustees of the 'folk faith' of England. Their ability to face both Rome and Canterbury while assuming a haughty profile to the humble citizenry makes them more like the Church of Janus Christ, than of Jesus Christ.

The patrician Dr Edward Norman, Dean of Peterhouse, takes the acerbic view that the Church of England has already discstablished itself by its willingness to indulge in ecumenical discussions at all. His view of the role of the C of E in relation to other churches seems to make it similar to the Royal Mail allowing other mail firms to share its facilities. But as always the shrewd Dr Norman has a point – albeit one he has stretched. The C of E does have the right under the 1944 Education Act to sit on the committees which determine the syllabus in religious education at local level in state schools. The same Act prescribes a collective act of worship (in 1944 it was taken for granted this would be Christian and so it was not made explicit). Yet the woeful condition of religious education in state schools has been the subject of much debate in recent years. In a report by the Educational Research Trust in 1988 Baroness Cox wrote in the foreword:

> As a nation we are in danger of selling our spiritual birthright for a mess of secular pottage. Many of our children are in schools where they are denied the experience of religious worship at all and where teaching about Christianity has either been diluted to multi-faith relativism or has become little more than a secularized discussion of social and political issues ... It is ironic that in one Church of England voluntary controlled school, no Christian act of worship was provided for any of the pupils. How has the Anglican Church allowed such a situation to develop?

How indeed, if it has not abrogated its responsibilities, Baroness Cox and those of like mind gained support from the conservative Bishop of London in the Lords for their attempts to strengthen the provision for Christianity within the Education Act, eliciting from a government spokesman the remark that Britain was no longer a Christian country (the Educational Trust dispute this, saying that 85 per cent of Britons claim to be Christian and less than 5 per cent belong to other faiths). If the C of E was fulfilling its role properly as a national Christian trustee, then it would have highlighted such a state of affairs long ago. There is some evidence that the C of E does not want to appear to act evangelically in a pluralistic society. Whatever the reason, this attitude does not qualify them to act as the guardians of religious interests in education for the rest of the Christian community. That role does not apparently belong to the churches alone. 'I believe politicians must see that religious education has a proper place in the school curriculum. The Christian religion which of course embodies many of the great spiritual and moral truths of Judaism – is a fundamental part of national heritage.' The words are those of Margaret Thatcher in her address to the General Assembly of the Church of Scotland in May 1988. This was a key speech. It was an outline of how one of the most significant politicians of the century sees her personal faith and how it has shaped her policies. It attracted widespread coverage, even being reprinted in the *Wall Street Journal* and occasioned churlish dissent before it was even uttered. The speech has been the subject of scathing attacks by senior churchmen in Scotland and England, which, had they been made by politicians, would have been considered ill-mannered and arrogant. It is worth quoting in full what Prime Minister Thatcher had to say about church/state interaction, for it is likely to be significant in interpreting her reaction to possible moves to disestablish the Church of England:

When Abraham Lincoln spoke in his famous Gettysburg speech of 1863 of 'government of the people', he gave the world a neat definition of democracy which has since been widely and enthusiastically adopted. But what he enunciated as a form of government was not in itself especially Christian, for nowhere in the Bible is the word democracy mentioned. Ideally, when Christians meet, as Christians, to take counsel together their purpose is not (or should not be) to ascertain what is the mind of the majority but what is the mind of the Holy Spirit – something which may be quite different.

Nevertheless I am an enthusiast for democracy. And I take that position not because I believe majority opinion is inevitably right or true – indeed, no majority can take away God-given human rights. But because I believe it most effectively safeguards the value of the individual, and, more than any other system, restrains the abuse of power by the few. And that is a Christian concept.

But there is little hope for democracy if the hearts of men

and women in democratic societies cannot be touched by a call to something greater than themselves. Political structures, state institutions, collective ideals are not enough. We parliamentarians can legislate for the rule of law. You the church can teach the life of faith.

When all is said and done, a politician's role is a humble one. I always think that the whole debate about the church and the state has never yielded anything comparable in insight to that beautiful hymn 'I vow to thee my country'. It begins with a triumphant assertion of what might be described as secular patriotism, a noble thing indeed in a country like ours: 'I vow to thee my country all earthly things above; entire, whole and perfect the service of my love.' It goes on to speak of 'another country I heard of long ago' whose King cannot be seen and whose armies cannot be counted, but 'soul by soul and silently her shining bounds increase'.

Not group by group or party by party or even church by church – but soul by soul – and each one counts.

The theology of that speech has been criticized because it did not place sufficient stress on the idea of community and society, and put excessive stress on the individual, but whatever its shortcomings theologically it is a definite assertion that the churches have a role to play in the life of the nation, not as a shadow political debating chamber but as the spiritual reservoir. Nor is Mrs Thatcher's view to be isolated as specifically Tory and therefore politically partisan. In the weekly journal of the House of Commons[7] in December 1988, the socialist peer, the Rev the Lord Soper wrote:

As a generalization, the Church is the corporate nature and practise of Christianity. It is 'what the Christian does with his loneliness'. Similarly, the State is the political setting in which its members organize their corporate life. It is what the citizen does with his privacy, or to use the contemporary word, his privatization. Were the Church and State the obverse and reverse of the same medal, the question of the freedom of non-establishment would not arise. The brute fact is that far from expressing anything that could be called unity they have an almost irresistible tendency to collide.

If I as a Methodist claim the freedom of non-establishment, and I would claim so to do, it is because I believe it wrong

7. No 425, Vol. 14,

to invest the State in which I live with official Christianity. We are not a Christian State, though there is much of Christianity in our laws and practices. Therefore a Church which belongs to an establishment that identifies the two is in my judgement flawed. In all fairness, on the other hand, Christian communities (like the Methodist Church) which have exercised their freedom in disassociating themselves from the established Church, are only justified in so doing on two grounds. First, to represent elements of what they believe to be essential Christianity and which the established Church either tends to ignore or obscure. Second, to contribute towards an ecumenical churchmanship which serves the true interest of a world community, rather than the State which as at present constituted is the most predatory and violent association of human beings.

A similar point of view in the same publication was taken by Labour MP Eric Heffer, who sees his Christianity as synonymous with his socialism:

The Church cannot and must not avoid or reject politics. It should not of course ally itself to any particular party and it should avoid what has happened in Europe and some other parts of the world where the Church has become identified with one political party, such as the Christian Democrats. When that happens it is a great mistake and the Church usually becomes the bulwark of the Establishment and ruling class of the country concerned.

The Church should and must be free of the State and any ruling political party. At the same time it should and must side with the oppressed, the downtrodden, the poor and fight for justice and peace.

I believe the time has come to ensure that the Church stands on its own two feet, that it again gets back to arguing and working for the early Christian teachings and is once again biased to the poor. That can be done best if it is free from any State interference or control.

Thus from two distinctly different political wings there is support for the idea that the prophetic witness of the church is necessary – but not necessarily from the position of establishment. This is a crucial point because it has always seemed to me as a Scot, somewhat strange that English Christians both within and outside the Church of England have not challenged the established position before now.

The answer may be that there has been no crisis to focus the issue. (The abdication crisis of the thirties involved the person of the king rather than the status of the church). There is another reason which is less admiring in its view of the English character. This view sees the somewhat haughty, class-ridden church of the *Barchester Chronicles* as a product of the English class system. This is the Church of the establishment and the establishment do not surrender their power or influence easily. This church is not a church of the people but a feudal overlord who behaves benignly towards them. It is a church which has much to fear from the meritocratic individualism of Mrs Thatcher and the egalitarian socialism of Messrs Benn and Heffer. It survives in an established role because of history. Beyond that it cannot appeal to the Bible or a divinely appointed pope or to scholastic reasons as to why one denomination should be preferred to another. We are because we are, seems to be the response of those anti-disestablishmentarians who fudge the difference between national status for the Christian religion and the privileged protection of one particular church. But instinct or tradition is not a strong enough justification upon which to base the national establishment of religion. As we have seen, the democratic argument from membership statistics does not give the Church of England a mandate to speak on behalf of British Christians.

One factor which has not been considered so far is the financial foundation upon which the Church of England rests. 'Christ is made the sure foundation . . . Christ the head and cornerstone,' runs the hymn. But the foundation stone of many of the historic C of E churches is also sure (of 16,582 in use, 12,000 have been declared listed buildings). Annually the C of E spends £50–60 million on its churches (excluding cathedrals) and receives currently only £4–5 million under the State Aid Scheme which has now been made permanent. On the face of it, this is an extraordinary burden for the C of E to bear without state funding, and indeed the state does not finance the Church of England.

The parochial income in the Church of England in 1986 was £167 million, excluding cathedrals. The average attending member gives £2 per week. That seems a reasonably satisfactory state of affairs until the bills start coming in. The Church Commissioners, who act as stewards of the C of E's money paid out in the same year £93 million on clergy pay; £39 million in pay and pensions; £20 million on clergy houses. Add to that £6 million on episcopal administration, £3 million on buildings, and the Commissioners' own running expenses of £8½ million and we have a total of £170 million, which begins to make the financial situation of the Church of England look precarious.

But there are hidden treasures (which are not shouted about too loudly lest it act as a disincentive for members to contribute generously). The Church lands seized by the Crown at the English Reformation did not pass to the nobles, as happened in Scotland. The C of E is still rich in property, land and stock. The income of the Church Commissioners in 1987 from the Stock Exchange was £53 million; from land and property £54.5 million; from Mortgages £9.6 million; from Trust income and from diocese and parishes towards stipend £56 million – a grand total of £173 million. Then there are £251 million in an Investment Fund; £31 million in a fixed interest subscribers fund; and £217 million in a Deposit Fund.

The Commissioners also pursue a hard-nosed policy of maximising their investments and getting the best market price for their assets. A church which has taken the majority shareholding in the £64 million St Enoch Shopping Centre which opened in Glasgow in 1989 can hardly be accused of being as timid or as poor as its church mice.

The bottom line of this balance sheet is that the Church of England is not as poor as its church mice. Its Church Commissioners draw no income from the state and, with such a low proportion of its building costs coming from outside funds, there is no risk, in the event of disestablishment, of it being landed with listed building cornerstones around its neck in a sea of insolvency. The assets of the C of E would not only survive privatization but would thrive on it.

The tensions between the Conservative government which took office in 1979 and the Church of England have caused irritation to both bodies. Their expectations of one another were mismatched. When the church attacked the prime minister's policies, her first reaction was to feel betrayed. But the dispute has been going on long enough for it to have assumed a much larger perspective. It is not a matter of a short-term tiff between trendy bishops and a schoolmarmish premier. Mrs Thatcher made clear in her 'Sermon on the Mound' (see p 199) that her political philosophy rests on a moral and religious basis akin to the Protestant work ethic, and she certainly does not justify the role of capitalist anti-Christ which her critics seem to want to force upon her. The mistake would be to see the situation as an English church/state conflict. It is, as the former Dean of Canterbury, Victor de Waal, points out, 'that suddenly in England, as has been the case for a generation in other parts of the world, the qualifications of those in political power to make in effect moral judgements about wealth, about human rights (I am thinking of immigrants) and about war and peace have been challenged and challenged for the first time by the institutional church.'[8]

The debate has exposed atrophied muscles in the body politic. It has shown that our pride in English history and pageantry must be modified in the realization that history has reshuffled the ecclesiastical cards in this country. The joker in the pack may prove to be the Archbishop of Canterbury. Dr Robert Runcie is seventy in October 1991 and his successor will be appointed by the prime minister. When Robert Runcie became primate in 1980, a paltry 2.7 per cent of the population attended Anglican services and since then it has fallen. Lips are being licked in an anticipation of a church/state confrontation if Mrs Thatcher should decline to appoint the person acceptable to the Church of England Appointments Commission. Another option being discussed is that a leading Anglican from overseas might be appointed, such as the Irish primate, Archbishop Eames. This would emphasize the world-wide nature of the Anglican communion but would at the same time raise in an acute form the absurdity of a British prime minister who might be a non-Christian, selecting the head of a worldwide communion. The more likely ground on which the shaking of the foundations of the Church of England establishment will take place is over the ordination of women priests. As mentioned previously, there are Anglo-Catholic members of parliament who would want to block the measure. The conflict escalated when Barbara Harris, a black divorcee, was ordained Bishop of Boston and many Church of England priests, led by the Bishop of London, promptly declared themselves to be out of communion with her. Their argument is that not only are women priests theologically unsound but that the office of bishop is a symbol of unity in the church and that by ordaining her the US Episcopal Church was adding insult to injury. This has created an absurd situation in which clergy of the same communion are treating each other as pariahs. It could be tolerated within a private organization but can hardly be allowed to continue, within an established church. Should such internal splits continue, the cracks will spread down to the foundations

8.   Ibid. p 55.

and, if a schism occurred over women priests within the Church of England, it is almost certain that the state would be compelled to disestablish the Church in a judgement of Solomon. When Solomon was confronted with two mothers claiming the same child he had cunningly advised them to cut it in half, whereupon the real mother gave up her claim in order to save the life of her child.

There are some who argue that if disestablishment went through, the ordinances of religion would no longer be available to Englishmen and women, that is, the right to be baptised, married and buried by the church. The Church would then have thrown away the baby with the baptismal water. But it need not be so. There is an analogous situation in Scotland where the Church of Scotland pledges itself to provide the ordinances of religion on a national basis. This is a promise, not a legal requirement by the state. Following disestablishment there is nothing to prevent the Church of England pledging to baptise, marry and bury on a national basis and to guarantee the rights which at present exist. It might be argued that the Church of England would then be undertaking pastoral responsibilities for those who in no way might contribute to its funding, a somewhat impractical way to do 'business'. It would be open to the Church to charge a fee for weddings and baptisms or, in cases of funerals where there might be hardship, to have the death grant increased to cover costs. In practice, it is doubtful whether the church would want to put this on a formal basis, but I state it in order to demonstrate that rights to the rites of passage need not be affected.

A more serious objection to disestablishment is that it would remove from the British system of government specific acknowledgement that there is a moral law which rulers are called to observe. The Church of England provided that role within the British Constitution. Clifford Longley, Religious Affairs correspondent of *The Times* has argued that the unwritten constitution of Britain can only work if there is a moral basis to society so deep rooted and universally shared that there is no need to state it. 'If the British Constitution contains a special temptation to those who take part in working it, it is a temptation to commit hubris among parliamentarians by their assumption that they have been elected to frame morality to their own convenience or prejudice and not merely to reflect it.'[9]

9. *The Times*, 15 June 1987.

The traditional guardian of the moral law written in men's hearts and in the gospel was the established church. Disestablishment would, however, not necessarily create a problem. The adherence of the state to the Christian faith and traditions is contained in the coronation oath which could be amended to include a statement acknowledging the fundamental doctrines of the Christian religion (perhaps either the Nicene or Apostles Creed to which no mainstream church can take exception). This would leave the way clear for agents of that religion, that it, the churches, be given legal status without the state assuming control over their doctrine or practice. They in turn would be free to criticize the actions of the state and remind it of the duty to conform to the moral law.

In recent years there has been a process of what has been called 'creeping disestablishment'. It has been leisurely and controlled, marked by church/state commissions which allowed such developments as the production of an Alternative Service Book, a way of circumventing parliamentary approval for changes to the liturgy by making its use optional. Another change was in the way in which bishops' names were recommended to the prime minister before being passed to the queen. Upon this last custom hangs the justification for the twenty-six senior bishops of the Church of England having a seat in the House of Lords. Since it is the second chamber of the legislature, the prime minister retains control of who goes there, as is the case with life peerages. In the present circumstances, it is unlikely that there could be a form of disestablishment which would free the Church of England from parliamentary control of doctrine and appointments and would allow it twenty-six ex-officio seats for bishops in the upper chamber. It will be all or nothing. However, in a wholescale reform of the House of Lords, it is not inconceivable that there would be built into the proposals representation for the Christian Church. That would give comfort to those who might fear disestablishment would remove the voice of conscience from the corridors of power, and it would enable the church representatives to be chosen on a more equitable basis.

The case for disestablishment need not be party political or theological. The Anglo-Catholic would be free to found his schismatic church without women priests which could join with Rome. The Low Church Evangelical would be free of the panoply of state pageantry and canonical oppression which would make him feel his relationship to God was more direct, not channelled through parliament. The Tory would be happy to see the Church of England take up some of the privatized welfare opportunities and cost-sharing with other denominations, providing a wider caring service for citizens without resorting to the state. The socialist could rejoice in the new liberation which freed the church to preach against the corruption of power by the state and identify with the poor and the oppressed in society, rather than the grandees. The other churches would surely welcome the ecumenical equality which disestablishment would bring. It would free the C of E to speak internationally rather than as the servant of a particular state. Nor, as we shall see, need the place of Christianity in the nation's life be sacrificed by such a move. If the churches took the opportunity, it could be enhanced. The erosion of religious belief by secular forces may be tempting many Christians to cling to establishment as a last straw lest the church blow away entirely in the wind of change. But to keep the status of establishment on that basis is not only dishonest to the secular majority but cowardly and unchristian in its vision.

The case for disestablishment is now both historical and constitutional, statistical and equitable, moral and theological – but it is also practical and political on the basis that it is better to make the change willingly from strength, and from faith in the future, than unwillingly from weakness.

8 Conclusion: The High Road and The Low Road

The Scots are a religious nation with a special affinity for the Old Testament. Not simply because they can identify with the mountains of the Lord and the clan chieftans of the tribes of Israel, but because of a special regard for the law. It was a Scot, Rutherford, who in his succinct phrase *Lex Rex* declared that the law was king, in answer to the Divine Right pretensions of the Stuart monarchs.

The national church is Presbyterian and the way it does its business in 'courts' of the church is rigorously legalistic. The church history of Scotland is peppered with 'cases' and the documents of its disputes are framed with the grandiloquence of judges appearing before the bar of heaven. We – and I speak as a minister of the Church of Scotland as well as a journalist/broadcaster – have a tendency to think that our system had a head start on others because of its heavily democratic nature and that the prevailing church/state bond in Scotland is a model which affords the best of both worlds.

It would be nice to be swallowed by the Scots myths and believe that. But the erosion of Christian faith and practice in Scotland parallels that of England. Neither is an island and the tide of secularism is making inroads into the once dominant position of the Church of Scotland. There are several important differences between the national churches of north and south Britain. The most obvious is that the queen is not head of the Church of Scotland (that role being assigned to Jesus Christ) but a member of it. Its government consists of presbyteries, roughly corresponding to a diocese, composed of equal numbers of ministers and elders who can be male or female. The supreme governing body is the General Assembly held annually in Edinburgh which 1,250 commissioners attend. Its agenda is more flexible than the General Synod, its debates less predictable and its decisions require no ratification by parliament. All ministers are of equal rank and there are about sixty women ministers.

The Kirk has a higher percentage of the population in its membership than the Church of England. Out of a Scottish population of 5.6 million, 850,000 adults are members of the national church, outnumbering Roman Catholics by about two to one. All other denominations combined have less than 100,000. The Kirk used to get its income from land taxes but is now mainly dependent on voluntary offerings which makes it more vulnerable to falling membership and rising inflation than its neighbour south of the border with its vast resources in property and investments.

If there has been a trend in recent years it has been falling inexorably downward in membership. Against this trend is an increase in the number of Evangelicals coming into the ministry who have also begun to be appointed to key posts. The other significant development is that those who see the church's duty to speak out on political issues have become more outspoken against the Conservative government in recent years. There have been a number of reports indicting Thatcherite policies and early in 1989 the moderator, Professor James Whyte (who had presided over the 1988 Assembly at which Mrs Thatcher spoke) in February 1989 accused the prime minister in her speech of having 'a defective view of human nature' because she seemed to ignore the importance of community. It meant, he said, that there was 'a great hole in the theology by which we are governed'. The remarks were as pungent as anything the Bishop of Durham has said about the Thatcher government and illustrate the Kirk tradition of speaking out on public issues.

The reasons for the anti-Thatcher tone of many recent Kirk pronouncements are complex. It is not simply that leftist theologians have now assumed prominent spokesman roles, or that the theology of individual responsibility and work-ethic advanced by Mrs Thatcher in her 'Sermon on the Mound' to the Kirk's Assembly in May 1988, is deeply heretical. It is partly a reflection of the decline in Tory support in Scotland as a whole in recent years, and partly Scots antipathy of her Sassenach suburban style. Whatever the reasons, the fact is that church and state are in as much discord north of the border as they are south of it. Whether this will lead to the Kirk backing calls for independence is highly debatable. Consistent Kirk support for devolution has never led its ministers to play the nationalist card in substantial numbers and despite attempts in 1989 to underwrite the strongly devolutionist 'Claim of Right' and Scottish Convention, my intuition is that the national church will be wary of plunging itself in the muddy waters of the devolution/independence debate. The Scottish Labour Party is already showing signs of strain over the issue and without an external threat to its cultural dominance, the Kirk is unlikely to prove a focus for militant nationalism.

Scotland provides much in the way of lessons to be learned when it comes to considering the best basis for a new church/state relationship in Britain. From the Celtic Age when it was a fertile ground for Irish missionaries, Scotland has nurtured a different ecclesiastical system from that of England. The Scots Reformation was influenced by Luther's sermons from Germany finding their way into the east coast ports such as Dundee, where they were preached with fervour by George Wishart. Nearby, in Scotland's ecclesiastical capital of St Andrews, a revolt against the despotic Cardinal Beaton after he burned Wishart resulted in the deportation of young John Knox who returned from exile embracing the ideas of the Calvinist Reformation in Geneva. In 1560 these ideas helped erect a bulwark against the power of Mary Stuart, Queen of Scots, who was imbued with all the pretensions to divine authority of the French court. The nobles, or lairds, were only too happy to establish a Calvinistic system. This gave the Kirk a partnership with the state. In the cities the state appointed and paid the ministers. In the country the laird paid taxes (*teinds*) to the church.

Initially the old church stayed in existence, unable to function and with its property unclaimed, until 1567 when the Church Act confirmed the reformed church as 'the only trew and haly kirk of Jesus Christ within this realme'. The next step was the Church Jurisdiction Act of 1567 which declared no other ecclesiastical jurisdiction than that of the Church of Scotland. The third Act was also passed in 1567 – the Coronation Oath which required future monarchs to swear to protect the Kirk as established and to root out those opposed to its teaching. All three were incorporated into the 1592 Act establishing the Presbyterian government of the Church of Scotland. But the king tried to establish ascendancy over the church on the English model, largely by using Crown patronage of bishoprics. When the Union of the Crowns in 1603 made James VI of Scotland King of England also, he introduced episcopacy to confirm his authority over the intransigent Presbyterians.

In 1638 the imposition of an English liturgy was too much for the Scots. Many signed the National Covenant, the charter which sparked off a bitter half-century of religious strife and civil war. The Revolution Settlement of 1688 restored the position of the Kirk as master in her own house and Presbyterianism as 'agreeable to the word of God', a mild term considering the fury of the previous half-century. It goes some way to explain the Scottish hostility to episcopacy that has passed into the Scots' racial memory. By an irony, it was during this period that the English Puritans produced the Westminster Confession of Faith which was adopted as the standard of the Scots Kirk until it was relegated to the position of 'subordinate standard' in the less anti-Catholic atmosphere of the twentieth century.

The next milestone in church/state relations came with the Union of the Parliaments in 1707. The Kirk, fearing its position would be disturbed, made sure there was a clause in the Act appointing the Scots negotiators and forbidding them to discuss anything with their English colleagues affecting the church 'as now by law established'. In 1706, the Protestant Religion and Presbyterian Church Act was inserted in the Treaty of Union and secured the Protestant religion, worship and discipline of the Kirk 'to continue without alteration to the people in this land in all succeeding generations'. But there was a trade-off. In 1711 toleration of alternatives to Presbyterianism allowed a minority of episcopalians to re-assert themselves and in 1712 the Patronage Act permitted the principal landowner to choose the minister in rural parishes.

Up to this point, the idea of a church which did not need sanction for its institutions and decisions was implicit in the Acts and in the early Books of Discipline drawn up by Knox and his sterner successor Andrew Melville. But throughout the eighteenth century the idea of a single sovereign source of state authority was growing. A church/state collision occurred when the evangelical revival in the first half of the nineteenth century stirred the Kirk in 1834 to pass the Veto Act (which allowed parishioners to veto a patron's choice of minister) and the Chapel Act which gave seats on presbyteries to the ministers of the churches planted in new population areas.

The Ten Years' Conflict (1834–43) culminated in the Disruption, a peaceful religious revolution in which a third of the ministers of the Church of Scotland forsook their parishes and the security of their stipends to found a Free Church of Scotland. It was a 'shadow' establishment whose leaders shared the Tory politics of most top Kirk figures. Like its established elder brother, its aim was to have a school in every parish and under its patriarch Thomas Chalmers, a distinguished preacher and political free marketeer, to 'quit a vitiated establishment in order to return to a pure one'. This church/state battle was ecclesiological, not political, since all three churches accepted without dissent the prevailing social order, including the dark satanic mills which would have certainly been the subject of Church censure today.

Two other churches were growing at this time: the Roman Catholic Church, mainly through Irish immigrations; and the United Presbyterian (UP) Church funded on the voluntary principle, i.e. offerings on a collection plate. To an English outsider, the C of S, Free and UP churches must have looked like Scots versions of C of E, Methodists and Congregationalists. In 1900 the Free and UP churches formed the United Free Church, leaving a rump of theologically conservative members (mostly in the Highlands) who were entitled by a House of Lords ruling in 1904 to retain all the property and holdings of the Free Church because they had adhered to its principles.

The tremors caused by the Disruption had caused the state to abolish patronage in 1874. The Kirk has also lost its powers to summon people to meetings of the Kirk Session to be cross-examined on moral offences and rebuked publicly on the 'cutty stool' in front of the congregation, as was common in the eighteenth century. By the end of the nineteenth century the process of disestablishment was gathering force. The theological qualification for university chairs was abolished in 1854, and in 1872 the Church of Scotland lost its control of schools to the state. (Until 1861 the local presbytery had the right to inspect schools and require teachers to profess the Westminster Confession of Faith and the Established Church.) In 1918, the Education Act gave the right to the Roman Catholic Church to have its own schools paid for out of state funds and to veto appointments to these schools of those deemed to be unacceptable in their Catholic practice or faith.

It is significant that all these changes were made on the initiative of the state. What Caesar had given, Caesar then took away. By 1920 the Church of Scotland was still the declared national church of Scotland, but had been disestablished in all but name. There was a general wish to preserve the historic place of Presbyterianism in the nation but the painful lessons of the past century had taught the Kirk that, while all along it had thought itself to be master in its own house, parliament and the Court of Session still ruled. The classic compromise which stands to this day was the Declaratory Articles of 1921 which paved the way for the reunification of the United Free Church with the Kirk in 1929 and restored the unity of Presbyterianism. Effectively this document, passed by parliament, makes the Church of Scotland its own judge in matters of doctrine and practice and forbids the state to interfere. For example, a sacked minister has no redress in civil law since the General Assembly is supreme.

The first Article, which roughly corresponds to the Nicene Creed, is the doctrinal standard and defines the substance of the faith held by the church and is not capable of being changed by church or parliament. The General Assembly and no other body may amend all articles with the exception of Article I, thus bringing into being a national church which is responsible for its own doctrine, protected by law from state interference and guaranteed Royal protection. The sovereign is a member of the Church while in Scotland but need not be Presbyterian to uphold the pledge. The Lord High Commissioner represents the sovereign at the annual meeting of the Assembly which by its representative membership from every corner of Scotland has, since 1707, taken on the role of a quasi-parliament in its debates on social issues.

The Declaratory Articles commit the Church of Scotland to 'part of the Holy Catholic or Universal Church'; 'the Word of God as contained in the Scriptures of the Old and New Testaments as the supreme rule of faith and life' (I); 'as a national church . . . acknowledges its distinctive call and duty to bring the ordinances of religion to the people in every parish of Scotland through a territorial ministry' (III); 'the right and power, subject to no civil authority, to legislate and to adjudicate finally in all matters of doctrine, worship, government and discipline in the church' (IV); 'the inherent right . . . to frame or adopt its subordinate standards . . . of which agreement the church shall be sole judge and with due regard to liberty of opinion in points which do not enter into the substance of the faith' (V); 'This church acknowledges the divine appointment and authority of the civil magistrate within his own sphere, and maintains its historic testimony to the duty of the nation acting in its corporate capacity to render homage to God . . . and to honour his church . . . The church and state owe mutual duties to each other . . . and have the right to determine each for itself all questions concerning the extent and right and the continuance of their mutual relations in the discharge of these duties' (VI).

This is, I believe, an ideal basis upon which the Christian Church might build a new relationship with the British state. The type of 'establishment' in Scotland affects neither the civil nor the religious rights of Catholics (indeed with their denominational schools one might say that the Roman Catholics have greater state privileges than the Church of Scotland members). But the ecumenical dimension has changed the landscape not only of Scotland but also of Britain. Apart from doctrinal differences which are internal matters of validation, the Anglican, Roman Catholic, Methodist and Presbyterian Churches recognize each other's baptism as valid. There are World Council of Churches reports ('Baptism, Eucharist and Ministry', Lima 1982) which imply that mutual recognition of ministries and Eucharist may be around the corner. The British churches share moral stances on most of the great social issues of our time and often issue joint statements on matters such as nuclear weapons, unemployment and education. They were all members of the Inter-Church process in 1986–7 which culminated in a conference at Swanwick at which the mainstream Christian Churches pledged themselves to become members of a new ecumenical 'instrument' which would act like a turbo-charged British Council of Churches. (For the first time it would include the Roman Catholic Churches of Scotland, England and Wales who were not BCC members.) These kinds of developments are evolutionary, but lack real expression if the anomaly of one denomination being the 'state' church remains.

An appendix to the Anglican-Presbyterian conversation of 1966 defines 'establishment' as 'recognition of some particular religious body as the "state church", that is, as the body to which the state looks to act for it in matter of religion and which it expects to consecrate moments of national life by liturgical or official ministrations'. That definition could just as easily apply to a Council of Churches as to one particular denomination.

There would be nothing to stop parliament passing a law acknowledging the Christian faith as the historic faith of the United Kingdom and disestablishing the Church of England. Indeed, Tony Benn MP published such a Private Member's Bill in May 1988 known as the English Church Act 1988. It was brief, and simply called for the legal establishment of the Church of England to cease and for a bar on future appointments by the monarch or her ministers to ecclesiastical office. Whether or not Mr Benn incorporates this proposal into a Bill of Rights he is preparing, it is a straw in the wind. The signatories are all well-known left-wingers in the Labour Party but, as Mr Benn told me, cross-party support will be forthcoming for such a measure, although not all reasons for supporting disestablishment will appeal to Mr Benn. The Thatcher government might see disestablishment as an opportunity to take revenge on the troublesome priests who have been criticizing it. Fervent supporters of the free market might view it as a kind of 'privatization' of religion, although they would presumably stop short of selling shares in the Church of England!

There is, however, a serious side to the argument that the churches, as voluntary bodies in the field of welfare and caring services, are well placed to develop that role. Already the national churches run homes and hostels for all kinds of social problems. At present, the Church of Scotland Social Responsibility Department has a £13 million annual budget, most of it from state sources, for use in operating a wide range of homes and hostels. These are run from a central bureaucracy but there are good reasons for encouraging local initiatives and what better unit than the parish? It is about the right size to sustain homes for dementia sufferers, the elderly and infirm, and to promote community care, particularly for mental illness or additional problems. The burgeoning numbers of homeless and unemployed people have put burdens on the statutory services which they cannot sustain. Giving part-funding to religious bodies at a local level could not only ease this burden by providing caring services for the benefit of all but would release the churches or religious bodies to create a co-operative role which would not require any body to be licensed by the state at a national level. It would combine the best of the old system and yet take account of the new pluriform religious situation. It would rely on the best of free market principles while retaining the welfare state socialist ideas of community. Truly a Godly commonwealth.

To effect this at a national level it would be necessary for parliament to set up a National Religious Council for the United Kingdom. Assuming that it is the democratic will to retain Christianity as the historic faith of the nation (and I believe that any poll would back such a view), then the majority of places on this Council would go to the Christian churches. It would of necessity include the Archbishops of Canterbury and York; the Moderator of the Kirk's General Assembly; the Presidents of the Roman Catholic hierarchies of England (and Wales) and of Scotland. It would have places for the principal non-Christian faiths such as Islam, Judaism and Sikhism and could act as a liaison body between parliament and the religious bodies. In order to preserve as much as possible the independence of the religious bodies such a body should perhaps be consultative, but it could carve an influential role for itself by organizing assemblies on subjects of common concern to those of religious faith. This would simply be to give institutional form to a process which has been gathering force over the years, resulting in greater fraternity and joint action on subjects of social concern. As a guardian of harmony and humanity for its citizens, no democratic state should see such a body as a threat.

I would prefer to see the debate on disestablishment begun on such lines rather than precipitated by some disgruntled Anglicans who cannot stomach the thought of receiving communion from a woman priest and taking up parliamentary time with an issue which does not properly belong to the state. Yet that is the prospect which looms for the Church of England. Disestablishment would make the matter an internal doctrinal dispute between those of the Anglican communion, not something upon which Irish Free Presbyterians, Welsh Methodists and a Scots Jew decide. Already there have been signs that the Anglo-Catholic wing in the Church of England will play the parliamentary card, as it did over the ordination to the priesthood of divorcees.

Another illustration that this issue is not one of fanciful theory or of historical irrelevance was the controversy over Salman Rushdie's novel *The Satanic Verses* which protrayed a fictitious Mohammed figure who toyed with the idea of agreeing to recognize three goddesses in addition to Allah in order to protect his followers from persecution before finally rejecting it. In some ways it has parallels with the novel and film *The Last Temptation of Christ* in which Christ on the cross dreams of what life might have been like had he had a sexual relationship with Mary Magdalene. There was perhaps some irony in the fact that the distress and anger aroused among Muslims by Rushdie's book merited a sympathetic press release from the British Council of Churches whereas the revulsion of Christians for the Scorsese film went unchampioned. I remark on this if only to show that already the British churches are aware of the sensitivity of the Muslim community and that this will not be the last clash of culture and religious freedom which we will see in Britain. It is better by far to plan ahead of such events and enunciate the framework of tolerance and democracy which must be applied to any church/state bond rather than be forced to decide the issue over controversial cases.

Until a few years ago, for instance, a candidate for the Woolsack was barred from taking up the office of Lord Chancellor if he was a Roman Catholic. As it was, it was not necessary to change the law in order to accommodate a particular individual, always a less satisfactory way of reforming law. The present occupant of the Woolsack is a Free Presbyterian and despite a much publicised rebuke from hardline Calvinists within his robustly Protestant church for attending a requiem mass for a former colleague, Lord Mackay of Clashfern does not need allegiance to any church to do his job. However, as a committed Christian he has a view on the way in which church and state should co-exist, expressed in a lecture on 'Authority in Church and Nation' delivered in the Scottish context. There were, he said, two forms of authority which co-exist — 'the authority of Her Majesty to rule and administer justice derived from God and the authority of the church to rule in matters spiritual derived from God. Neither subordinate in its own sphere to the other . . . and yet the authority for each flowing ultimately from the same source.' Lord Mackay went on to distinguish between the coercive character of the state's authority with sanctions available to enforce it and the different character of church authority. He claimed that although the church may impose the threat of excommunication:

> The purpose of the church's existence is to win the hearts of people for her Head. The morality which the Bible teaches may be summed up in these two great commandments on which hang all the law and the prophets: thou shalt love the Lord thy God with all thine heart, with all thy strength and with all thy mind and thy neighbour as thyself. Love, though it appears in commandments, is something which cannot be forced or coerced. Insofar as authority is thought of as coercive, it cannot be the basis of a morality founded upon love. The authority of the church is therefore an authority to call for a willing obedience, not an enforced obedience.

These words were uttered before Lord Mackay became Lord Chancellor, the government member who would be crucial to guiding through legislation to disestablish the Church of England. But they contain in embryo form the principle which it has been the purpose of this book to tease out, namely that Christianity is most capable of furthering the kingdom of God when it persuades those in power rather than colludes with the state. Lord Mackay's remark on the basis of authority is clearly derived from Paul's words in Romans Chapter 13 with which I began, but they are balanced with Paul's other words in I Corinthians Chapter 13 on the nature of love. Had Christian history qualified, more often, the divine authority of the state, some of the worst excesses of church and state might have been avoided. One only needs think of the craven attitude of the Protestant church in Germany to Hitler and the shabby appeasement practised towards the Nazis by Pope Pius XI.

There is less excuse in our own times for failing to learn the lessons of the past. We also have contemporary examples of how Christians in communist and Third World countries are facing up to state oppression. Their heroic witness echoes that of the early Christians in Rome under Nero, who did not have the luxury of interpreting Paul's thirteenth chapter in the light of history, and in isolation it is an inadequate critique of the way in which the church should relate to the state. Fortunately the church of the twenty-first century has a chance to learn from history and not to repeat it.

Index

Adrian, Patriarch 92-3
Afghanistan 96, 98
Africa 11, **12-13**, 13-14, 16, **106-38**
   see also individual countries
African National Congress (ANC)
   116-21, 135, 136
Albania 25, 130
Alexei, Patriarch 97
Alexis, Tsar 91-2
'alternative theology' 172
Alves, Ruben 76
Ambrose, Saint, Bishop of Milan 21
Ambrosiano, (Banco) 157-8, 159
America, North *see* United States
America, South/Central *see* Latin
   America
Amin, President Idi 122
Anabaptists 57, 106, 177
ANC *see* African National Congress
Angelica, Mother 81
Anglicanism 10, 15-16, **173-96**, 202-3
   Africa/S. Africa 12-13, 109, 116,
     132
   Clergy Disqualification 184-5
   'creeping disestablishment' 194-5
   ecumenism 187
   High/Low churches 179; *see also*
     Anglo-Catholicism
   international churches 176-7, 179,
     180, 193
   Ireland 152, 155
   Monarchy 183-4, 191
   religious education 187-8
   US (Episcopalianism) 5, 65, 193
   women's ordination 180, 181-2,
     186, 193

Anglo-Catholicism 177, 179, 186-7,
   205
apartheid, origin 106, 108
Apostolic Revival Movement
   (Zimbabwe) 134
Aquino, Cory 53
Arap Moy, President Daniel 109, 131
Argentina 37, 40, 41, 43, 51
Arius/Arians 20
Armenia 88, 89, 96
Armstrong, Gerry 84
Arns, Cardinal Archbishop Paulo
   Evaristo 10, 13, 39-40, 46, 50
   Brazil — Never again! 36-7
   Easter sermon 37-8
   interviewed 47-9
Ascherson, Neal 147
Athanasius, Bishop 20
Augustine, Saint (of Hippo) 21, 167
Avvakum, Archpriest 91-2

Bakker, Jim/Tammy 73, 79
Banana, President Canaan 133-4, 137
Banco Ambrosiano 157-8, 159
Banda, Dr Hastings 131, **132**
Bando y Bravo, Cardinal 51-2
Baptists

   UK 175
   US 65, 71-2
   USSR 95, 97, 98
Barrett, David 175-6
base community (CEB) 29, 37, 41, 44,
   48
   Ecclesiogenesis 46
   Hungary 144
BCC *see* British Council of Churches

Beaton, Cardinal 199
Belize 56
Belli, Humberto 52
Benn, Tony, MP 191, 203
Bennett, Canon Gareth 179
Berryman, Phillip 42-3
Beyerhaus, Professor Peter 120
Beza, Théodore 167
Bhagwan Shri Rajneesh 82
Bhekuzulu, King Goodwill 136
Bible/Scriptures 37
   church taxes 6, 167-8
   England 176
   fundamentalists 77, 80
   Greece 141
   liberation theology 44-5, 46
   Lutheranism 161
   Moral Majority 76
   Orthodox churches, 90, 100
Black Muslims 69
Black Theology/Black Power (Boesak)
   122
Boesak, Reverend Dr Allan 109, 113,
   119, 136, 138, **121-7**
Boff, Clodovis 13, 43, 44
Boff, Leonardo 13, 35-6, 37, 46-7, 53
   suspension 13, 45-6, 49
Bolivia 41
Boniface VIII, Pope 18, 23-4
Bonino 43
Bordeaux, Reverend Michael 102-3,
   105
'born again' movement 59, 65, 74, 76,
   77
Boshoff, Carel 128
Botha, President P W 108, 113, 115,
   116-18, 121
Botha, Pik (S. African Foreign
   Minister) 120-21
Bradstock, Andrew 52
Brazil 10, 13, 16, **27-51**, 161
   Archbishop of Rio *see* Sales
   Bishops Conference (CNBB) 50-51
Brazil — Never Again! (Arns) 36-7
Brezhnev, Leonid 95, 100
Britain *see* United Kingdom
British Council of Churches (BCC)
   182, 203, 205
'broad church' concept 179
Broadley, John 186
Bulanyi, Father 144
Bulgaria 89, 142, **143**

Bush, President George 66
Buthelezi, chief M.G. 136

'Cadillac theology' 80
Caesaro-papism 90, 143
   'papo-Caesarism' 149
Call for an End to Unjust Rule, A
   (Boesak) 123-4
Calvi, Roberto 157
Calvin, John 123, 137, **167-8**
Calvinism 23, 57, 124, 199
Camara, Bishop Helder 13
Canterbury, Archbishop of *see* Runcie
   etc
capitalism, as oppressor 41-2
Carballo, Monsignor Bismark 52
Cardenal, Father Ernesto 45, 52
Cardenal, Father Fernando 52
Carroll, Charles 58
Carter, President Jimmy 59
Casaroli, Cardinal 159
Catholicism 10
   Africa 12-13, 132-3, 134-5
   Celtic Church 152, 176, 199
   concordate 149-60
   Czechoslovakia 145-6
   Denmark 162
   Eastern rite 96
   Hungary 144-5
   Ireland 14-15, 151-6
   Italy 14-15, 156-60
   Latin America 10, 26-54
   Netherlands 10, 107
   Norway 163
   Poland 18, 146-8
   Scotland 15-16, 198, 199-200,
      200-201, 202-3, 204
   Spain 14-15, 149-51
   Sweden 163
   Switzerland 17-18, 168-72
   UK 15-16, 175, 179, 186-7, 205;
      monarchy 15, 16, 177, 183-4;
      Reformation 176; *see also*
      Scotland *above*
   'Universal Church' 8-10
   US 10, 58, 60, 65, 66, 70, 71, 72;
      secularization 17; *Presidency* 59,
      60, 72; *tele-evangelism* 81
   USSR 88, 95, 96-7, 104
   W Germany 165-7
   Yugoslavia 146

CBN (Christian Broadcasting
  Network) 57
Ceaucesçu, President Nicolae 142
CEB *see* base community
CELAM (Latin American bishops'
  conference) 50
  see also Medellin; Puebla
Celtic Church 152, 176, 199
Chalcedon, Council of 21-2, 80
Chalmers, Thomas 200
Charismatic churches (USA) 77
Charlemagne, Emperor 22, 140, 156
Charles I, King of England 177
Charles II, King of England 177
Charles, Prince of Wales 183
'Charter 77' group 145
Chikane, Reverend Frank 111-15
Children of God organization 81
Chile 37, 41
Christendom concept 11, 19-25, 42-3,
  139
Christian III, King of Denmark 162
Christian Bill of Rights (Falwell) 77
Christian Broadcasting Network
  (CBN) 57
Christian Committee for the Defence
  of Believers' Rights (USSR) 98, 104
Christianity, surveyed 5-25
Christian Manifesto (G. North) 65, 73
Christian Reconstructionists 65
Christian Seminar (USSR) 99
Christ in a Pancho (Esquivel) 43-4
Church, Charism and Power (L. Boff)
  45-6
Church and Nation in a Secular Age
  (Habgood) 185
*Church-State relations: Tensions and
  Transitions* (Robbins) 81
Citizen and Churchman (Temple) 185
City of God, The (Augustine) 21
'civil religion' 42, 63-4, 65
CNBB *see under* Brazil
colonialism, religious 35-6, 54
Colson, Charles 84, 85
Comblin, Joseph 42, 43
communism *see* Marxism
Congregationalism 58, 109
conscientización 44, 45-6
Constantine I the Great, Emperor 5-6,
  14, 20-21, 25, 90
'contextual theology' 120
Contras (Nicaragua) 51-4, 56-7

Coptic Church 89
Council for Religious Affairs (USSR)
  101-2
Cox, Caroline, Baroness 187
Cox, Professor Harvey 68
CPK (Church of Province of Kenya)
  132
Cranmer, Archbishop Thomas 177
Creationist theory 60, 70-71, 74
Crete 141
Crockford's Clerical Directory 179
Cromwell, Oliver 177-8
crusades 23
Cuba 56, 64
Cult Observer 83-4
cult religions (US) 81-4, 85
Cupitt, Reverend Don 176, 181
Cyprus 89
Cyril, Saint (of Alexandria) 21
Cyril, Saint (Apostle of the Slave) 88
Czechoslovakia 145-6

'death, theology of' 54
de Waal, Victor 192
Denmark 17, 160-61, 162
Dimitrios I, Metropolitan 89
'disappeared ones' 36-7
Divine Light organization 82
*Domination or Liberation; The Place
  of Religion in Social Conflict* (Kee)
  35-6, 77
Donatists 20
Dopper Kerk (South Africa) 128
Dors, Traian 142
Douglas, Justice (US Supreme Court)
  69
Dubček, Prime Minister Alexander
  145
Dudko, Father Dmitri 101
Dukakis, Governor Michael 73
Dutch Reformed Church 107
  South Africa *see* Nederduitse
    Gereformeerde Kerk dyophysites
    89

Eames, Archbishop 193
Easter 37-8, 80
*Ecclesiogenesis; Base Communities
  Re-invent the Church* (L. Boff) 46
ecclesiology, defined 19
Economist 149-50
Ecuador 41

ecumenism 9, 10-11
 liberation theology 47; *see also*
  Wright *etc*
 UK 202-3, 204
EEC (European Economic
 Community) 140, 142, 151, 154
Eire *see* Ireland, Republic of
EKD (Evangelische Kirche in
 Deutschland) 166
Electronic Church *see* tele-evangelism
El Salvador 13
Elizabeth I, Queen of England 177
Elizabetch II, Queen of England 183-4
Engele v. vitale 69
England 173-96, 203
 Reformation 23
 see also United Kingdom
England, Church of *see* Anglicanism
Episcopalianism (US) 5, 65, 193
 see also Anglicanism
Escoto, Father Miguel d' 52, 53
Escriva, monsignor 151
Esquivel, Adolfo Perez 43-4
EST (cult) 84
Eternal Word Television Network 81
Ethiopia 89, 109
Europe 11, 16-17, 57, **139-72**
 see also individual countries
European Economic Community
 (EEC) 140, 142, 151, 154
Eusebius of Caesarea 20, 21
evangelicalism 115, 198
 USA 60-61, 65, 77-8
  see also Lutheranism *etc*
Evangelische Kirche in deutschland
 (EKD) 166
evangelism 26, 54, 72
 see also tele-evangelism
evolution theory 71, 74

'Faith and Protest' (S. African
 schismatics) 128
Faith in Struggle (Haslam) 54
Falwell, Reverend Jerry 66-7, 73, 77-8,
 79-80
Far From the Madding Crowd (Hardy)
 179
Fatima (Spain), prophecies at, 96
favela 28, 29-34
Fedor III, Tsar 92
Feet-on-the-Ground Theology (C.
 Boff) 13, 44

Ferraro, Geraldine 60
Filaret, Abbot (Kiev) 100
Filaret, Patriarch 90
Finland 17, **162**
Fox, George 179
France 24, **160**
Franco, General Francisco 150
Free Church (Scotland) 200
Free Churches (UK) 186
Frelimo party (Mosambique) 135
fundamentalism, Protestant
 African front-line states 135
 Latin America 54
 US 60-61, 65, **77-81**

Gandhi, Mahatma 7, 122
GDR (German Democratic Republic)
 18-19, 166, 167
Georgia 87-8, 89
Germany
 East (DDR/GDR) **18-19**, 166, 167
 West 18, 19, 161, **165-7**
 Reformation 23, 165
'Gideon syndrome' 24-5
glasnost 14, 18, 86, 102-5, 148
Glasnost (journal) 102
Glemp, Cardinal 148
Gomulka, Prime Minister 147
Gorbachev, President Mikhail 14, 87,
 96, 100, 148-9
Gorbachev, Raisa 86
Graham, Dr Billy 78
Great Schism 23, 88, 92, 140
Greece 14, 89, 100, **140-42**
Guatemala 56
Gustavus Adolphus, King of Sweden
 162
Gútiérrez, Gustavo 34, 43, 44, 49

Habgood, Archbishop John 178, *note*,
 185
Hadrian IV, Pope 176
Harare Declaration 117
Hardy, Thomas 179
Hare Krishna (ISKCON) 82
Harris, Bishop Barbara 193
Haslam, David 54
Hatfield, Mark 77-8
Heffer, Eric, MP 190, 191
Helsinki Accord 97, 98
Henry VII, King of England 177

Henry VIII, King of England 23, 176, 183
Heritage USA organization 79
Heyns, Reverend Professor Johan 128, 128-30, 137
Hieronymous, Archbishop 141
High Noon (film) 62
Hitler, Adolf/Nazism 61, 166, 206
Hochhut, Rolf 159
Honduras 56
Hoskins, Professor 104
house church movement 175
Hubbard, L. Ron 82, 84
Huddleston, Bishop Trevor 116
Hungary 144-5
Hurd, Douglas 182-3
Hurley, Archbishop Denis 120, 136
Husák, President Gustáv 145

If This is Treason — I am Guilty! (Boesak) 122
India 89, 161
Initsiativniki 95, 98
Inkatha 135-6
Institute per l'Opere di Religione *see* IOR
Inter-Church movement (UK) 203
IOR (Institute per l'Opere di Religione) (Vatican Bank) 156-8, 159
IRA (Irish Republican Army) 154
Iran 95
Iraneus 44
'Irangate' scandal 54, 56
Ireland
    Northern 16, **152-5**, 175; *see also* UK
    Republic of (Eire) 14-15, 149, **151-6**
Irish Republican Army (IRA) 154
ISKCON (International Society for Krishna Consciousness) 82
Islam 22-3
    Black Muslims 69
    Satanic Verses 205
    Spain 149, 151
    Uganda 132
    UK 204, 205
    USSR 88, 95-6
    W. Germany 166
    Yugoslavia 146
Israel 56, 62

Istoe 46-7
Italy 14-15, 149, **156-60**

Jackson, Justice (US Supreme Court) 70
Jackson, Reverend Jesse 59-60, 72
Jacobites 58
James VI and I, King 199
Jaruzelski, General W. 148
Jefferson, President Thomas 58-9, 71, 74
'Jefferson Wall' 59, 66-7
Jehovah's Witnesses 69, 132
Jenkins, Bishop David 176, 181
Jews *see* Judaism
Job, Patriarch 90
John Paul I, Pope 159
John Paul II, Pope 10, 41
    Hungary 145
    IOR 157-8
    'Laborem et Exercens' 49
    Latin America 13, 39, 45-6, 49-50, 52-3; *Puebla conference* 41, 42
    married priests 150
    Netherlands 107
    Poland 145, 147, 148
    South Africa 120-21
    US 72
    USSR 96-7
Johnson, Paul 110-11
Jones, Jim 81
Judaism/Jews 6, 11
    UK 184, 188, 204
    US 56, 61, 65, 66, 69
    USSR 97
Julian the Apostle, Emperor 21
Justin, Patriarch 142
Justinian, Patriarch 142

Kairos Document 117, 119-20
Kaunda, President Kenneth 131
Kee, Alistair 35-6, 37
Kennedy, President John F. 59, 72
Kenya 109, **131-2**
Kenyatta, President Jomo 131
Kerk en Samelewing (NGK *verligten*) 127
Keston College (UK) 98, 102
Khrushchev, Nikita 93-5
King, Coretta 75
King, Martin Luther 72-3, 122

Kingdoms in Conflict (Colston) 84
Kipling, Rudyard 8
Kirk *see* Presbyterianism: Scotland
Knox, John 199, 200
Kolbe, Blessed Maximilian 148
Ku Klux Klan 61
Küng, Professor Hans 166
Kwazulu 135

Lamont, Bishop Donal 134
Lang, Archbishop Cosmo 185
Last Temptation of Christ, The (film)
    205
Lateran Agreements 158
Latin America 11, 13-14, 26-54, 72,
    80
Latinamerica Press 29
Laud, Archbishop William 177
Lefevre, Archbishop 10
Lekai, Cardinal 144
Lenin, Vladimir Ilyich 93
Leo I, Pope 21
liberation theology 13, 26-54
    summarized 43-5
    Zimbabwe 133-4
Liberation Theology (Berryman) 42-3
Liberty Broadcasting Network 73-4
Liberty Foundation 74
Liberty University (USA) 76
Lithuania 95, 96-7
Licinius, Emperor 20
Lollard movement 176
Longley, Clifford 194
Lord's Army 142-3
Lorscheider, Cardinal 47
Lubbe, Professor Willie 128
Lusaka Statement 117, 119, 120
Luther, Martin 18, 23, 161, 199
Lutheranism 161
    Brazil 161
    Czechoslovakia 146
    Germany 18-19, 161, 166
    Hungary 144
    India 161
    Reformation 23, 161
    Scandinavia 17, 160-65
    South Africa 109
    Tanzania 161
    US 65, 161
Luthuli, Chief Albert 118
Luwum, Archbishop Janani 12, 132

Macarius, Patriarch 91
McCarthy, Senator Joseph 54, 63
McGuire, Father John 30-34
Machel, President Samora 135
Mackay (of Clashfern), James, Baron
    205-6
Macleod (of Fuinary), Very Revd
    George, Baron 184
Madison, President James 58
Madsen, Mette 162
Maharaji, Guru 82
Maksim, Patriarch 143
Malawi 131, 132
Mandela, Nelson 118
Mandela, Winnie 136
Marcinkus, Archbishop Paul 157-8
Marxism/communism 25, 206
    Africa: *front-line states* 133-5;
    S. Africa 116-17, 119, 120
    Eastern bloc churches 142-9
    Greece 141
    Italy 159
    liberation theology 29, 35, 36, 44,
        45-6; *Puebla conference* 41-2
    'populorum progressio' 40
    Sandinistas 52-3
    South Africa 116-17, 119, 120
    US 53-4, 63
    see also Union of Soviet Socialist
        Republics
Mary, Queen of Scots 199
Mary I, Queen of England 177
Mboya, Tom 131
Medellin conference 40-41
Melville, Andrew 200
Mennonites 57, 170
Merwe, Brigadier Johan van der 122
Methodism
    Argentina 43
    Mozambique 134, 135
    South Africa 109
    UK 175, 184, 187, 188-90, 202-3
    US 65
    Zimbabwe 134
Mexico 56
Michael, Tsar 90
Michael, Prince, of Kent 183
Milingo, Archbishop Emmanuel 10,
    133
Milvian Bridge, Battle of 5-6
Mindszenty, Cardinal 144, 145

MM *see* Moral Majority
Mokoena, Bishop Isaac 116, 136
monophysites 89
Montefiore, Dr Hugh 186
Moonies (Unification Church) 81
Moral Majority movement (MM) 59,
   65, 66-7, **73-81**, 84
Mormon Church 71
Moy, President Daniel Arap 109, 131
Mozambique 133, **134-5**
Mugabe, Prime Minister Robert 133,
   134
Muge, Bishop Alexander 132
Musa, Pastor N.B. 134
Musey, Mathieu 170
Muslims *see* Islam
Mussolini, Benito 156, 159
Muzorewa, Bishop Abel 134

Napoleon I, Emperor 160
'national security ideology' 41-2
Naude, Dr Beyers 111
Nazism/Hitler 61, 166, 206
Nederduitse Gereformeerde Kerk
   (NGK) (Dutch Reformed Church)
   109, 111
   new directions 121, 127-31, 136-7
Nero, Emperor 206
Nestorius 21
Netherlands 10, 50, **106-7**, 138
Neuhaus, Reverend Richard 68
Neves, Prefect Luiz Carlos 31-2
Newman, Cardinal John Henry 179
New Religious Movements *see* cult
   religions
New Right, The (Vigeurie) 77
NGK *see* Nederduitse Gereformeerde
   Kerk
NHK (Nederduitse Hervormde Kerke)
   128
Nicaragua 42, 45, **51-4**, 56-7, 63, 64
   priests in government 13, 52-3
Nicea, Council of/Nicene Creed 20, 89
Nicholas II, Tsar 93
Nikodim, Metropolitan 101
Nikon, Metropolitan 91-2
Nims, Jerry 73-6, 79
Njonjo, Charles 131
Norman, Dr Edward 187
North, Dr Gary 65
North, Colonel Oliver 54, 56
Norway 17, **162-3**

O'Connor, Sister Gabriela 29
O'Flaich, Cardinal Tomás 153, 154
O'Hare, Father Joseph 68
Okullu, Bishop Henry 131
Old Believers 92
Opus Dei organisation 149, 151
Orthodox churches 14, **87-95**, 95-105
   Armenia 88, 89, 96
   autocephaly 89
   monasteries 89, 141
   Bulgaria 89, 143
   Ecumenical patriarchate (Phanar)
      89, 141
   Finland 162
   Georgia 87-8, 89
   Greek 89, 100, **140-42**
   Lord's Army 142-3
   monasteries/convents 86, 89, 91, 99-
      100, 141
   Old Believers 92
   Oriental 89
   Phanar (Ecumenical patriarchate)
      89, 141
   priesthood 99, 100
   Russian 86-105
   UK 184
   US 89
   women 99
   Yugoslavia/Serbian 89, 146
   see also Union of Soviet Socialist
      Republics

PAC (Pan African Congress) 108,
   121
'Pacem in Terris' organization 145
Padin, Bishop Candido 41
Paisley, Reverend Ian 152, 184
Palladius, Saint 152
Palme, Prime Minister Olof 164
Pan African Congress (PAC) 108,
   121
Panama 56
papacy *see* Vatican
Papadopoulos, General 141
Papandreou, Prime Minister 141,
   142
Paraguay 37
Parrales, Father Edgar 52
Paton, Alan 107
Patrick, Saint 152
Paton, Alan 107
Patrick, Saint 152

Paul, Saint 206
Paul VI, Pope 40, 47, 157
Paul of Aleppo 91
Paulke, Bishop 65
Paulo, Dom *see* Arns
Pentecostalism 12, 72, 77, 97, 109, 116
'people, church of the' 45
'people of the poor' 42
Peru 41
Peter the Great, Emperor 14, 92
Peter's Pence 158
PF (People's Front) (Zimbabwe) 134
Phanar (Ecumenical Patriarchate) 89, 141
Philippines 53, 64
Pilgrim Fathers 57
Pimen, Patriarch 90, 98, 101, 102
Pius XII, Pope 159, 206
Poland 18, **146-9**
Polanyi, Michael 12
'poor, option for' 41, 42
'poor, people of the' 42
praxis
    liberation theology 27, 29, 34-5
    South Africa 115
Presbyterianism **197-8**
    Hungary 144
    Ireland 152, 155
    Latin America *see* Wright
    Mozambique 135
    Scotland 15-16, **197-202**
    South Africa 109
    UK 175, 205
    US 58, 63-4, 65
Presbyterianism, United (UP) 201
Presbyterian Survey 64
Pro Life movement 66-70, 85
Protestantism 8
    Germany 206
    Hungary 144
    Italy 159
    Latin America 26
    'non-violent revolution' 137-8
    Poland 147
    Sweden 163
    Switzerland 17-18, 167-72
    UK 175
    US 55-8, 69
    see also Reformation; and individual sects
Protestantism and Repression (Alves) 76

Protestants and Other Americans United for Separation of Church and State (POAU) 69
PTL (Praise the Lord organization) 79, 80
Puebla conference 41-2

Quakers (Society of Friends) 179

Rajneesh, Bhagwan Shri 82
Randall, Claire 67-8
'rapture' concept 81
Rastafarians, UK 184
Ratzinger, Cardinal 10, 45-6, 49
RC (Roman Catholicism) *see* Catholicism
RDP (Right Doctrine Protestantism) 76-80
Reagan, President Ronald 61, 71, 72, 81
    fundamentalists 59-60, 66
Reconstructionism, Christian 65
Reeves, Bishop Ambrose 111, 113
Reformation 11, 23, **23-4**, 57, 106
Rehnquist, Chief Justice William 71
religion
    'civil' 42, 63-5
    'popular' 44
    world statistics 24
Religion in Communist Lands 98
Representative, The (Hochhut) 159
Richard, Pablo 42, 43
Right Doctrine Protestantism (RDP) 76-80
Robbins, Harold 81
Roberts, Oral 79
Robertson, Reverend Pat 57, 60, 61, 78-9
Robinson, Bishop John 176
Roe v. Wade 70
Rogers, Dr Isobel 63-4
Roman Catholicism (RC) *see* Catholicism
Romania 89, **142-3**
Rome *see* Vatican
Romero, Archbishop 13, 39, 44
Rosedale, Herbert 82-3
Rossi, Cardinal Archbishop 40
Runcie, Archbishop Robert 111, 179-8, 193
Rushdie, Salman 205
Rushdoony, R. J. 65

Russia *see* Union of Soviet Socialist
  Republics
Rutherford, Samuel 197

SACC *see* South African Council of
  Churches
SACP (South African Communist
  Party) *see* Marxism/communism,
  South Africa
SADF (South African Defence Force)
  118
Saints and Sandinistas (Bradstock) 52
Sakharov, Andrei 97
Sales, Archbishop (of Rio de Janeiro)
  40, 50
Salvador, Republica de 13
samizdat 95, 99
Samoza family 51, 56
San Salvador 39
Sanctuary movement 64
Sandinistas 57
Sandino, Augusto 51
Santer, Bishop Mark 186
Sarney, President 28, 50-51
Satanic Verses, The (Rushdie) 205
Scandinavia 17, **160-65**
Scorsese, Martin 205
Schaeffer, Dr Francis 73
Schindler, Rabbi Alexander 61
Scientology 82, 83-4
Scopes trial 60, 66
Scotland **15-16**, 175, 183, 186, 193,
  197-202
  clergy disqualification 184
  social welfare 204
  Thatcher government 182, 188
  see also United Kingdom
Scotland, Church of 132
Segundo 43
Sendinkerk (S. Africa) 128
Seraphim, Archbishop 141, 142
Serbia/Yugoslavia 89, 146
'700 club' 79
Seventh Day Adventists 69
Shakers 57
shanty towns 109
  see also favela
Sharpeville shootings 108, 111, 118,
  125-6
Shaw, Dr Duncan 182
Shenouda, Pope 89
Shepherd, William 83

Siberian Seven 97
Sikhs, UK 184, 204
Sin, Cardinal Jaime 53
Sindona, Michele 157, 158
Sinn Fein 154
Smith, Prime Minister Ian 134
Smith, Reverend Nico 127
Sobrino 43, 44
'social gospel' 13
Soderblom, Archbishop 164
Solidarity movement (Poland) 146,
  148
Solzhenitsyn, Alexander 97
Soper, Reverend Donald, Baron 184,
  189-90
Sophia, Regent 92
South Africa **106-31**, 135-8
  Afrikaner National Party 107-8, 127
  banned organizations 108, 111-15
  Broederbond 107
  Constitutions 108-9
  'critical involvement' 111
  front-line states 110, 131-5
  Independent churches 109, 116, 136
  racial composition, 108, 135-6
  religious statistics 109, 128
  republic formed 108
  Sharpeville shootings 108, 111, 118,
    124-5
  socio-economic conditions 110, 130
  Soweto 109, 118, 120, 125
  'state terrorism' 112, 120, 124-5
  trade sanctions 110-11
  tverligtent 127
  Zulus 107, 135-6
South Africa International 110-11
South African Council of Churches
  (SACC) 111, 113, 116-18, 120
South African Defence Force (SADF)
  117
Southern, R.W. 22
Soviet Peace Fund 101
Soweto (S. Africa) 109, 118, 120, 125
Spain **14-15**, **149-51**
spiritism 12, 50, 133
Stalin, Joseph 93, 94, 99
Star (S. Africa) 122
'state terrorism' (S. Africa) 120, 124-5
Stendahl, Bishop Krister 164-5
Sudan 109
Sun (UK) 179
Sun Yung Moon 82

Sweden 17, 161, **163-5**
Swaggart, Timmy 54, 56, 79
Switzerland 17-18, 23, **167-72**
Sykes, Professor Stephen 181
Synanon organization 84
Syria 89

Tambo, Oliver 118-19
Tanzania 131, 161
'tele-evangelism' ('Electronic Church')
   17, 55-6, 66, **78-81**, 84, 85
   Latin America 54, 56-7, 80
   Nims 73-6
   Robertson 57, 60, 78-9
Temple, Archbishop William 185
Terre Blanche, Eugene 128
'Testimony of Faith' (Romania) 142-3
Thaddeus, Apostle 88
Thatcher, Prime Minister Margaret/
   Government 15, 178, 182, 191, 192,
   198, 203
   bishops appointed 178
   Scottish speech (1988) 188-9, 192,
   198
'Theological Rationale' (Boesak *et al*)
   119
theology
   'alternative' 172
   'Cadillac' 17, 80
   'contextual' 120
   'of death' 54
   'upside-down' 26
Theology of Promise (Banana) 134,
   137
Tikhon, Patriarch 93
Time 66-8, 101
Tito, President 146
Tomasek, Cardinal 145
Torrance, Reverend Professor James
   136-7
To Secure the Blessing of Liberty . . .
   (Shepherd)83
Transcendental Meditation 82
transformationism 84
*Trial of Faith, The: Theology and the
   Church Today* 10
Trinity, Orthodox view 89
Trujillo, Bishop Lopez 50
Turkey 14, 89
Tutu, Archbishop Desmond 13, 111,
   113, 115, 122, 136
   Botha speech 116-18

UDF *see* United Democratic Front
Uganda 131, **132**
UK *see* United Kingdom
UK Christian Handbook 175
ultramontanism 18
UN (United Nations) 110
Unification Church (Moonies) 82
Union of Soviet Socialist Republics
   (USSR) 14, **86-105**
   Christian Committee for the
      Defence of Believers' Rights 98,
      104
   Christian Seminar 99
   Council for Religious Affairs 94,
      101-2
   Czechoslovakia 95, 146
   dissident-religious conflation 95, 97-
      9
   Finland 162
   forest churches 96
   Holy Governing Synod 93
   monasteries/convents 86, 91, 99-
      100
   nationalist-religious links 95-7, 99,
      104
   religious statistics 87-8, 89, 93-4,
      95-6
   Revolution 93
   seminaries 99
   state-Church collusion 101-2
   statutory restriactions 87, 93-5
   Zagorsk 86-7, 99
United Democratic Front (UDF)
   (S. Africa) 108, 120, 121, 136
United Free Church (Scotland) 201
United Kingdom (UK) **15-16, 173-207**
   ecumenism 202-3, 204
   Monarchy 15
   multiculturalism 173-4, 183, 186,
      187-8
   'National Religious Council/
      Conference of Churches' 15-16,
      204
   religious statistics 175, 187-8
   see also Anglicanism
United Nations Organization (UN)
   110
United Presbyterianism (UP) 201
United Reformed Church (UK) 187
United States of America (US) **17, 55-
   85**
   African front-line states 135

Anglicanism (Episcopalianism) 5, 65, 193
  blacks 72-3
  Catholicism 10
  Constitution/1st Amendment 59, 60-61, 62
  education 60-61, 68-9, 70-71
  Irish 155
  Latin America 51, 53-4, 56-7, 62, 64
  Marxism/communism 53-4, 63
  Philippines 53, 64
  religious statistics 65, 161
  Revolution 24
  Virginia Statute 58-9
'upside-down theology' 26

van der Merwe, Brigadier Johan 122
van der Walt, Reverend Dr Ernst 108
Vatican/papacy 8, 9, 22-4, 149, 156-60
  concordats 16-17
  Czechoslovakia 146
  Holy Roman Emperor 140
  Hungary 144-5
  Italy 156-60
  liberation theology 26
  Nicaragua 51-4
  non-conforming Catholics 10, 13, 14-15, 50, 107, 132-3
  Orthodox view of 88-9
  Poland 146
  US 72
  see also individual popes
Vatican Council, Second (1962-4)
  Curia 149
  France 160
  Ireland 153
  Latin America 26-7, 37-8, 40
  Netherlands 107
  US 72
verseiling 106
Viguerie, Richard 77
Vischer, Professor Lukas 168-72
Vladimir I the Saint, Prince of Kiev 38, 90
Vlok, Adriaan 12

Waal, Victor de 192
Wales 175, 185, 203, 204
  see also United Kingdom
Wallis, Reverend Jim 85
Wall street Journal 40, 188

Wals, Pastor Peter 170
Walt, Reverend Dr Ernst van der 108
WARC *see* Alliance of Reformed Churches
WCC *see* World Council of Churches
Welsh v. USA 69-70
Wesley, Charles/John 179
Westphalia, Peace of 165
Whitby, Synod of 152
Whyte, Professor James 198
Willebrands, Cardinal 96
Wishart, George 199
Witherspoon, John 58
Wojtyla, Karol *see* John Paul II
World Alliance of Reformed Churches (WARC) 121, 127, 172
World Christian Encyclopaedia (Barrett) 175-6
World Council of Churches (WCC) 9, 43, 172, 203
  South Africa 120
  USSR 98, 101
Wright, Dr Jaime 36-9
Wyclif, John 176, 178
Wyszinski, Cardinal 147

Yakunin, Father Gleb 97-8, 101
Yugoslavia/Serbia 89, 146

Zabolotsky, Professor 103-4
Zambia 131, 132-3
ZANU (Zimbabwe African National Union) 134
Zimbabwe 109, 133-4
Zwingli, Huldreich 167, 169